AMERICA'S
TEST KITCHEN

Also by America's Test Kitchen

More Mediterranean

The New Cooking School Cookbook: Fundamentals

Cooking with Plant-Based Meat

The Savory Baker

The Complete Autumn and Winter Cookbook

Five-Ingredient Dinners

One-Hour Comfort

The Complete Plant-Based Cookbook

Cook for Your Gut Health

Foolproof Fish

The Complete Salad Cookbook

Meat Illustrated

Vegetables Illustrated

Bowls

The Ultimate Meal-Prep Cookbook

The Chicken Bible

The Side Dish Bible

The Complete One Pot

Cooking for One

How Can It Be Gluten-Free Cookbook Collection

The Complete Summer Cookbook

100 Techniques

Easy Everyday Keto

Everything Chocolate

The Perfect Pie

The Perfect Cake

The Perfect Cookie

How to Cocktail

Spiced

The Ultimate Burger

The New Essentials Cookbook

Dinner Illustrated

America's Test Kitchen Menu Cookbook

Cook's Illustrated Revolutionary Recipes

Tasting Italy: A Culinary Journey

Cooking at Home with Bridget and Julia

The Complete Mediterranean Cookbook

The Complete Vegetarian Cookbook

The Complete Cooking for Two Cookbook

The Complete Diabetes Cookbook

The Complete Slow Cooker

The Complete Make-Ahead Cookbook

Just Add Sauce

How to Braise Everything

How to Roast Everything

Nutritious Delicious

What Good Cooks Know

Cook's Science

The Science of Good Cooking

Bread Illustrated

Master of the Grill

Kitchen Smarts

Kitchen Hacks

100 Recipes: The Absolute Best Ways to Make the True Essentials

The New Family Cookbook

The Cook's Illustrated Baking Book

The Cook's Illustrated Cookbook

The America's Test Kitchen Family Baking Book

The Best of America's Test Kitchen (2007–2022 Editions)

America's Test Kitchen Twentieth Anniversary TV Show Cookbook

The Complete America's Test Kitchen TV Show
    Cookbook 2001–2022

Healthy Air Fryer

Healthy and Delicious Instant Pot

Mediterranean Instant Pot

Cook It in Your Dutch Oven

Vegan for Everybody

Sous Vide for Everybody

Toaster Oven Perfection

Air Fryer Perfection

Multicooker Perfection

Food Processor Perfection

Pressure Cooker Perfection

Instant Pot Ace Blender Cookbook

Naturally Sweet

Foolproof Preserving

Paleo Perfected

The Best Mexican Recipes

Slow Cooker Revolution Volume 2: The Easy-Prep Edition

Slow Cooker Revolution

The America's Test Kitchen D.I.Y. Cookbook

THE COOK'S ILLUSTRATED ALL-TIME BEST SERIES:

All-Time Best Brunch

All-Time Best Dinners for Two

All-Time Best Sunday Suppers

All-Time Best Holiday Entertaining

All-Time Best Soups

COOK'S COUNTRY TITLES:

Big Flavors from Italian America

One-Pan Wonders

Cook It in Cast Iron

Cook's Country Eats Local

The Complete Cook's Country TV Show Cookbook

FOR A FULL LISTING OF ALL OUR BOOKS:

CooksIllustrated.com

AmericasTestKitchen.com

Praise for America's Test Kitchen

Selected as the Cookbook Award Winner of 2021 in the General Cookbook Category

INTERNATIONAL ASSOCIATION OF CULINARY PROFESSIONALS (IACP) ON *MEAT ILLUSTRATED*

Selected as the Cookbook Award Winner of 2021 in the Health and Nutrition Category

INTERNATIONAL ASSOCIATION OF CULINARY PROFESSIONALS (IACP) ON *THE COMPLETE PLANT-BASED COOKBOOK*

"The book's depth, breadth, and practicality makes it a must-have for seafood lovers."

PUBLISHERS WEEKLY (STARRED REVIEW) ON *FOOLPROOF FISH*

"Another flawless entry in the America's Test Kitchen canon, *Bowls* guides readers of all culinary skill levels in composing one-bowl meals from a variety of cuisines."

BUZZFEED BOOKS ON *BOWLS*

"Diabetics and all health-conscious home cooks will find great information on almost every page."

BOOKLIST (STARRED REVIEW) ON *THE COMPLETE DIABETES COOKBOOK*

"*The Perfect Cookie* . . . is, in a word, perfect. This is an important and substantial cookbook. . . . If you love cookies, but have been a tad shy to bake on your own, all your fears will be dissipated. This is one book you can use for years with magnificently happy results."

THE HUFFINGTON POST ON *THE PERFECT COOKIE*

"Here are the words just about any vegan would be happy to read: 'Why This Recipe Works.' Fans of America's Test Kitchen are used to seeing the phrase and now it applies to the growing collection of plant-based creations in *Vegan for Everybody*."

THE WASHINGTON POST ON *VEGAN FOR EVERYBODY*

"True to its name, this smart and endlessly enlightening cookbook is about as definitive as it's possible to get in the modern vegetarian realm."

MEN'S JOURNAL ON *THE COMPLETE VEGETARIAN COOKBOOK*

"Filled with complete meals you can cook in your Instant Pot. Next time you're thinking of turning to takeout or convenience foods, prepare one of these one-pot meals instead."

NBC NEWS ON *MEDITERRANEAN INSTANT POT*

"If you're a home cook who loves long introductions that tell you why a dish works followed by lots of step-by-step hand holding, then you'll love *Vegetables Illustrated*."

THE WALL STREET JOURNAL ON *VEGETABLES ILLUSTRATED*

"A one-volume kitchen seminar, addressing in one smart chapter after another the sometimes surprising whys behind a cook's best practices. . . . You get the myth, the theory, the science, and the proof, all rigorously interrogated as only America's Test Kitchen can do."

NPR ON *THE SCIENCE OF GOOD COOKING*

"The 21st-century *Fannie Farmer Cookbook* or *The Joy of Cooking*. If you had to have one cookbook and that's all you could have, this one would do it."

CBS SAN FRANCISCO ON *THE NEW FAMILY COOKBOOK*

"The go-to gift book for newlyweds, small families, or empty nesters."

ORLANDO SENTINEL ON *THE COMPLETE COOKING FOR TWO COOKBOOK*

"Some books impress by the sheer audacity of their ambition. Backed by the magazine's famed mission to test every recipe relentlessly until it is the best it can be, this nearly 900-page volume lands with an authoritative wallop."

CHICAGO TRIBUNE ON *THE COOK'S ILLUSTRATED COOKBOOK*

"The America's Test Kitchen team elevates the humble side dish to center stage in this excellent collection of 1,001 recipes. . . . Benefiting from the clarity that comes from experience and experiments, ATK shows off its many sides in this comprehensive volume."

PUBLISHERS WEEKLY ON *THE SIDE DISH BIBLE*

BOARDS

STYLISH SPREADS FOR CASUAL GATHERINGS

FOOD STYLING & EXPERT ADVICE BY
ELLE SIMONE SCOTT

PHOTOGRAPHY BY
STEVE KLISE

THE EDITORS AT AMERICA'S TEST KITCHEN

CONTEN

TS

Welcome to America's Test Kitchen   x

Get on Board
Cheese, Charcuterie, and More   xii

First Things First
Breakfast Boards for Any Time of Day   38

Snacks and Sips
Grazing Boards for Cocktail Parties and Beyond   74

Bring Your Appetite
Dinner-Sized Boards to Fill You Up   142

Sweet Things
Dessert Boards to Satisfy Your Sweet Tooth   224

Nutritional Information for Our Recipes   258

Conversions and Equivalents   264

Index   266

Library of Congress Cataloging-in-Publication Data
Names: America's Test Kitchen (Firm), author. |
    Scott, Elle Simone, author. | Klise, Steve, photographer.
Title: Boards : stylish spreads for casual gatherings / food
    styling & expert advice by Elle Simone Scott ;
    photography by Steve Klise ; America's Test Kitchen.
Description: First edition. | Boston, MA : America's Test
    Kitchen, [2022] | Includes index.
Identifiers: LCCN 2021062497 (print) | LCCN 2021062498
    (ebook) | ISBN 9781954210004 (hardcover) |
    ISBN 9781954210011 (ebook)
Subjects: LCSH: Appetizers. | Food presentation. |
    Entertaining. | LCGFT: Cookbooks.
Classification: LCC TX740 .A6578 2022 (print) | LCC
    TX740 (ebook) | DDC 641.81/2--dc23/eng/20220103
LC record available at https://lccn.loc.gov/2021062497
LC ebook record available at https://lccn.loc.gov/2021062498

AMERICA'S TEST KITCHEN
21 Drydock Avenue, Boston, MA 02210

Printed in Canada
10 9 8 7 6 5 4 3 2 1

Distributed by Penguin Random House Publisher Services
Tel: 800.733.3000

Pictured on front cover **Crudités Board (page 33)**

Pictured on back cover **Steak Frites (page 205), Dessert Cheese Board (page 253), Oktoberfest (page 165)**

Photography by **Steve Klise**
Food Styling by **Elle Simone Scott**

Editorial Director, Books **Adam Kowit**

Executive Food Editor **Dan Zuccarello**

Deputy Food Editor **Stephanie Pixley**

Executive Managing Editor **Debra Hudak**

Project Editor **Brenna Donovan**

Senior Editors **Valerie Cimino and Sara Mayer**

Digital Test Cook **Samantha Block**

Assistant Editors **Emily Rahravan and Sara Zatopek**

Design Director **Lindsey Timko Chandler**

Deputy Art Director and Designer **Katie Barranger**

Photography Director **Julie Bozzo Cote**

Photography Producer **Meredith Mulcahy**

Senior Staff Photographers **Steve Klise and Daniel J. van Ackere**

Staff Photographer **Kevin White**

Food Stylist **Elle Simone Scott**

Contributing Food Stylists **Catrine Kelty and Chantal Lambeth**

Photoshoot Kitchen Team

   Photo Team and Special Events Manager **Alli Berkey**

   Lead Test Cook **Eric Haessler**

   Test Cooks **Hannah Fenton, Jacqueline Gochenouer, and Gina McCreadie**

   Assistant Test Cooks **Sāsha Coleman, Hisham Hassan, and Christa West**

Make-up Artist **Luiz Filho**

Senior Manager, Publishing Operations **Taylor Argenzio**

Senior Print Production Specialist **Lauren Robbins**

Production and Imaging Coordinator **Amanda Yong**

Production and Imaging Specialists **Tricia Neumyer and Dennis Noble**

Copy Editor **Deri Reed**

Proofreader **Ann-Marie Imbornoni**

Indexer **Elizabeth Parson**

Chief Creative Officer **Jack Bishop**

Executive Editorial Directors **Julia Collin Davison and Bridget Lancaster**

Welcome to America's Test Kitchen

This book has been tested, written, and edited by the folks at America's Test Kitchen, where curious cooks become confident cooks. Located in Boston's Seaport District in the historic Innovation and Design Building, it features 15,000 square feet of kitchen space, including multiple photography and video studios. It is the home of *Cook's Illustrated* magazine and *Cook's Country* magazine and is the workday destination for more than 60 test cooks, editors, and cookware specialists. Our mission is to empower and inspire confidence, community, and creativity in the kitchen.

So many people across the company worked together to make this book possible. In the studio is where the boards came to life. It's a testament to the great teamwork between food stylist Elle Simone Scott, photographer Steve Klise, and art director Katie Barranger that this process was so successful. None of this would have been possible without photography director Julie Bozzo Cote, photography producer Meredith Mulcahy, and the entire photoshoot kitchen team: Alli Berkey, Eric Haessler, Hannah Fenton, Jacqueline Gochenouer, Gina McCreadie, Sāsha Coleman, Hisham Hassan, and Christa West, who sourced the ingredients and cooked all of the food on set. Thanks to Catrine Kelty and Chantal Lambeth, who each styled two boards in this book. Luiz Filho was Elle's makeup artist.

Brenna Donovan was the project editor and worked closely with Elle from the studio to the page, ensuring all the different editorial pieces came together. Executive food editor Dan Zuccarello oversaw the recipe side of things and provided invaluable culinary consultation, making sure there was a balance of something simple and homemade to add as well as recipes to take your board to the next level. Sam Block, Sara Mayer, and Stephanie Pixley also contributed to this project. Thanks to Sara Zatopek, Emily Rahravan, and Valerie Cimino for stepping in to provide editorial support, and thanks especially to Jack Bishop and Adam Kowit for their guidance overseeing the entire editorial process.

Along with art direction, Katie Barranger designed the entire book, from the cover to the endsheets, conceiving of the look and feel of the book and making the layout as approachable and fun as the boards felt. Design director Lindsey Chandler provided guidance with design every step of the way, and assisted greatly with visual direction of the photography, at times acting as extra hands and providing ideas on set.

We also appreciate the hard work of the production team, Lauren Robbins, Amanda Yong, Tricia Neumyer, and Dennis Noble, who ensured that the photos look as good in print as they do on-screen. The book was copyedited by Deri Reed, proofread by Ann-Marie Imbornoni, and indexed by Elizabeth Parson, who all thankfully have keen eyes for detail. We particularly would like to recognize the contributions of Taylor Argenzio and Debra Hudak, who kept the book schedule on track thanks to their top-notch project management and organizational skills and helped tie up the many loose ends that present themselves at the end of a project.

To see what goes on behind the scenes at America's Test Kitchen, check out our social media channels for kitchen snapshots, exclusive content, video tips, and much more. You can watch us work (in our actual test kitchen) by tuning in to *America's Test Kitchen* or *Cook's Country* on public television or on our websites. Listen to *Proof*, *Mystery Recipe*, and *The Walk-In* (AmericasTestKitchen.com/podcasts) to hear engaging, complex stories about people and food. Want to hone your cooking skills or finally learn how to bake—with an America's Test Kitchen test cook? Enroll in one of our online cooking classes. And you can engage the next generation of home cooks with kid-tested recipes from America's Test Kitchen Kids.

Our community of home recipe testers provides valuable feedback on recipes under development by ensuring that they are foolproof. You can help us investigate the how and why behind successful recipes from your home kitchen. (Sign up at AmericasTestKitchen.com/recipe_testing.)

However you choose to visit us, we welcome you into our kitchen, where you can stand by our side as we test our way to the best recipes in America.

🅕 facebook.com/AmericasTestKitchen
🅞 instagram.com/TestKitchen
▶ youtube.com/AmericasTestKitchen
♪ tiktok.com/@TestKitchen
🐦 twitter.com/TestKitchen
🅟 pinterest.com/TestKitchen

AmericasTestKitchen.com
CooksIllustrated.com
CooksCountry.com
OnlineCookingSchool.com
AmericasTestKitchen.com/kids

GET ON BOARD

Cheese, Charcuterie, and More

SO WHAT IS A **BOARD**, ANYWAY?

Let me guess. The first thing that came to mind when you opened this book was a larger-than-life-size wooden board overflowing with giant hunks of cheeses, cascading grapes, and more cured meats than you would know what to do with. Am I right? Be honest, we're all friends here. If so, you're not entirely off base—you'll find plenty of stunners (and cheese) here. But these days, a board is so much more than just cheese and cured meat—it's an interactive and low-key-yet-elegant way of presenting food for a wide range of occasions.

Boards are tailor-made for parties. They instantly make your gathering looser than a seated dinner, and there's no real set meal time so guests will serve themselves, eat with their hands, and continue snacking until they're full. When you're serving a board, it gets the party started. In fact, the food is the party.

But boards aren't just for entertaining; don't wait to break out your best board until you have a large group coming. It's just as fun serving a board as dinner to your family of four, or even scaling a board down for a perfect date-night-in option.

From grazing boards to steak dinners and everything in between (you can even turn your cocktail bar setup into a board complete with snacks!), you'll find plenty to inspire you in the pages of this book. Now let's get started.

Hi, I'm Elle.

I have worn many hats in my career (as culinary producer, showrunner, caterer, and production cook) and I'm proud of all of them. But the one that wakes me up in the morning is food stylist. In nonkitchen language, I get to play with food and make it look impressive enough so you either want to devour it, or at the very least take a photo of it. The greater part of that is getting to decide what to do with the gorgeous bounty when all the work is done . . . that's where my "entertaining enthusiast" side comes in.

As a food stylist, most of my days consist of deciding what food should look like on camera. But once we wrap, that's when friends get to benefit from the hard work. In my early days as a food stylist, in an effort to avoid food waste, I started bringing leftovers home from shoots and planning small gatherings in my apartment. Inspired by the work of American fashion icon and model turned entertaining icon and restaurateur B. Smith, I set up tablescapes repurposing the leftovers into game-night meals or whatever the theme had been for the day. Eventually, I became quite popular, as you can imagine. And you can be, too. Food styling isn't just for the professionals—anyone can do it at home to impress their friends (or even yourself). Creating boards is really the best introductory experience into food styling. It can be a great exercise in creating shapes with food and experimenting with color palettes, and a way to really lose your inhibitions and find your "style" of styling. Odds are that if you're reading this it's because you have already been thinking about how to play with your food. I hope you'll find inspiration in these pages.

This book is unique compared to others created here at ATK and thus it had to be approached in a way that was new and challenging. We began by exploring what readers and home cooks enjoy about boards and entertaining. We weren't surprised to learn that it was not merely about how the food looked, but how it makes guests *feel,* and feeling seen and considered is always top priority when someone is in my care. Boards are a perfect opportunity to use what you know about all of your guests' likes and dislikes to build a winning board that can please the crowd while still maintaining a personal touch. This could also serve as a way to get your guests trying new and exciting things. And it's perfectly OK if some of those "new things" are new to you as well; sharing food adventures makes for great party memories.

Speaking of creating moments to remember, teaming up with photographer extraordinaire Steve Klise to create this book has been the ultimate joy. Every morning upon entering the studio, Steve and I would meet with art director Katie Barranger and get strategic about the boards we were creating that day; sometimes that involved sketching ideas on paper, or seeking inspiration from our favorite social media food influencers, or just creating something we've never seen before. Somehow our minds are completely in sync when we work together; the synergy flows. It could be a testament to our true camaraderie and friendship, but also to Steve's photographic genius, which is unique and special. I'm grateful to have built this book's full aesthetic with him and the team that held us down the whole way. I'm also grateful for the contributions from fellow food stylists Catrine Kelty and Chantal Lambeth.

Through it all, we had an amazing time strumming through some of our most current and diverse recipes to include in these boards; it was so important to us that you all know that a board can be created simply from the parameters of your market aisles but could also be elevated with some snazzy recipes and drink pairings to boot. So I hope that you will use this book to inspire your cooking genius within, that you'll be adventurous and create some unique boards that will make you famous amongst your friends, and maybe you'll put it on your coffee table where it will spark conversations about the beauty of food and food styling. Either way, have fun. Eat well, and entertain from your heart and soul.

IN FOOD & LOVE,

Elle

HOW TO USE THIS BOOK:

Every board starts with a dashboard, pointing out the items in the photo. While every board may look ambitious, the dashboard is separated into two sections—"Start with" and "If you want, add"—to help you dial up or down based on how much time you have. The "Elle's Strategy" section highlights the things that are important for you to know about making the board, from make-ahead ideas to styling tips. And of course, there are recipes with every board so you can add your homemade touch.

The important thing to remember here is that these boards should serve as an inspiration for your own creations. You can follow them exactly, or use the photos as a jumping-off point. If you see something that could easily be store-bought, go for it! You can make or buy as much or as little as makes sense for you.

WHAT'S YOUR TYPE?

BOARDS, BUFFETS, AND SPREADS

There are a whole range of boards in this book—from more classic styles to out-there ideas—but all of them can be classified into three main categories.

TRADITIONAL BOARDS

These are the ones that most likely come to mind when you think "board." You arrange all of the elements like a mosaic on one board, whether shingling Spanish cheeses and pulling back the tops of tinned fish just so in Tapas (page 109), or organizing chicken wings into sections surrounded by a bouquet of crudités in Wings (page 89).

BUFFET BOARDS

The ultimate interactive board is a buffet-style board featuring lots of components and topping options in little dishes. Set out a big bowl of greens and a plethora of toppings for the Chopped Salad board (page 171) or a few pints of ice cream and an assembly line of add-ons for Ice Cream Sundaes (page 227).

SPREADS

When a board is feeling too full, or there are multiple distinct themes you want to highlight, it helps to break things up into a couple separate boards. On the Baked Potatoes board (page 185) this technique helps to give people ideas for topping combinations while still encouraging mixing and matching across the boards. These boards often end up fitting into one of the above two categories, too.

BOARD BASICS

Here's how to get started making a beautiful board, from selecting just the right one to useful entertaining equipment to keep around.

CHOOSING YOUR BOARD

Finding the right board is like trying on clothes in a fitting room; you take a few sizes in there with you to see what fits. I like to take out a few options and arrange them on my counter to see what works best. These are the two main things I think about when in the selection process:

The vibe: Consider what type of board you're hoping to put together. Is it a sophisticated spread? Maybe a ceramic platter is your best bet. Or is it a casual cheese plate for a night in with friends? A wooden cutting board could do the trick (bonus: it's easier to cut on). Think about color: are you going for a moody setting or something bright and cheerful?

The size: Before I even start assembling the board, I like to leave items in their packages and block out where I want things to go. I've even used a clean, dry sponge to hold the place of something I want to add later. You don't want the board to feel crowded, but you don't want it to look sparse either. This mock-up technique never fails me; I use it on set and at home.

SCALING YOUR BOARD

The number of servings is given with every board in the book, but you may want to adjust the amounts if you have more or fewer people coming over. Here are some general guidelines for the most common board components, but take into consideration what meal you're serving and adjust accordingly. So if you're serving a board as an appetizer to a bigger meal you may want to scale back a bit—or dial it up if people will be snacking on the board all night.

BOARD ITEM	AMOUNT
Cheese	2 to 3 ounces per person
Meats	2 to 3 ounces per person
Nuts	2 to 3 tablespoons per person
Crackers or bread	4 to 6 ounces per person
Vegetables or crudités	4 to 8 ounces per person
Dips	½ cup per person

Shopping Your House

When furnishing your board with utensils and containers, you might be tempted to run out and purchase every cute knife in existence. But first, take stock of what you already own (hint: it might not be in your kitchen). If you do have an itch to shop that needs to be scratched (I feel you), hit up thrift stores, flea markets, and the sale section of a favorite store for the most interesting pieces. Restaurant supply stores are also great for scoring things like quarter sheet pans and cute bottles.

• Muffin tins are perfect for organizing small toppings such as sprinkles (see page 245) and other garnishes.

• Cake stands add height to your tablescape.

• Sheet pans and trays can easily serve as a board (see page 197).

• Drinking glasses make everything you display look like a bouquet (see pages 69 and 137).

• Break out the fancy silverware, glassware, or serving utensils to add a sophisticated look. This is the special occasion you've been waiting for!

• Look around your house to see what you have on display in other rooms and incorporate pottery or textiles from your travels.

EQUIPMENT TO HAVE ON HAND (BEYOND THE BOARD):

• **Serving utensils:** No matter what you're setting out, you'll need a selection of big forks, spoons, spatulas, and/or tongs to make serving easier.

• **Tiny knives, forks, and spoons:** Cocktail-size utensils make serving small bits so much easier.

• **Toothpicks and skewers:** These are great for serving small items like olives and little snacky things. Be sure to have a "discard" bowl and put a used toothpick in it before the party even starts so people know what it's for.

• **Straws:** If you're serving drinks, you need straws; they're always a hit. Look for colorful or patterned straws to add a fun touch.

• **Cocktail napkins:** Have more napkins than you think you might need. They're just as good as serving as an impromptu plate as they are for cleaning up accidental (and inevitable) spills.

• **Tweezers:** A food stylist's secret weapon! You can find giant tweezer tongs online—they're great for moving something on your board when you don't want to disturb what's around it.

• **A spray bottle filled with water:** Give your greens a good spritz to keep them looking fresh; it mimics the mister at the grocery store!

• **Mason jars:** Perfect for shaking up salad dressings—or for serving up store-bought items so people will think they're homemade. (I won't tell if you don't.)

Every Board Needs to Have

A UNIFYING THEME

To really be a board, it should be centered around an overall concept. Sometimes that concept is an event such as a day at the ballpark (see page 151) or an afternoon tea (see page 129). But more often I prefer a food-focused board, such as the build-your-own martinis on page 137, pulled pork on page 197, or gorgeous grilled vegetables on page 179.

A FOCAL POINT

This is the star of the show, the thing you want everyone to remember once the party's over. Maybe it's the fluffiest scrambled eggs around (see page 65), shatteringly crisp chicken wings (see page 92), or something as easy as a pretty dish with luxurious burrata balls smack dab in the center of a grilled veggie board (see page 179).

SOMETHING HOMEMADE

You don't have to go overboard (sorry) with homemade food; buy as much as you'd like. But for a special touch, I'll include at least one homemade item on my boards, even if it's as simple as a compote to add to granola parfaits (see page 45), mini frittatas to bring life to a brunch spread (see page 50), or a lemony vinaigrette (see page 175).

SOMETHING STORE-BOUGHT

This is the real secret to success: Lean into store-bought items. I like to start with one or two homemade options and fill out the board with things I pick up at the store. Hit up the olive bar or take a trip down the specialty aisle in your supermarket and see what you find.

ACCENTS THAT MAKE IT PRETTY

This could be as simple as a sprig of fresh herbs or strategically scattered dried apricots, but adding that final layer of something special takes your board to new heights.

SOMETHING HOMEMADE

ACCENTS THAT MAKE IT PRETTY

SOMETHING STORE-BOUGHT

A FOCAL POINT

GET GORGEOUS

When I'm styling, there are some back-pocket tricks I use to take things from simple to special. Here's the inside scoop on making your board beautiful, no matter what's on it.

THE SPRINKLE

Once you're finished with your board, scatter accent items (think: nuts, olives, capers, dried fruit) all over the board instead of limiting them to one section. This adds another dimension to your board and helps it feel more whimsical.

THE SWIRL

For a no-fail way to make dips look delicious, use the back of a spoon to press into the dip (or hummus) in a swirling, back-and-forth motion with varying degrees of pressure. Then, drizzle with olive oil to fill in the wells, and/or sprinkle with chopped herbs or cracked black pepper.

THE SMEAR

Instead of peppering small dishes of condiments all over your board, add a more organic, casual touch by dolloping it right onto the board and using the back of a spoon or a small knife to smear it into a long line.

THE TRAIL

Create boundaries by arranging things in long trails across the board. This helps section space off but also adds a visual distinction.

THE LIFT

When I've got something that I don't want to stick to the board (hello, smoked salmon), I prop it up on a bed of leafy greens or sprouts. It gives definition, makes things easier to pick up, and adds softness to the board.

THE HERB GARNISH

Your first instinct might be to chop herbs and sprinkle them across the board, but put the knife down. Instead, leave the herbs whole and use the sprigs as garnish. This works especially well with herbs with long stems you can tuck between pieces on the board, but basil also makes a beautiful "flower" (see page 83).

KEEP IT FRESH:

Here are some ways to keep your boards looking beautiful, no matter when your guests arrive.

- Keep any veggies in an ice water bath as you're assembling the board to keep them crisp.

- Brush a little oil on the vegetables to keep them from looking dried out.

- Once your board is made, cover it with some damp paper towels. If you do this, be sure to leave the crackers and other soggy-prone items off until you're ready to serve.

Stages of a Board

Whether I'm putting together a cheese board or a bagels and lox spread (see page 55), I always break the construction up into four stages. This helps keep me organized, and ensures a balanced and looks-good-enough-to-eat board. Follow these steps (plus a few bonus styling ideas!) to set up like a stylist.

1

START WITH A FOCAL POINT

This is usually the "star" or the ingredients that set the tone for the board's theme. If there's no theme, just start with the largest item (or items). Sometimes for larger boards these focal points are more spread out (such as strategically placed dips).

2

CREATE SECTIONS

Use bread, crackers, and/or fruit as section dividers, creating zones on your board. (You'll fill them in next!)

3

FILL IN SPACE

Fill in the sections with hearty items like meats, olives, or fruit. This is also the time to add anything you might have in small dishes.

4

ADD FINISHING TOUCHES

It's all about the garnishes here. Sneak some dried fruit into the empty spaces and use fresh herbs or even edible flowers to take your board into a new dimension.

WHAT'S THE OCCASION?

No matter what kind of party you're planning, there's a board to help you celebrate.

	Board	Type of Board	Page
BABY/BRIDAL SHOWER	Granola Parfaits	Spread	41
	Low-Lift Brunch	Traditional Board	47
	Bruschetta	Traditional Board	83
	Afternoon Tea	Spread	129
	Pavlovas	Spread	233
	Cookie Decorating	Buffet	245
BIRTHDAY	Cheese Board	Traditional Board	19
	Charcuterie Board	Traditional Board	27
	Afternoon Tea	Spread	129
	Martinis	Buffet	137
	Pizza Parlor	Buffet	145
	Ballpark	Buffet	151
	Clambake	Traditional Board	217
	Ice Cream Sundaes	Buffet	227
	Cookie Decorating	Buffet	245
GAME DAY	Bloody Mary Bar	Buffet	69
	Hummus	Traditional Board	77
	Wings	Traditional Board	89
	Nachos	Buffet	97
	Ballpark	Buffet	151
	Oktoberfest	Traditional Board	165
	Baked Potatoes	Spread	185
	Chocolate Fondue	Traditional Board	239

	Board	Type of Board	Page
ELEGANT COCKTAIL PARTY	Bruschetta	Traditional Board	83
	Tapas	Traditional Board	109
	Raw Bar	Traditional Board	115
	Pâté	Traditional Board	123
	Martinis	Buffet	137
CASUAL HANG WITH FRIENDS	Hummus	Traditional Board	77
	Wings	Traditional Board	89
	Nachos	Buffet	97
	Movie Night	Spread	103
	Pizza Parlor	Buffet	145
	Grilled Vegetable Platter	Traditional Board	179
BEGINNER BOARDS	Crudités Board	Traditional Board	33
	Granola Parfaits	Spread	41
	Low-Lift Brunch	Traditional Board	47
	Bloody Mary Bar	Buffet	69
	Movie Night	Spread	103
	Afternoon Tea	Spread	129
	Chopped Salad	Buffet	171
	Ice Cream Sundaes	Buffet	227
	Chocolate Fondue	Traditional Board	239
MOSTLY SHOPPING	Granola Parfaits	Spread	41
	Low-Lift Brunch	Traditional Board	47
	Bagels and Lox	Traditional Board	55
	Bruschetta	Traditional Board	83
	Movie Night	Spread	103
	Tapas	Traditional Board	109
	Chopped Salad	Buffet	171
	Baked Potatoes	Spread	185
	Ice Cream Sundaes	Buffet	227
	Chocolate Fondue	Traditional Board	239
	Dessert Cheese Board	Traditional Board	253

THREE ESSENTIAL BOARDS

CHEESE BOARD

Serves 6 to 8

ON THIS BOARD:

1–2 pounds cheese (Cheese Log with Herbes de Provence on page 24, Manchego, cheddar, blue, and Brie)

Crackers (store-bought and homemade on page 25)

Dried fruit (apricots, dates, and figs)

Fresh fruit (grapes, blackberries, and apples)

Nuts (pecans and almonds)

Fig-Balsamic Jam (page 24)

Honey

→

BUILDING YOUR CHEESE BOARD

Whether you're making an over-the-top showstopper or a pared-down version for simple snacking, cheese boards are always welcome to the party. But as adaptable as they are, the best cheese boards hit the same main categories to strike a perfect balance of textures and flavor, from cheese to accompaniments. Read on for a step-by-step process to getting cheesy.

CHOOSE YOUR CHEESES

Start by choosing three to five cheeses with different textures and flavors. It's helpful to think of cheese in the following categories: sharp and crumbly (like aged cheddar or Parmesan), soft and bright (like chèvre), firm and nutty (like Gruyère), tangy and funky (like blue), ripe and oozy (like Brie). Plan on serving 2 to 3 ounces of cheese per person, and let the cheese sit at room temperature, covered, for 1 to 2 hours before serving to take the chill off. In a pinch, you can quickly soften creamy varieties such as Brie by placing them in a zipper-lock bag and letting them sit in 80-degree water.

CRACK THE CRACKER CODE

The cheese really is the star of the show here, so choose carby accompaniments that let the cheese shine. Make sure you have mild-tasting crackers and bread (like water crackers and baguette) that don't step on the cheeses' toes. If you do want to add some interest, include just one or two flavored options (such as the Seeded Pumpkin Crackers on page 25) to keep it simple.

ADD EXTRAS

This is the point where you can really make your board as over-the-top (or as streamlined) as you want. Think about the cheeses you're offering, and select your extras intentionally. You can either go complementary, like zesty onion relish with tangy goat cheese, or contrasting, like sweet fig jam with a sharp, bracing blue cheese.

When deciding on your extras, you should have each of the following categories represented at least once on the board:

- **Something sweet:** Honey, spicy honey, dried fruit, chocolate squares, yogurt-covered pretzels

- **Something snacky:** Nuts, olives, cornichons, crudités, fresh fruit, sesame sticks, grissini (think about texture here!)

- **Something spreadable:** Mustard, jam, caramelized onions, chutney, pesto

---

LEFTOVERS? DON'T PANIC.

I firmly believe it's better to have too much cheese than not enough. So if you went a little overboard, be sure to store your cheeses properly so they don't go to waste. It can be tricky: As cheese sits, it releases moisture. If this moisture evaporates too quickly, the cheese dries out. But if the moisture is trapped on the cheese's surface, it encourages mold. To let cheese breathe without drying out, wrap it tightly in waxed or parchment paper and then loosely in aluminum foil. Or, buy specialty cheese bags or cheese paper (check out the brand Formaticum) that has a two-ply construction that mimics this.

Dial It Back

Not all boards have to be overflowing displays. Sometimes all you need is a small spread for noshing. But that doesn't mean it should be an afterthought. Here are some ideas for dialed-back boards that still check all the boxes.

← **MINIMALIST**

Choose three cheeses, making sure to still have a range of texture and intensity to keep everyone happy. This one has blue cheese, simple cubed cheddar, and a wedge of Brie. A nice jam brings something sweet and spreadable (here I used fig) and walnuts and apples are perfect for nibbling. Pantry-friendly store-bought crackers round it out.

SOMEWHERE IN BETWEEN →

Just a couple of homemade touches can take a board from simple to special. Here, I toasted up some sliced baguette and made a Blue Cheese Log with Walnuts and Honey (page 24). For additional cheeses I went with Gruyère and Brie. Dried fruit and jam bring a sweet element, and cornichons, pearl onions, almonds, and grapes give guests something to snack on.

SLICING CHEESES
(IT'S DIFFERENT DEPENDING ON THE TYPE!)

My colleague and former cheesemonger and all-around resident cheese expert Kate Shannon gave me the skinny on slicing cheese. As she puts it, you wouldn't cut a pizza the same way that you portion a tray of lasagna, right? (Good point, Kate.) The way you slice the cheese actually impacts each bite—many cheeses change in flavor and texture from edge to center. With each slice, you want to keep a roughly equal ratio of interior and exterior (or rind). And from a styling perspective, different cuts add visual interest and make the board easier to navigate. Here's how to slice it right.

SMALL BARK-WRAPPED WHEELS

Cheeses: Harbison (pictured), Vacherin Mont d'Or, Winnimere, Rush Creek Reserve

What to do: Using paring knife, start by making a shallow cut around the perimeter of the rind on top of the cheese, then make a shallow cut down the center of the wheel. Peel back both halves of the rind so guests can scoop out the cheese with a spoon or rounded knife.

SOFT WHEELS AND WEDGES

Cheeses: Camembert, triple-crème cheeses such as Sugar Loaf (pictured, wheel), Brie Jouvence Fermier (pictured, wedge)

What to do: Small wheels can be cut into equal-size wedges (imagine cutting a small cake). For larger wedges, make slices along the sides of the cheese that angle out from the tip of the wedge.

SEMISOFT AND HARD WEDGES

Cheeses: Blue (pictured, semisoft), Manchego (pictured, hard), Drunken Goat

What to do: Place the cheese cut-side down on the board. Make parallel slices off the sides, working towards the center. If you cut thick slices (like the blue), you can cut smaller pieces from each one.

RECTANGLES, SQUARES, AND BLOCKS

Cheeses: Cheddar, softer cheeses such as Robiola, Taleggio (pictured, top), or Brebirousse d'Argental (pictured, bottom)

What to do: If the cheese is fairly firm and relatively uniform in texture (like the Taleggio), you can simply slice straight across it, cutting each piece in half if you'd like.

If the cheese is softer and you can't get the whole cross section in a bite or two (like the Brebirousse d'Argental), start by cutting the cheese in half diagonally and then cut each half in half again to form triangles. Make small slices from the sides, from the exterior to the center, working towards the middle of the triangles.

LOGS

Cheese: Goat (pictured)

What to do: Slice the log into coins. For larger logs, position the coin so that it's flat and then cut into half-moons or little wedges.

LARGER FIRM AND SEMIFIRM WEDGES

Cheeses: Alpine-style cheeses such as Challerhocker (pictured) and washed rind cheeses such as Morbier

What to do: Place the cheese cut-side down on the board. Begin by cutting slices across the width of the cheese. When you work halfway or three-quarters of the way through the wedge, begin making slices along the length of the cheese instead. These wide wedges can be cut into smaller pieces.

Small Bark-Wrapped Wheels

Soft Wheels and Wedges

Semisoft Wedges

Hard Wedges

Rectangles, Squares, and Blocks

Logs

Larger Firm and Semifirm Wedges

LEVEL UP YOUR CHEESE BOARD

Goat Cheese Log with Herbes de Provence
Serves 10 to 15

Chilling the cheese log in the freezer makes it much easier to roll in the herbes de Provence when firm. Once the cheese log has been garnished, it can be wrapped tightly in plastic wrap and refrigerated for up to 2 days. This recipe can be easily halved; shape cheese mixture into 4-inch log in step 2.

- 6 ounces goat cheese, crumbled (1½ cups)
- 6 ounces cream cheese
- 2 tablespoons extra-virgin olive oil, plus extra for drizzling
- 1 small garlic clove, minced
- ½ teaspoon pepper
- 3 tablespoons herbes de Provence

1. Process goat cheese, cream cheese, oil, garlic, and pepper in food processor until smooth, scraping down sides of bowl as needed, about 1 minute.

2. Lay 18 by 11-inch sheet of plastic wrap on counter with long side parallel to counter edge. Transfer cheese mixture to center of plastic and shape into approximate 9-inch log with long side parallel to counter edge. Fold plastic over log and roll up. Pinch plastic at ends of log and roll log on counter to form tight cylinder. Tuck ends of plastic underneath. Freeze until completely firm, 1½ to 2 hours.

3. Spread herbes de Provence on large plate. Unwrap cheese log and roll in herbes de Provence to evenly coat. Transfer to serving dish and let sit at room temperature for 1 hour. Drizzle with extra oil before serving.

VARIATIONS

Blue Cheese Log with Walnuts and Honey
Combine ¼ cup toasted and chopped walnuts and ¼ cup chopped dates. Substitute 1½ cups crumbled mild blue cheese for goat cheese and walnut-date mixture for herbes de Provence. Omit oil and increase pepper to 1 teaspoon. Drizzle cheese log with 2 tablespoons honey before serving.

Cheddar Cheese Log with Chives
Be sure to buy refrigerated prepared horseradish, not the shelf-stable kind, which contains preservatives and additives.

Substitute 1½ cups shredded extra-sharp cheddar cheese for goat cheese and ½ cup minced fresh chives for herbes de Provence. Omit oil. Add ¼ cup mayonnaise, 1 tablespoon drained prepared horseradish, and 2 teaspoons Worcestershire sauce to processor with cheddar.

Fig-Balsamic Jam
Makes about 1 cup

Combining fresh figs with balsamic vinegar and spices makes a sweet-savory jam that is perfect for cheese and delicious with canapés.

- 12 ounces fresh figs, stemmed and quartered
- ½ cup sugar
- ¼ cup balsamic vinegar
- ¼ cup water
- 1 tablespoon lemon juice
- 1 teaspoon yellow mustard seeds
- ¾ teaspoon minced fresh rosemary
- Pinch table salt
- Pinch pepper

1. Bring all ingredients to simmer in 10-inch nonstick skillet over medium-high heat. Reduce heat to medium-low and cook, stirring occasionally, until rubber spatula leaves distinct trail when dragged across bottom of skillet, 25 to 30 minutes.

2. Transfer jam to food processor and pulse until uniformly chunky, 4 to 6 pulses. Let jam cool to room temperature, about 1 hour, before serving. (Jam can be refrigerated for up to 2 months.)

Seeded Pumpkin Crackers

Serves 8

If you can't find baharat, substitute a combination of
½ teaspoon ground cumin, ¼ teaspoon pepper, ¼ teaspoon
ground coriander, pinch ground cinnamon, and pinch ground
clove. This recipe is best made in two 5½ by 3-inch loaf pans.
You can use one 8½ by 4½-inch loaf pan instead; bake the loaf
for the same amount of time, then slice the frozen loaf down
the center before slicing crosswise. Crackers will continue to
crisp as they cool.

- 1 cup (5 ounces) all-purpose flour
- 1 teaspoon baking powder
- ¼ teaspoon baking soda
- 1 cup canned unsweetened pumpkin puree
- 1 teaspoon baharat
- ½ teaspoon table salt
- ¼ cup (1¾ ounces) sugar
- 5 teaspoons vegetable oil
- 2 large eggs
- 1 tablespoon grated orange zest
- ⅓ cup dried apricots, chopped
- ⅓ cup sesame seeds
- ⅓ cup shelled pistachios, toasted and chopped
- 2 tablespoons coarse sea salt

1. Adjust oven rack to middle position and heat oven to
350 degrees. Grease two 5½ by 3-inch loaf pans. Whisk flour,
baking powder, and baking soda together in large bowl; set
aside. Combine pumpkin puree, baharat, and table salt in
10-inch skillet. Cook over medium heat, stirring occasionally,
until reduced to ¾ cup, 6 to 8 minutes; transfer to medium
bowl. Stir in sugar and oil and let cool slightly, about 5 minutes.

2. Whisk eggs and orange zest into pumpkin mixture then
fold into flour mixture until combined (some small lumps
may remain). Fold in apricots, sesame seeds, and pistachios.

Scrape batter into prepared pans, smoothing tops with rubber
spatula. Bake until skewer inserted in center comes out clean,
45 to 50 minutes, switching and rotating pans halfway
through baking.

3. Let loaves cool in pans on wire rack for 20 minutes. Remove
loaves from pans and let cool completely on rack, about
1½ hours. Transfer cooled loaves to zipper-lock bag and freeze
until firm, about three hours.

4. Heat oven to 300 degrees and line rimmed baking sheet
with parchment paper. Using serrated knife, carefully slice
each frozen loaf crosswise as thin as possible (about ¼ inch
thick). Arrange slices in single layer on prepared sheet and
sprinkle with sea salt. Bake until dark golden, 25 to 30 minutes,
flipping crackers and rotating sheet halfway through baking.
Transfer sheet to wire rack and let crackers cool completely,
about 30 minutes. Serve.

CHARCUTERIE BOARD

Serves 6 to 8

ON THIS BOARD:

1–2 pounds meats (mortadella, 'nduja, chorizo, soppressata, Genoa salami, prosciutto)

Mustards (whole-grain and Dijon)

Olives

Caper berries

Sliced baguette

Fresh thyme

Quick Pickled Fennel (page 30)

Stuffed Pickled Sweet Peppers (page 30)

Bacon Jam (page 31)

→

BUILDING YOUR CHARCUTERIE BOARD

Cured meats so often play second fiddle to cheeses, why not give them their own spread? This decadent board is a crowd-pleaser, and though it seems elegant, almost all of the components are store-bought.

CHOOSE YOUR MEATS

To ensure a balance of texture and flavor, I like to choose a spreadable meat (such as pâté or 'nduja), a hard meat (such as pepperoni or chorizo), something soft and creamy (try mortadella), and a salty option (prosciutto is always a hit).

MAKE IT PRETTY

Here's how to add interest to a board that's mostly just meat. See pages 10–13 for more general board styling tips.

- **The Pile:** Take one slice and create a small nest, letting it fold over itself. Repeat with other slices and either group together or use to fill in empty spaces on the board. Perfect for prosciutto and other paper-thin cuts.

- **The Fold:** Folding pieces in either half or quarters and then fanning them out on the board not only makes it look attractive, the pieces are also easier to pick up. This is best for circular slices like deli salami and mortadella.

- **The Wrap:** Wrap thinly sliced meat around bread sticks, pretzel rods, figs, or melon slices. (Bonus: This strategy also keeps the wrapped item from rolling around the board.)

ADD EXTRAS

Add snackable items that provide contrast to the rich, fatty flavors. Include something neutral to serve the meats on (such as sliced baguette or crackers), mustard is a must (include a couple of varieties such as Dijon and whole-grain), and then fill out the rest of the board with briny things for contrast (the supermarket olive bar is your friend here—olives, caper berries, and pickled peppers are all great options).

CURED AND FERMENTED MEAT PRIMER:

Prosciutto: Made by seasoning, curing, pressing, and air-drying a pork thigh for as long as two years, this charcuterie board staple has an incredibly dense, silky texture and a delicate, nutty flavor.

Serrano ham: The Spaniards call it jamón serrano, literally "mountain ham," because the sheds where it's hung to dry are at high elevations. It's woodsy, earthy, and oh-so tender.

Capicola: Made from the shoulder or neck of a pig, capicola is seasoned with wine, garlic, herbs, and spices before it's cured and hung for months.

Salami: Salamis are a huge family of cured, boldly seasoned sausages (including pepperoni). Softer, larger salamis can be sliced at the deli like sandwich meat, while small, hard ones are usually sold whole.

Mortadella: Hailing from Bologna, Italy, this far-from-Oscar-Mayer meat is like an herby high-end baloney studded with pistachios and creamy chunks of fat.

'Nduja: Named for its resemblance to French andouille, this spreadable sausage is often made from a mix of pork shoulder, belly, and fatback as well as various less valuable cuts. It's liberally spiced to a fiery brick red and slow-fermented so it takes on a notable tangy funk.

MAKING A SALAMI ROSE:

1. Layer pieces of salami around the rim of a glass, working your way around the glass and overlapping the pieces as you go, until you have multiple layers.

2. Flip the glass and meat over onto your board to create a rose.

LEVEL UP YOUR CHARCUTERIE BOARD

Quick Pickled Fennel

Makes about 2 cups

At its peak, from fall through early spring, fennel is available when other vegetables commonly used for pickling (such as pickling cucumbers) are not. Fennel for pickling should be free of blemishes and soft spots; choose bulbs that are firm, small, and bright white in color.

- ¾ cup seasoned rice vinegar
- ¼ cup water
- 1 (1-inch) strip orange zest
- 1 garlic clove, peeled and halved
- ¼ teaspoon fennel seeds
- ⅛ teaspoon black peppercorns
- ⅛ teaspoon yellow mustard seeds
- 1 fennel bulb, stalks discarded, bulb halved, cored, and cut crosswise into ¼-inch-thick slices

1. Bring vinegar, water, zest, garlic, fennel seeds, peppercorns, and mustard seeds to boil in medium saucepan over medium-high heat.

2. Place one 1-pint jar under hot running water until heated through, about 1 minute; shake dry. Pack fennel into hot jar. Using funnel and ladle, pour hot brine over fennel to cover. Let jar cool to room temperature, about 30 minutes.

3. Cover jar with lid and refrigerate for at least 2½ hours before serving. (Pickled fennel can be refrigerated for up to 6 weeks; fennel will soften significantly after 6 weeks.)

Stuffed Pickled Sweet Peppers

Makes 25 peppers

I always pick these up at the olive bar, but they're almost just as easy to make yourself. Sweet cherry peppers are sold in jars and at the deli counter alongside the olives. If placing the peppers on a platter, help them stand upright by using a paring knife to trim the bottom of the peppers level.

- 3 tablespoons extra-virgin olive oil
- 1 tablespoon minced fresh parsley or basil
- 2 teaspoons lemon juice
- 1 garlic clove, minced
- ⅛ teaspoon table salt
  Pinch pepper
- 16 ounces pickled sweet cherry peppers (25 peppers)
- 6 ounces fontina cheese, cut into ½-inch cubes
- 7 ounces thinly sliced prosciutto, cut in half lengthwise

1. Whisk oil, parsley, lemon juice, garlic, salt, and pepper together in bowl; set aside.

2. Remove stem and core of peppers with paring knife. Rinse peppers well and pat dry with paper towels. Roll each piece of cheese inside 1 piece prosciutto and stuff inside cored peppers. Whisk dressing to recombine, then drizzle over peppers. (Dressing and peppers can be assembled and refrigerated separately for up to 24 hours. Bring to room temperature and drizzle peppers with dressing before serving.)

Bacon Jam

Makes about 1¼ cups

This supersavory jam is a perfect unexpected spreadable element. Do not use thick-cut bacon in this recipe. Cider vinegar is best here, but you can experiment with other vinegars if you like. You can use more or less cayenne to suit your preferences; the ⅛ teaspoon called for provides just a hint of heat.

- 1   pound bacon, cut crosswise into ½-inch-wide strips
- 2   cups thinly sliced onions
- 4   sprigs fresh thyme
- 2   garlic cloves, smashed and peeled
- 4   cups water
- ⅓   cup cider vinegar
- ⅓   cup maple syrup
- ⅛   teaspoon cayenne pepper

1. Cook bacon in 12-inch nonstick skillet over medium heat until crispy, 15 to 18 minutes. Using slotted spoon, transfer bacon to paper towel–lined plate; set aside. Pour off all but 2 tablespoons fat from skillet.

2. Heat fat left in skillet over medium heat until shimmering. Add onions, thyme sprigs, and garlic and cook until onion is softened and browned, 5 to 7 minutes. Stir in water, vinegar, maple syrup, cayenne, and reserved bacon. Increase heat to medium-high and bring to boil. Cook, stirring occasionally, until nearly all liquid has evaporated and mixture begins to sizzle loudly, 22 to 28 minutes.

3. Remove from heat and let cool for 15 minutes. Discard thyme sprigs. Transfer bacon mixture to food processor and pulse until minced, 15 to 20 pulses. Serve warm. (Jam can be refrigerated for up to 4 days. To serve, cover and microwave for 1 minute, stirring once halfway through microwaving.)

MORE THINGS TO ADD TO YOUR CHARCUTERIE BOARD:

- Candied nuts (see page 256)
- Pâté (see page 123)
- Cheese straws (see page 140)
- Prosciutto-wrapped dates (see page 140)
- Pickled red onion (see page 58)
- Cooked sausage
- Fresh figs or sliced melon to wrap prosciutto around
- Arugula or shaved celery tossed with lemon juice, EVOO, and flake sea salt

CRUDITÉS BOARD

Serves 4 to 6

ON THIS BOARD:

1½–3 pounds mixed vegetables
(see page 34)

Green Goddess Dip (page 36)

Whipped Cashew Dip with Roasted
Red Peppers and Olives (page 36)

Beet Tzatziki (page 36)

Prosciutto-Wrapped Asparagus
(page 37)

→

BUILDING YOUR CRUDITÉS BOARD

Once the days start getting longer and the snow starts to melt, I'm ready for any excuse to celebrate (New England winters are no joke). And the arrival of warmer weather can only mean one thing: farmers' market season. I love putting together this board with whatever I happened to have lugged home from the market in my overstuffed tote bag, plus some creamy, herby dips to kiss winter goodbye in style.

CHOOSE YOUR VEGGIES

This board is all about the veggies, so be sure to use the most gorgeous looking produce possible. I like to do my vegetable shopping at the farmers' market—not only can you find the freshest stuff, it's where you can score interesting veggie varieties (like purple cauliflower!). This board can easily be switched up depending on the season—try a roasted vegetable board in the colder months. Plan on 4 to 6 ounces of vegetables per person.

GET DIPPING

What's a crudités platter without the dip? I've listed a few of my favorites on page 36, but any combination of homemade and store-bought will do just fine. Hummus (store-bought or the homemade recipe on page 79) is a fail-safe option, and so are ranch (see page 95), blue cheese (see page 95), and pesto. And of course, who doesn't love French onion dip? Plan on approximately ½ cup of dip per person.

ARRANGE WITH CONFIDENCE

I find it easiest to put my dips down first and then build the veggies around them. Use longer vegetables (like green beans or carrots) along the edge to highlight the length of the board and provide a little structure, and put smaller pieces in the middle to show variety and color. Keep raw vegetables in an ice bath while you're arranging your board to crisp things up and keep it all looking fresh.

PERFECT PREP

Vegetables are the star of the show here, so it's important to get them looking their best. To store crudités, refrigerate raw vegetables wrapped in damp paper towels in a zipper-lock bag and blanched vegetables in an airtight container for up to 2 days. Here's how to treat each veggie right.

Asparagus: To remove the tough, fibrous ends of the asparagus, bend the thick end of each stalk until it snaps off. Blanch the asparagus for 30 to 60 seconds.

Broccoli and cauliflower: Cut broccoli and cauliflower florets into bite-size pieces (see page 94 for tips on how to do it without making a mess). Blanch broccoli and cauliflower (separately) for 1 to 1½ minutes.

Carrots and celery: Slice both celery and peeled carrots lengthwise into long, elegant lengths rather than short, stumpy pieces. Leave the tops on the carrots, and go to the heart of the celery to find the most tender, leafy stalks.

Cucumbers: Use Persian or English cucumbers (fewer seeds and more-tender skin) and cut them into both long spears and elongated coins for visual interest.

Green beans: Line beans up in a row and trim off inedible stem ends with just 1 cut. Blanch beans for 1 minute.

Peppers: Slice off top and bottom of pepper and remove seeds and stem. Slice down through side of pepper, unroll it so that it lies flat, then slice into ½-inch-wide strips.

Radishes: Choose radishes with green tops still attached so that each half has a leafy handle for grasping and dipping. Slice each radish in half through stem.

BLANCHING DIRECTIONS:

Bring 6 quarts water and 2 tablespoons table salt to boil in large pot over high heat. Cook vegetables, 1 variety at a time, until slightly softened but still crunchy at core, following times given for individual vegetables at left. Transfer blanched vegetables immediately to bowl of ice water to soak until completely cool, then drain and pat dry.

LEVEL UP YOUR CRUDITÉS BOARD

Whipped Cashew Dip with Roasted Red Peppers and Olives
Makes 2 cups

- 1½ cups raw cashews
- ½ cup jarred roasted red peppers, rinsed, patted dry, and chopped
- 3 tablespoons water
- 3 tablespoons extra-virgin olive oil
- 3 tablespoons lemon juice
- 1 garlic clove, minced
- ½ cup minced fresh parsley
- ½ cup pitted kalamata olives, chopped

1. Place cashews in bowl and add cold water to cover by 1 inch. Let sit at room temperature for at least 12 hours or up to 24 hours. Drain and rinse well.

2. Process soaked cashews, red peppers, water, oil, lemon juice, and garlic in food processor until smooth, about 2 minutes, scraping down sides of bowl as needed. Transfer cashew mixture to bowl, stir in parsley and olives, and season with salt and pepper to taste. Cover with plastic wrap and let sit at room temperature until flavors meld, about 30 minutes, before serving. (Dip can be refrigerated for up to 2 days.)

Beet Tzatziki
Makes 2 cups

- ½ cucumber (6 ounces), peeled, halved lengthwise, seeded, and shredded
- 6 ounces raw beets, peeled and grated
- ½ teaspoon table salt
- 1 cup whole-milk Greek yogurt
- 2 tablespoons extra-virgin olive oil
- 2 tablespoons minced fresh mint and/or dill
- 1 small garlic clove, minced

Toss cucumber and beets with salt in colander and let drain for 15 minutes. Whisk yogurt, oil, mint, and garlic together in bowl, then stir in drained cucumber. Cover and refrigerate until chilled, at least 1 hour or up to 2 days. Season with salt and pepper to taste and serve.

Green Goddess Dip
Makes 1¾ cups

- ¾ cup mayonnaise
- ¾ cup sour cream
- ¼ cup minced fresh parsley
- ¼ cup minced fresh chives
- 2 tablespoons minced fresh tarragon
- 1 tablespoon lemon juice
- 2 garlic cloves, minced
- ⅛ teaspoon salt
- ⅛ teaspoon pepper

Whisk all ingredients together in serving bowl until smooth and creamy. Cover with plastic wrap and refrigerate until flavors are blended, at least 1 hour or up to 2 days.

Prosciutto-Wrapped Asparagus

Serves 4 to 6

I like to incorporate a cooked component to my crudités board whenever I have the time. These warm prosciutto-wrapped spears are supersimple (and a great way to eat your veggies!). If necessary, you can substitute thin asparagus for thick: Just roll two thin spears into each bundle. Don't overcook the asparagus in step 3 or the prosciutto will turn tough and leathery; the spears should just be warmed through before serving.

 2   pounds thick asparagus, trimmed

 2   teaspoons extra-virgin olive oil

 1   (5.2-ounce) package Boursin Garlic & Fine Herbs
     cheese, room temperature

16   thin slices prosciutto (8 ounces), cut in half crosswise

1. Adjust oven rack 3 inches from broiler element and heat broiler. Toss asparagus with oil and lay in single layer on rimmed baking sheet. Broil until asparagus is crisp-tender, about 5 minutes, tossing halfway through broiling. Let asparagus cool slightly.

2. Spread Boursin evenly over each piece of prosciutto. Roll prosciutto around center of each asparagus spear and transfer to clean rimmed baking sheet.

3. Adjust oven rack to middle position and heat oven to 450 degrees. Bake prosciutto-wrapped asparagus until just warmed through, about 5 minutes. Serve warm.

FIRST THINGS FIRST

Breakfast Boards for Any Time of Day

41 **Granola Parfaits**

47 **Low-Lift Brunch**

55 **Bagels and Lox**

61 **Breakfast Tacos**

69 **Bloody Mary Bar**

GRANOLA PARFAITS

Serves 4 to 6

START WITH:

The Ultimate Granola Bark (page 43)

Yogurt (regular and/or Greek)

Fresh fruit (strawberries, bananas, blackberries, raspberries, blueberries, grapefruit, oranges)

Something sweet to drizzle (agave, honey, and/or maple syrup)

IF YOU WANT, ADD:

Strawberry Compote (page 45)

Dried fruit (cranberries, apricots, kiwis)

Chocolate chips

Fresh mint

Fig jam (or any type of jam)

$\longrightarrow$

GRANOLA PARFAITS

I love granola parfaits—the creamy yogurt tang plus sweet granola crunch is a match made in flavor heaven. Turning them into a board feels like such an impressively elegant breakfast to set out for guests, but the truth is it's so easy. And the parfaits really can be whatever you want. Got a lot of kiddos in your crew? Mix in some flavored yogurts and crunchy cereals. More of a health-conscious group? Go for plain Greek and plenty of nuts and seeds.

ELLE'S STRATEGY:

Set up shop. Having more than one place to access the yogurt is important—it keeps a bottleneck from happening. Break things up by having multiple trays, and arrange dishes of dried fruit and sweet stuff on one side, fresh fruit on the other (both add different elements, and if you're a dried fruit person, you're probably piling it on). Use fresh mint as a garnish and to fill out the tray. Set out a variety of glasses, and make sure you have enough spoons, for both serving and eating.

Get a head start. Granola can be made 2 weeks ahead of time, and compote 3 days ahead. Wash your berries right when you get home from the store so they're good to go; they'll keep in the fridge for 4 days. Make sure your pantry is stocked with dried fruit and other goodies.

Switch it up with the season. Try an apple butter–cinnamon-walnut version in the fall, or a blood orange–vanilla option to make the most of winter citrus season. Fruit looking a little lackluster? Toss it with jam or honey to give it new life.

Dial it back (if you want). Pressed for time? Keep things simple with store-bought granola and no-prep fruit (like berries) and other easy toppings (think dried fruit and honey).

Glass game strong. Don't feel tied to a traditional parfait glass—any vessel that can be accessed with a spoon is on the table. Set out a variety of sizes and shapes, from cups and juice glasses to small bowls and jars.

The Ultimate Granola Bark

I'm more of a "yogurt-as-a-garnish" person as far as parfaits are concerned, so it's all about the granola for me. And nothing impresses quite like the homemade stuff. This recipe bakes into one big sheet that you break up into shards as big (or as small) as you want after it's cooled a bit. The secret is to firmly pack the granola mixture into a rimmed baking sheet before baking, and don't touch it once it's in the oven (bonus points for the hands-off situation!).

Almond-Raisin Granola

Makes about 9 cups
Do not use quick oats here. Chopping the nuts, seeds, and dried fruit by hand ensures even texture and superior crunch; avoid using a food processor.

- ½ cup vegetable oil
- ⅓ cup maple syrup
- ⅓ cup packed (2⅓ ounces) light brown sugar
- 4 teaspoons vanilla extract
- ½ teaspoon table salt
- 5 cups (15 ounces) old-fashioned rolled oats
- 2 cups (10 ounces) raw almonds, chopped coarse
- 2 cups (10 ounces) raisins, chopped

1. Adjust oven rack to upper-middle position and heat oven to 325 degrees. Line rimmed baking sheet with parchment paper. Spray parchment with vegetable oil spray.

2. Whisk oil, maple syrup, sugar, vanilla, and salt together in large bowl. Fold in oats and almonds until thoroughly combined.

3. Transfer oat mixture to prepared sheet and spread across entire surface of sheet in even layer. Using stiff metal spatula, press down firmly on oat mixture until very compact. Bake until lightly browned, 35 to 40 minutes, rotating sheet halfway through baking.

4. Transfer sheet to wire rack and let granola cool completely, about 1 hour. Break cooled granola into pieces of desired size. Stir in raisins and serve. (Granola can be stored in airtight container for up to 2 weeks.)

VARIATIONS

Apricot-Orange Granola
Substitute 1 cup raw pepitas, chopped coarse, for almonds and dried apricots for raisins. Add 1 tablespoon grated orange zest to oil mixture in step 2.

Cherry–Chocolate Chip Granola
Substitute dried cherries for raisins. Add 1 cup mini semisweet chocolate chips to mixture with dried cherries in step 4.

Honey-Pecan Granola
Substitute honey for sugar and pecans for almonds. Add 1 tablespoon ground cinnamon to oil mixture in step 2.

Salted Caramel–Peanut Granola
Omit raisins. Increase salt to 1½ teaspoons. Substitute ¾ cup jarred caramel sauce for sugar and unsalted dry-roasted peanuts for almonds.

KEEP IT FRESH:

Nobody likes a mushy, moldy berry. Break out the vinegar to keep these summertime gems from spoiling:

1. Right when you get home from the store, wash the berries in a bowl of 3 cups water and 1 cup distilled white vinegar. Drain them in a colander and rinse under running water.

2. Place the berries in a salad spinner lined with three layers of paper towels. Spin for 15 seconds, or until the berries are completely dry. Store the berries in a loosely covered, paper towel–lined container at the front of the fridge for up to 4 days.

LEVEL UP YOUR BOARD

Strawberry Compote

Makes about 2 cups

This simple compote—like preserves without the hassle (no canning skills needed!)—is full of strawberry goodness. Try to buy smaller berries; they have better flavor than larger ones. Quarter any berries larger than a Ping-Pong ball. It's important to pull the strawberries from the heat as soon as the mixture begins to bubble and thicken in order to not overcook them.

⅓ cup (2⅓ ounces) sugar

1 tablespoon cornstarch

Pinch table salt

¼ cup water

1 pound strawberries, hulled and halved or quartered if large (2½ cups)

2 teaspoons lemon juice

1. Whisk sugar, cornstarch, and salt in medium saucepan until no lumps of cornstarch remain. Whisk in water. Stir in strawberries until evenly coated with sugar mixture.

2. Cook over medium heat, stirring occasionally, until bubbles begin to form around edge of saucepan and mixture thickens, about 5 minutes.

3. Immediately transfer compote to bowl. Stir in lemon juice. (Mixture will be very thick but will thin as strawberries sit and continue to release their juice.) Let cool completely, about 30 minutes. Serve. (Compote can be refrigerated for up to 3 days.)

VARIATIONS

Strawberry-Lime Compote

Substitute ½ teaspoon grated lime zest plus 2 teaspoons juice for lemon juice.

Strawberry-Vanilla Compote

Substitute 1 teaspoon vanilla extract for lemon juice.

GO FOR THE GRANOLA FIRST:

Build the perfect parfait by starting with a little granola in the bottom of your cup before adding yogurt and more toppings. It keeps you from having to scrape out yogurt from the bottom of the glass.

EVERYONE LOVES A THEME:

If you want to get all chichi froufrou with it, try these flavor combos to take things up a notch:

- **Chocolate covered strawberries:** Strawberry compote + chocolate chips

- **French toast:** Cinnamon Toast Crunch cereal + pecans + maple syrup drizzle

- **Go nuts:** Slivered almonds + toasted walnuts + chia seeds

- **Mai tai:** Fresh oranges + slivered almonds + lime zest

- **Monkeying around:** Sliced bananas + chopped peanuts

- **Piña colada:** Toasted coconut + pineapple + cashews

- **Raspberry lemonade:** Fresh raspberries + lemon zest

- **Shirley Temple:** Maraschino cherries + pomegranate seeds + fresh mint

- **Snack attack:** Crushed pretzels + peanut butter chips

LOW-LIFT BRUNCH

Serves 6 to 8

START WITH:

Muffin Tin Frittatas (page 50)

Store-bought pastries (scones, toaster pastries, biscuits, banana bread, croissants, coffee cake)

Toast

Jam (apricot, raspberry, mixed berry)

Butter

IF YOU WANT, ADD:

Hands-Off Bacon (see page 50)

Juice (orange, cranberry, and/or peach nectar)

Sparkling wine

Fruit for garnishing mimosas (oranges, frozen grapes)

→

LOW-LIFT BRUNCH

This classic brunch is always a hit with guests (and something I can put together before I've had my first cup of coffee). It's perfect for lingering over, which is why I always buy more pastries than I might think I need: People are always breaking off pieces of coffee cake or other delectables to nosh on; it's all about variety. The key here is getting high-quality baked goods, ideally from a local bakery. Balance all that sweetness with savory mini frittatas and crispy hands-off bacon for a few homemade touches that make this supersimple board feel a little extra special.

ELLE'S STRATEGY:

Set up shop. Keep the frittatas warm in the oven in a small baking dish, and have everything set up before your bring them out. Put toast in a bowl or basket lined with a clean dish towel to keep it warm. Set out mini knives with jam and butter. Cut the cakes and breads into slices and set out with the pastries. Use a large cutting board so people feel free to cut the pastries into smaller pieces and hot things can rest without needing a trivet.

Get a head start. Make frittatas up to 5 days in advance. Shop for your pastries and fruit the day before, so when the morning comes all you have to do is make the bacon. (Bonus: It'll make your kitchen smell brunchy.)

Keep it simple. You could serve up some homemade pastries, but it's easiest to head to your favorite local bakery and pick up some treats (the pictured pastries are from Joanne Chang's Flour Bakery + Cafe in Boston, a definite fave). It's a low-lift way to fill out the board without creating more work for yourself.

Expand your drink horizons. A mimosa bar is always a hit, but you can switch up your choice of beverages depending on your crowd's tastes. Try Bloody Marys (see page 71), coffee, tea, or even hot chocolate.

Muffin Tin Frittatas

Makes 12 frittatas

Easier than making eggs to order, and perfect for using up bits and bobs kicking around your fridge, these mini frittatas are customizable and crowd-friendly. The main recipe can easily be doubled (use two tins), or make both fillings but halve each recipe to make two different types in a single muffin tin.

 8 large eggs

 ¼ cup half-and-half

 ½ teaspoon pepper

 ¼ teaspoon table salt

 1 recipe frittata filling (recipes follow)

1. Adjust oven rack to lower-middle position and heat oven to 425 degrees. Generously spray 12-cup nonstick muffin tin with vegetable oil spray. Whisk eggs, half-and-half, pepper, and salt together in large bowl.

2. Divide filling evenly among muffin cups. Using ladle or liquid measuring cup, evenly distribute egg mixture over filling in muffin cups. Bake until frittatas are lightly puffed and just set in centers, 9 to 11 minutes. Transfer muffin tin to wire rack and let frittatas cool for 10 minutes. Run plastic knife around edges of frittatas, if necessary, to loosen from muffin tin, then gently remove and serve. (Frittatas can be refrigerated for up to 5 days. To reheat, place frittatas on greased, foil-lined baking sheet or 13 by 9-inch baking dish and bake in 350-degree oven for 10 minutes.)

HANDS-OFF BACON:

It's no fun to be tied to the stove, turning bacon until it's crispy. Instead, arrange 12 slices of bacon on a rimmed baking sheet (crucial to contain the rendered bacon fat) and cook in a 400-degree oven until the fat begins to render, 5 to 6 minutes. Rotate the sheet and continue to cook until the bacon is crispy and brown, 5 to 6 minutes longer for thin-cut bacon or 8 to 10 minutes longer for thick-cut. Transfer bacon to paper towel–lined plate, let drain, and serve.

Hosting a crowd? Double the amount of bacon and use two rimmed baking sheets. Just be sure to rotate the sheets and switch their oven positions about halfway through cooking.

Frittata Fillings

Each recipe makes enough filling for 12 frittatas. For a half-batch, halve the ingredients, use a 10-inch skillet, and reduce the sauté time to 8 to 10 minutes. You can prepare the egg and filling mixtures up to 24 hours in advance; refrigerate them separately.

Chorizo, Parsley, and Pepper Jack Filling

- 1 tablespoon extra-virgin olive oil
- 8 ounces Spanish-style chorizo sausage, quartered lengthwise and sliced thin
- 8 ounces Yukon Gold potatoes, unpeeled, quartered lengthwise and sliced thin
- 1 large onion, chopped fine
- ½ teaspoon table salt
- 2 garlic cloves, minced
- 6 ounces pepper Jack cheese, shredded (1½ cups)
- 3 tablespoons minced fresh parsley

Heat oil in 12-inch nonstick skillet over medium heat until shimmering. Add chorizo, potatoes, onion, and salt and cook, stirring occasionally, until potatoes are tender, 10 to 15 minutes. Stir in garlic and cook until fragrant, about 30 seconds. Transfer to bowl and let cool for 15 minutes. Stir in pepper Jack and parsley.

Asparagus, Dill, and Goat Cheese Filling

- 2 tablespoons extra-virgin olive oil
- 8 ounces Yukon Gold potatoes, unpeeled, quartered lengthwise and sliced thin
- 1 large onion, chopped fine
- ½ teaspoon table salt
- 8 ounces asparagus, trimmed and sliced thin
- 2 garlic cloves, minced
- 6 ounces goat cheese, crumbled (1½ cups)
- 1 tablespoon minced fresh dill

Heat oil in 12-inch nonstick skillet over medium heat until shimmering. Add potatoes, onion, and salt and cook, stirring occasionally, until potatoes are tender, 10 to 15 minutes. Stir in asparagus and garlic and cook until fragrant, about 30 seconds. Transfer to bowl and let cool for 15 minutes. Stir in goat cheese and dill.

LEVEL UP YOUR BOARD

Mimosa

Makes 1 cocktail

- 2½ ounces orange juice, plus orange slice for garnishing (optional)
- ¼ ounce orange liqueur
- 3 ounces dry sparkling wine, such as prosecco or cava, chilled

Add orange juice and liqueur to chilled wine glass or flute glass and stir to combine. Add wine and, using spoon, gently lift juice mixture from bottom to top of glass to combine. Garnish with orange slice, if using, and serve.

VARIATION

Bellini

Substitute peach juice or nectar for orange juice, and peach schnapps for orange liqueur. Garnish with thin slice of peach instead of orange slice, if desired.

Orange-Thyme Spritzer

Makes 1 drink

For your guests who may not want to indulge in a boozy breakfast, offer this mimosa-like option.

- 4 ounces orange juice, plus orange slice for garnishing (optional)
- ½ ounce Herb Soda Syrup made with thyme (see page 107)
- 4 ounces seltzer, chilled

Fill glass halfway with ice. Add orange juice and herb syrup and stir to combine using spoon. Add seltzer and, using spoon, gently lift orange mixture from bottom of glass to top to combine. Top with additional ice. Garnish with orange slice, if using, and serve.

VARIATION

Grapefruit-Rosemary Spritzer

Substitute grapefruit juice for orange juice and Herb Soda Syrup made with rosemary for thyme syrup. Garnish with grapefruit slice instead of orange slice, if desired.

SETTING UP A BRUNCH COCKTAIL BAR:

If you don't want to make your drinks to order, set out an array of juices, chilled sparkling wine, and fun garnishes so your guests can help themselves to a mimosa, Bellini, or spritzer. Here's what you need to pop bottles like a pro.

Sparkling wine: The MVP of the mimosa. The juice hides the nuances of the wine, so don't bother shelling out for the good stuff. Be sure to keep the wine chilled, either in the fridge or an ice bucket. A 750-ml bottle yields 5 glasses and 8 cocktails. (You know your crowd best, but I usually plan on at least 2 cocktails per person.) Include seltzer for those who prefer spritzers.

Juices: The sky is the limit. Classic orange is essential, but beyond that, try cranberry, grapefruit, and even nectars like peach or mango. Fresh squeeze it if you feel like getting fancy. Plan on about ¼ cup per cocktail.

Glasses: Flutes are best, but if you don't have them, really, any glass will work. We're mixing champagne with juice here, there's no need for pretenses.

Great garnishes: It's fun to add a little flair to your glass. For an orange wedge, cut your oranges along the equator into thin slices, then cut each wheel into quarters. Add a slit starting at the point and perch it on your glass. (Or, see page 141 for tips on making citrus twists. Use an orange instead of a lemon.) But my all-time favorite garnish is frozen grapes. Pop one in your drink to keep it extra cold without watering it down like ice would.

LEFTOVERS? DON'T PANIC.

Once you've popped open a bottle of bubbly, it's a race against the clock to finish it before it goes flat. If you opened one too many for your party, here's how to use it up (beyond the obvious... just drink it).

Store it. Seal the bottle with plastic wrap and secure tightly with a rubber band to preserve bubbles for a couple of days. Even better, use a champagne saver (try the Cilio brand) to keep leftover sparkling wine fresh and fizzy for up to a week.

Get fruity. Make an elegantly easy dessert: Toss berries and sliced peaches with sugar and lemon zest and let marinate in the fridge. Just before serving, pour sparkling wine over the top. Or, add sparkling wine to a fruit topping for pavlovas (see page 236).

Cook with it. If you waited too long and now it's flat, use it as you would wine in any recipe.

BAGELS AND LOX

Serves 4 to 6

START WITH:

Bagels and/or bialys

No-cook toppings (avocado, Bibb lettuce, capers, cucumbers, fresh dill, lemon wedges, olives, radishes, red onion, alfalfa sprouts, tomatoes)

Lox and/or smoked salmon

Easy Cream Cheese Spreads (page 57)

IF YOU WANT, ADD:

Everything Bagel Seasoning (page 58)

Pickled Red Onion (page 58)

Easy-Peel Hard-Cooked Eggs (page 176)

Bagel Chips (page 58)

More smoked fish (see page 57)

→

BAGELS AND LOX

My great-grandmother was the food service director for a Jewish nursing home and I was a kosher private chef when I lived in New York, so I've made (and eaten) my fair share of bagel boards. It's all about shopping here, so go for the good stuff. Look for high-quality bagels with a glossy exterior and good chew, and don't stop with lox—add other smoked fish like whitefish, sturgeon, mackerel, or sable (my favorite!) to mix things up.

ELLE'S STRATEGY:

Set up shop. Bagels take up a lot of real estate, so start by arranging them on one end and build the other components up to them so you don't run out of room (replenish as needed). Create a lettuce or sprouts nest for the fish, folding up the salmon so the slices don't stick together, and arrange the other toppings in long trails for easy access. Sprinkle the board with capers and olives. Set out the cream cheeses along with small knives for spreading and some small forks for the fish and toppings.

Get a head start. I like to freeze bagels so I'm always ready for a bagel party; just be sure to slice them first. The everything bagel seasoning can be made up to 3 months ahead of time, and the cream cheeses and pickled red onion can each be made up to 1 week ahead of time.

Paper thin, please. Slicing the toppings superthin looks prettier, and makes your towering bagel concoction easier to eat. Use a serrated knife for the tomatoes.

Up your schmear game. You can never go wrong with crowd-pleasing plain cream cheese, but I usually like to add one or two homemade versions for my board. If you want, skip the pieces of fish altogether and make the smoked salmon cream cheese.

Beyond the bagel. People usually want seconds, but might not want another bagel. Slice bagels into smaller pieces so people can scoop up some cream cheese. Or suggest guests make a salad with the toppings (you could even include a balsamic drizzle, see page 148).

Easy Cream Cheese Spreads

These light, fluffy, flavored cream cheeses are fresher than anything you can get in the store, and they come together in less than 30 seconds. Whipping them in a food processor ensures the flavorings are evenly dispersed and the texture is nice and smooth. For the creamiest results, let the cream cheese come to room temperature before processing. Forgot to take it out of the fridge in time? Never fear. Just microwave it in a large bowl for 20 to 30 seconds. All of the spreads can be refrigerated in an airtight container for up to 1 week.

Garlic and Herb Cream Cheese Spread
Makes 1 cup

- 8 ounces cream cheese, softened
- ½ cup fresh parsley leaves
- ¼ cup fresh basil leaves
- 1 teaspoon lemon juice
- 1 small garlic clove, minced to paste
- ¼ teaspoon table salt
- ¼ teaspoon pepper

Process all ingredients in food processor until smooth, about 20 seconds, scraping down sides of bowl as needed. Serve.

VARIATIONS

Olive and Scallion Cream Cheese Spread
Reduce cream cheese to 6 ounces. Omit lemon juice, garlic, and salt; increase pepper to 1 teaspoon. Instead of parsley and basil, use ½ cup pitted kalamata olives (patted dry) plus 2 teaspoons brine and 4 chopped scallions.

Smoked Salmon and Chive Cream Cheese Spread
Omit garlic and salt. Substitute ¼ cup chopped fresh chives for parsley and basil and add 2 ounces sliced smoked salmon, torn into 2-inch pieces.

Honey-Rosemary Cream Cheese Spread
Omit lemon juice and garlic. Instead of parsley and basil, use 2 tablespoons honey and 1 tablespoon minced fresh rosemary.

Cinnamon-Sugar Cream Cheese Spread
Omit lemon juice, garlic, salt, and pepper. Instead of parsley and basil, use 2 tablespoons packed brown sugar and 1 teaspoon ground cinnamon.

A SALMON BY ANY OTHER NAME:

Brush up on your fishy vocabulary to get your bagel game on like a pro. For your board, plan on 2 to 3 ounces of fish per person.

Smoked salmon: Can be either hot- or cold-smoked. (Hot-smoked salmon is also called kippered salmon.) Cold-smoked salmon—what you probably associate with smoked salmon—is technically not cooked, as the fish usually never gets hotter than 85 degrees, but the combination of the smoke and a presmoke cure (in salt and sugar) makes it safe to eat.

Lox: Comes from the belly of the salmon and is salt-cured but not smoked. **Nova lox,** which also comes from the belly of the salmon, is traditionally made from Nova Scotia–fished salmon, and is cold-smoked after curing (although you can now buy "nova lox" fished and smoked in other parts of the world).

Gravlax: Similar to lox, gravlax is salt-cured and not smoked, but it is traditionally seasoned with dill and often includes sugar and other seasonings (such as juniper, horseradish, pepper, and/or liquor) in the cure. Gravlax is weighted during curing; this speeds up the curing process and gives it a more compact texture. Traditional Scandinavian methods call for burying the salmon in the ground; in Swedish, *grav* means "grave" and *lax* means "salmon."

LEVEL UP YOUR BOARD

Everything Bagel Seasoning

Makes about ½ cup

You can find bagel seasoning pre-mixed in most stores, but if I'm feeling extra, I mix up my own batch. Serve in a bowl with a spoon for your guests to sprinkle, or scatter this magic dust over your toppings for an extra dose of seasoning. (Furikake on page 121 and Za'atar are also great sprinkling options.) But the fun doesn't have to stop there; it's also delicious on macaroni and cheese (page 202), hummus (page 79), pizza, and even instant ramen. Toast the seeds in a dry skillet over medium heat until fragrant (about 1 minute), then remove the skillet from the heat so the seeds won't scorch.

- 2 tablespoons sesame seeds, toasted
- 2 tablespoons poppy seeds
- 1 tablespoon caraway seeds, toasted
- 1 tablespoon kosher salt
- 1 tablespoon dried minced onion
- 1 tablespoon dried minced garlic

Combine all ingredients in bowl. (Seasoning can be stored in airtight container for up to 3 months.)

Pickled Red Onion

Makes about 1 cup

Quick pickling mellows out the harshness of red onion and brings a little zing to everything it touches. You can also add these to breakfast tacos (page 61), nachos (page 97), sandwiches, and salads. Be patient while the mixture cools— that time is essential for the flavors to meld together.

- 1 cup red wine vinegar
- ⅓ cup sugar
- ⅛ teaspoon table salt
- 1 red onion, halved and sliced thin through root end

Microwave vinegar, sugar, and salt in medium bowl until steaming, 1 to 2 minutes. Stir in onion and let sit, stirring occasionally, for 45 minutes. (Pickled onions can be refrigerated for up to 1 week.)

LEFTOVERS? DON'T PANIC.

If you've got some extras but you're all bageled out, turn them into brunchy chips and dip. The exact measurements for the dip may vary based on how much you have left over, but it's good to stick to a 2:1 cream cheese-to-salmon ratio.

Make bagel chips. Slice bagels vertically, ¼ inch thick, and arrange in a single layer on a rimmed baking sheet. Brush tops with oil and sprinkle with salt; flip slices and repeat on other sides. Bake in a 350-degree oven until crisp and light golden brown, 13 to 17 minutes. (Chips can be stored in airtight container for up to 3 days.)

Make smoked salmon dip. Process cream cheese, smoked salmon, lemon zest and juice, and pepper in food processor until smooth, about 30 seconds, scraping down sides of bowl as needed. Transfer to serving dish and spread into even layer. Sprinkle with minced red onion, capers, minced dill, and/or Everything Bagel Seasoning. Drizzle with extra-virgin olive oil and serve with bagel chips or extra sliced cucumber.

BREAKFAST TACOS

Serves 4 to 6

START WITH:

Scrambled Eggs (page 65)

Tortillas (flour or corn)

Cheese (shredded cheddar, pepper Jack, Monterey Jack, or cotija)

Fresh toppings (scallions, avocado, pickled jalapeños, cilantro, lime wedges)

Hot sauces

IF YOU WANT, ADD:

Salsa Roja (page 66)

Sautéed Poblanos, Beans, and Corn (page 66)

Chorizo and/or bacon (see page 50)

Potatoes (frozen hash browns or tater tots)

→

BREAKFAST TACOS

Whenever I cook breakfast for a crowd, I'm usually the last person to eat. There's nothing fun about feeling like a short-order cook, which is why I love making a breakfast taco spread. That way, I can get everything set up, scramble some eggs, and dig in with everybody else. Plus, it's the perfect excuse to display my hot sauce collection. You could add any of your Southwest favorites here, like guacamole (see page 99), pickled red onion (see page 58), and crema (see page 101).

ELLE'S STRATEGY:

Set up shop. I like using a really long serving board here because it functions like an assembly line (tortillas and eggs first, followed by toppings, and finally sauces). But any shape board will do, or even small dishes of toppings set out in a logical layering order. Be sure to keep the tortillas warm (see page 64), and leave the eggs in the skillet so as much heat is contained as possible.

Get a head start. Salsa Roja can be made up to 3 days ahead of time, and your no-cook toppings (except for avocados) can be prepared the night before. You can even set everything up on the board, cover it in plastic wrap, and let it sit in your fridge overnight.

Mix it up. Take this equation and turn it into a breakfast sandwich bar. Keep the eggs the same, but swap English muffins for tortillas and include different types of toppings like arugula, smoked salmon, prosciutto, sliced cheeses, pesto, aioli, or even chili crisp.

Timing is everything. Nothing is worse than cold eggs, so get everything set up before you scramble them. Once you're ready to go, char the tortillas and set them aside, then scramble the eggs. Let everyone know it's time to eat just before the eggs are finished, so once you set the eggs down people can dig in.

CHARRING TORTILLAS:

1. If you have a gas stove, hold one tortilla with tongs over the flame, turning every few seconds to get an even char. If you have an electric stove, heat a little oil in a skillet and warm the tortilla over medium-high heat, turning every few seconds.

2. Wrap the tortillas in a clean dish towel to keep warm. Or, get a tortilla warmer (look for the brand Imusa's cloth version).

Scrambled Eggs

Serves 4 to 6

Be sure to follow the visual cues when making the eggs as your pan's thickness will affect the cooking time. If you're using an electric stovetop, heat a second burner on low and move the skillet to it when it's time to adjust the heat.

- 12 large eggs
- ½ teaspoon table salt
- ¼ teaspoon pepper
- 2 tablespoons unsalted butter

1. Whisk eggs, salt, and pepper in bowl until thoroughly combined and mixture is pure yellow, about 1 minute. Melt butter in 12-inch nonstick skillet over medium heat. Add egg mixture and, using heat-resistant rubber spatula, constantly and firmly scrape along bottom and sides of skillet until eggs begin to clump and spatula leaves trail on bottom of skillet, 1½ to 2½ minutes.

2. Reduce heat to low. Gently but constantly fold egg mixture until clumped and slightly wet, 30 to 60 seconds. Season with salt and pepper to taste. Serve immediately.

VARIATION

Migas

Omit butter. Heat 3 tablespoons vegetable oil in 12-inch nonstick skillet over medium-high heat until shimmering. Cut 6 (6-inch) corn tortillas into 1 by ½-inch strips, then add to the pan and cook, stirring occasionally, until golden brown, 4 to 6 minutes. Add 1 finely chopped onion, 1 finely chopped bell pepper, and 1 tablespoon minced jalapeño and cook until vegetables are softened, 5 to 7 minutes. Add egg mixture to tortilla mixture and proceed with recipe as directed. Before serving, gently fold in ⅓ cup shredded Monterey Jack and 1 tablespoon chopped fresh cilantro.

HOW TO MAKE PERFECT EGGS:

Scrambled eggs may seem simple enough, but follow these tips to really up your game.

Salt your raw eggs. Adding salt to the raw eggs makes for more-tender curds. In the same way that soaking a piece of pork in a brine denatures its proteins so that it's better able to hold on to moisture, salt dissolves egg proteins so that they're unable to bond as tightly when cooked.

Don't overbeat. Aggressively whisking the eggs can cause them to cook up tough. If you can't whisk with restraint, use a fork to break up the yolks and combine them with the whites. When everything in the bowl registers the same homogeneous color, you're done.

For richer, creamier eggs, add more yolks. To really take your eggs to the next level, whisk in a couple extra yolks. They not only enrich the egg flavor, but also provide extra fat and emulsifiers that raise the coagulation temperature to stave off overcooking.

Use a dual-heat cooking method. Adding the eggs to the skillet over medium-high heat will give the eggs a lift as soon as they hit the pan (and constantly stirring them will help achieve large, evenly cooked curds). Then, when your spatula leaves a trail through the eggs, turn the heat down to low until they're glossy, moist, and clumpy.

LEVEL UP YOUR BOARD

Salsa Roja

Makes about 1½ cups

This drizzle-able, slightly spicy, tomatoey sauce—meant to be served warm—brings breakfast tacos to life. To make the salsa spicier, reserve and add the jalapeño seeds to the blender before processing. Make sure to drain the tomatoes after microwaving them so that the salsa does not become too watery.

- 1 pound plum tomatoes, cored and chopped
- 2 garlic cloves, chopped
- 1 jalapeño chile, stemmed, seeded, and chopped
- 2 tablespoons chopped fresh cilantro
- 1 tablespoon lime juice
- 1 teaspoon table salt
- ¼ teaspoon red pepper flakes

1. Combine tomatoes and garlic in bowl and microwave, uncovered, until steaming and liquid begins to pool in bottom of bowl, about 4 minutes. Transfer tomato mixture to fine-mesh strainer set over bowl and let drain for 5 minutes.

2. Combine jalapeño, cilantro, lime juice, salt, pepper flakes, and drained tomato mixture in blender. Process until smooth, about 45 seconds. Season with salt to taste. Serve warm. (Salsa can be refrigerated for up to 3 days; cover and microwave briefly to rewarm before serving.)

Sautéed Poblanos, Beans, and Corn

Makes about 3 cups

Perfect for adding heft to your taco or even replacing eggs for vegan guests, this bean sauté comes together quickly and without a whole lot of planning thanks to canned beans and frozen corn.

- 1 tablespoon vegetable oil
- 2 poblano chiles, stemmed, seeded, and chopped
- 1 (15-ounce) can pinto beans, rinsed
- 1 cup frozen corn
- ½ cup chopped onion
- 2 teaspoons chili powder
- ¼ teaspoon table salt

Heat oil in 12-inch nonstick skillet over medium heat until shimmering. Add poblanos, beans, corn, onion, chili powder, and salt and cook until softened, 6 to 8 minutes.

BLOODY MARY BAR

Serves 6 to 8

START WITH:

Bloody Marys for a Crowd (page 71)

Pickle-y garnishes (cornichons, dilly beans, kimchi, olives, pickled asparagus)

Fresh garnishes (celery stalks and grape tomatoes)

Hot sauce

Horseradish

Lemon and lime wedges

IF YOU WANT, ADD:

Black Pepper Candied Bacon (page 72)

Rim Salts (page 72)

Poached Shrimp (page 117)

→

BLOODY MARY BAR

I'm usually not a huge Bloody Mary fan (I know, I know!), but when I do drink them, I'm a garnish girl all day—a good sip with the right bite is everything. I've even been known to stack on a couple of chicken wings (if you're like me, there's a great recipe on page 92). Celery is the classic garnish, but beyond that, if you're in the pickle world you really can't go wrong. This board satisfies the snackers and the sippers in your group, and just may cure a hangover or two in the process.

ELLE'S STRATEGY:

Set up shop. Pour the Bloody Marys into a big pitcher, then display your celery in a tall glass with a little bit of water at the bottom to keep it fresh. Set out other garnishes in smaller containers (any old jars you can't find the lids for will work just fine). Cut slits in citrus wedges and arrange in a larger glass jar or bowl. I like using a shot glass to corral the different skewer sizes. If you're making rim salts, put them in shallow saucers with enough room to twirl a glass.

Get a head start. Everything can be made a day or two before, and the rim salts can be made up to a month in advance.

Show 'em how it's done. Start a couple of skewers for your guests to give them pairing suggestions and encourage them to go as over-the-top as they want.

Customize it. Mix up your big batch of Bloodies, but also set out some of the ingredients (like horseradish and hot sauce) so people can dial up the heat if they want to.

Get in the spirit. Vodka is just the starting point here. Try tequila, whiskey, or even sake. Or, skip the booze altogether.

Bloody Marys for a Crowd

Makes 12 cocktails

Tabasco is best here, but if you're not a Tabasco person, you can use whatever hot sauce you like; be sure to adjust the amount according to your tastes. For tomato juice, Campbell's is classic, but you can substitute V8 if that's your thing. Be sure to buy refrigerated prepared horseradish, not the shelf-stable kind, which contains preservatives and additives; do not use horseradish cream.

48	ounces tomato juice
16	ounces vodka
4	ounces lemon juice (3 lemons)
1	ounce Worcestershire sauce
4	teaspoons prepared horseradish
2	teaspoons pepper
½–1	teaspoon hot sauce

1. Whisk all ingredients together in serving pitcher or large container. Cover and refrigerate until flavors meld and mixture is well chilled, at least 2 hours or up to 1 day.

2. Stir Bloody Marys to recombine, then serve over ice. Garnish to your heart's content.

TIPS FOR SUCCESSFUL SKEWERING:

Start with a sturdy skewer. These guys are going to be bearing the weight of a whole lot of garnishes, so you don't want a flimsy thing that'll snap under pressure. Set out a couple different sizes (I use 6- and 7-inchers) to give your guests options—some people just want a couple of olives to perch on the top of their drink, they don't need a whole fancy dancy.

Layer up. Turn the skewer so the pointy end is facing away from you, and layer on your garnishes starting with the lightest items first (you don't want a top-heavy skewer tipping over your glass).

Finish strong. Once you've got your garnishes just right, finish with a good anchor item (something solid that will stay put on the skewer, like a big olive) to keep everything from sliding down into your drink.

It's all about the angle. If you've got a particularly heavy skewer situation, don't just drop it in there and hope the ice will keep things in place. Instead, put it in at an angle, using the rim of your glass for support. And make sure your glass can handle the skewer weight; if you're offering a lot of really heavy garnishes (see page 72), include some beer mugs to help keep things structurally sound.

LEVEL UP YOUR BOARD

Black Pepper Candied Bacon

Makes 12 pieces

You could always make regular old bacon (see page 50) but salty, sweet, crispy, candied bacon really sets these Bloodies off. Don't use dark brown sugar here. This recipe calls for center-cut bacon because the strips are a more even thickness than regular bacon.

- 6 slices center-cut bacon, halved crosswise
- 2 tablespoons packed light brown sugar
- ½ teaspoon pepper

1. Adjust oven rack to middle position and heat oven to 350 degrees. Line rimmed baking sheet with aluminum foil. Arrange bacon slices on prepared sheet.

2. Combine sugar and pepper in bowl. Sprinkle sugar mixture evenly over bacon (do not flip and season second side). Use your finger to evenly spread sugar mixture over each slice.

3. Bake until bacon is dark brown and sugar is bubbling, 20 to 25 minutes, rotating sheet halfway through baking. Transfer bacon to wire rack and let cool for 5 minutes. Serve.

TAKE IT OVER THE TOP:

Want to get gaudy with your skewers? Try adding some of these extreme garnishes to your board to bring your Bloodies to new heights.

- Beef jerky sticks
- Chicken wings (see page 92)
- Chicken nuggets
- Grilled cheese squares
- Jalapeño poppers
- Sliders
- Lobster tail (see page 219)
- Mini bagels
- Mozzarella sticks
- Onion rings
- Tater Tots

RIM SALTS

Gussy up your glass with a salty punch to make your Bloody Mary sing. I've included two of my favorites here, but you could raid your cupboards and make your own concoction—kosher salt plus Old Bay and/or celery salt, anyone? Or, skip the salt altogether and use everything bagel seasoning (see page 58) instead. Don't substitute table or other salts for the kosher salt, as their additives may impart off flavors. These recipes make enough for up to 8 glasses, but they can easily be doubled if needed. If you have rim salt left over, you can store it in an airtight container for up to 1 month.

Herb Rim Salt

Makes about ½ cup

- ½ cup kosher salt
- ½ cup minced fresh basil, dill, or tarragon

Using your hands, rub salt and basil in large bowl until well combined. Spread mixture into even layer on parchment paper–lined rimmed baking sheet. Let sit at room temperature, away from direct sunlight, until completely dry, 36 to 48 hours, stirring every 12 hours to break up any clumps.

Sriracha Rim Salt

Makes about ½ cup

- ½ cup kosher salt
- ⅓ cup sriracha

Combine salt and sriracha in bowl, then spread onto large plate. Microwave, stirring occasionally, until only slightly damp, 6 to 8 minutes. Let cool to room temperature, about 15 minutes. Transfer mixture to food processor and pulse until finely ground, 5 to 10 pulses.

PUT A RIM ON IT:

1. Moisten about ½ inch of your glass rim by running a citrus wedge around the outer edge; dry any drips with a paper towel. If you want, moisten only a portion of the glass so that you can enjoy your Bloody Mary both with and without salt.

2. Spread ½ cup of rim salt (for up to 8 glasses) into an even layer on a small saucer, then roll moistened rim in salt to coat.

SNACKS AND SIPS

Grazing Boards for Cocktail
Parties and Beyond

77 **Hummus**

83 **Bruschetta**

89 **Wings**

97 **Nachos**

103 **Movie Night**

109 **Tapas**

115 **Raw Bar**

123 **Pâté**

129 **Afternoon Tea**

137 **Martinis**

HUMMUS

Serves 6 to 8

START WITH:

Ultracreamy Hummus (page 79)

Crackers and/or pita chips
(see page 81)

Classic crudités (radishes, beets,
carrots, snap peas, cucumbers,
mini sweet peppers)

Extra-virgin olive oil

IF YOU WANT, ADD:

Toppings to level up your hummus
(see page 80)

Store-bought crispy chickpeas

Olive bar goodies (stuffed grape
leaves, olives, cherry pepper
poppers, marinated artichoke
hearts, feta)

→

HUMMUS

This board is my go-to when I'm having vegetarian friends over—it's so simple to throw together at the last minute. The hummus recipe is really the creamiest one around, so it's worth making—but in a pinch I'll just pick hummus up at the store and focus on the toppings instead. They can be as simple as a whorl of olive oil and a sprinkle of spices, but making some leveled-up garnishes transforms hummus from just something to scoop into the main event (plus, the meat version keeps the carnivores happy).

ELLE'S STRATEGY:

Set up shop. Separating hummus into bowls enables you to use multiple toppings. Set out crackers and pita chips around each hummus bowl, then create a line of vegetables. Make sure your dipping offerings are sturdy enough to scoop up the hummus (like crackers and thick planks of cucumber).

Get a head start. Keeping your pantry stocked with crackers and other dippables means you're always ready for a hummus party. Hummus can be made up to 5 days ahead of time, and pita chips (if you're making them) can be made up to 3 days in advance. See page 34 for make-ahead crudités tips.

It's all about the swoosh. Using the back of a spoon, press into the hummus in a swirling, circular motion with varying degrees of pressure to create wells, then fill them with olive oil. It's a never-fail stylist's technique for keeping dips pretty.

Raise the (olive) bar. If you want to make your board a little heartier, head to your local market's olive bar for all the things that pair nicely with hummus (you can also usually find hummus, in a pinch).

Make it a meal. Take hummus from snack to supper by adding some more filling options that match the Middle Eastern vibe, like fattoush and tabbouleh.

Ultracreamy Hummus

Makes about 3 cups

Store-bought hummus is a never-fail last-minute entertaining snack, but to really pull out all the stops I like to make this velvety-smooth, perfectly balanced recipe. (And, it's much easier than you'd think.) The small tricks here are game-changers, from simmering the (canned!) chickpeas with baking soda until their skins slide right off, to steeping minced garlic in lemon juice and salt to temper its raw bite. Tahini that is lighter in color is best here—it means it hasn't been roasted as long (which can lead to bitterness). Some brands to look for are Ziyad, Roland, or Kevala.

 2 (15-ounce) cans chickpeas, rinsed

 ½ teaspoon baking soda

 4 garlic cloves, peeled

 ⅓ cup lemon juice (2 lemons), plus extra for seasoning

 1 teaspoon table salt

 ¼ teaspoon ground cumin

 ½ cup tahini, stirred well

 2 tablespoons extra-virgin olive oil

1. Combine chickpeas, baking soda, and 6 cups water in medium saucepan and bring to boil over high heat. Reduce heat and simmer, stirring occasionally, until chickpea skins begin to float to surface and chickpeas are creamy and very soft, 20 to 25 minutes.

2. While chickpeas cook, mince garlic using garlic press or rasp-style grater. Measure out 1 tablespoon garlic and set aside; discard remaining garlic. Whisk lemon juice, salt, and reserved garlic together in small bowl and let sit for 10 minutes. Strain garlic-lemon mixture through fine-mesh strainer set over bowl, pressing on solids to extract as much liquid as possible; discard solids.

3. Drain chickpeas in colander and return to saucepan. Fill saucepan with cold water and gently swish chickpeas with your fingers to release skins. Pour off most of water into colander to collect skins, leaving chickpeas behind in saucepan. Repeat filling, swishing, and draining 3 or 4 times, until most skins have been removed (this should yield about ¾ cup skins); discard skins. Transfer chickpeas to colander to drain.

4. Process strained garlic-lemon juice, ¼ cup water, cumin, and remaining chickpeas in food processor until smooth, about 1 minute, scraping down sides of bowl as needed. Add tahini and oil and process until hummus is smooth, creamy, and light, about 1 minute, scraping down sides of bowl as needed. (Hummus should have pourable consistency similar to yogurt. If too thick, loosen with water, adding 1 teaspoon at a time.) Season with salt and extra lemon juice to taste. (Hummus can be refrigerated in airtight container for up to 5 days. Let sit, covered, at room temperature for 30 minutes before serving.)

LEVEL UP YOUR BOARD

Baharat-Spiced Beef Topping

Makes about 1 cup

This hearty topping turns a simple appetizer into a dinner-worthy spread. Ground lamb can be used in place of the beef, if you'd like. Toast the pine nuts in a dry skillet over medium-high heat until fragrant, 3 to 5 minutes. This makes enough for ½ recipe of hummus, but can be easily doubled to top a whole recipe, if desired.

- 1 teaspoon water
- ¼ teaspoon table salt
- ⅛ teaspoon baking soda
- 4 ounces 85 percent lean ground beef
- 2 teaspoons extra-virgin olive oil
- ¼ cup finely chopped onion
- 1 garlic clove, minced
- ½ teaspoon hot smoked paprika
- ½ teaspoon ground cumin
- ⅛ teaspoon pepper
- ⅛ teaspoon ground coriander
- Pinch ground cloves
- Pinch ground cinnamon
- 3 tablespoons pine nuts, toasted, divided
- 1 teaspoon lemon juice
- 1 teaspoon chopped fresh parsley

1. Combine water, salt, and baking soda in bowl. Add beef and toss to combine. Let sit for 5 minutes.

2. Heat oil in 12-inch nonstick skillet over medium heat until shimmering. Add onion and garlic and cook, stirring occasionally, until onion is softened, 3 to 4 minutes. Add paprika, cumin, pepper, coriander, cloves, and cinnamon and cook, stirring constantly, until fragrant, about 30 seconds. Add beef and cook, breaking up meat with wooden spoon, until beef is no longer pink, about 5 minutes. Add 2 tablespoons pine nuts and lemon juice and toss to combine. After spooning topping on hummus, sprinkle with parsley and remaining 1 tablespoon pine nuts.

Herb and Olive Salad Topping

Makes about 1 cup

This herb salad freshens up hummus, but is delicious on its own, too. This makes enough for ½ portion of hummus, but can be easily doubled to top a whole portion, if desired.

- ⅓ cup coarsely chopped fresh parsley
- ¼ cup coarsely chopped fresh dill
- ¼ cup pitted kalamata olives, sliced thin
- 1 tablespoon extra-virgin olive oil
- 1 teaspoon lemon juice
- 1 tablespoon pepitas, toasted
- 1 tablespoon sunflower seeds, toasted
- 1 tablespoon white sesame seeds, toasted

Toss parsley, dill, olives, oil, and lemon juice together in small bowl. Season with salt to taste. After spooning herb salad on hummus, sprinkle with pepitas, sunflower seeds, and sesame seeds.

FAR FROM HUMDRUM HUMMUS:

Hummus is the perfect blank slate that becomes special when you add toppings. Those can be hearty (like I have here), but you can keep things simple, too. A drizzle of extra-virgin olive oil is a must, but beyond that, try:

- A sprinkle of herbs and/or spices (smoked paprika, cumin, curry powder, sumac, or za'atar)
- Chopped preserved lemons
- Crispy chickpeas
- Everything bagel seasoning (see page 58)
- Fresh herbs (try parsley, mint, or basil)
- Pomegranate seeds
- Sun-dried tomatoes (plus the oil!)
- Toasted nuts (almonds, walnuts, or pine nuts)

Olive Oil–Sea Salt Pita Chips

Serves 6 to 8

Both white and whole-wheat pita breads will work well here. The larger crystal size of sea salt or kosher salt is best; if using table salt, reduce the amount of salt by half.

4 (8-inch) pita breads
½ cup extra-virgin olive oil
1 teaspoon sea salt or kosher salt

1. Adjust oven racks to upper-middle and lower-middle positions and heat oven to 350 degrees. Using kitchen shears, cut around perimeter of each pita and separate into 2 thin rounds.

2. Working with 1 round at a time, brush rough side generously with oil and sprinkle with salt. Stack rounds on top of one another, rough side up, as you go. Using chef's knife, cut pita stack into 8 wedges. Spread wedges, rough side up and in single layer, on 2 rimmed baking sheets.

3. Bake until wedges are golden brown and crisp, about 15 minutes, switching and rotating sheets halfway through baking. Let cool before serving. (Pita chips can be stored at room temperature for up to 3 days.)

BRUSCHETTA

Serves 4 to 6

START WITH:

Toasted Bread for Bruschetta (page 85)

Tomato-Basil Topping (page 85)

Spreads (ricotta, Boursin Garlic & Fine Herbs cheese, jam)

Drizzles (extra-virgin olive oil, balsamic reduction on page 148)

Crunchy finishers (crispy pancetta, toasted pine nuts)

IF YOU WANT, ADD:

Port-Caramelized Onions (page 86)

Smashed Peas with Lemon and Mint (page 86)

Fruit (sliced peaches, cantaloupe, honeydew melon)

More easy toppings (artichoke hearts, fresh mozzarella, shaved Parmesan, prosciutto)

Fresh basil

→

BRUSCHETTA

This board will transport you to a summertime patio no matter the time of year. And as impressive as it looks, it doesn't have to be complicated. I love hitting up the specialty foods aisle of my grocery store and grabbing a few jarred fancy spreads or jams—it's all about giving your guests options. But it's the low-lift homemade touches like the garlic-rubbed toasts and a simple stir-together topping that take it to new heights. Set it all out on a board big enough for people to gather around and let the grazing commence.

ELLE'S STRATEGY:

Set up shop. Build little neighborhoods for your toppings, keeping like items together—toasts in one area, spreads in another. Set out tongs for the toasts and small knives for spreads and cheeses. Make the board look more bountiful by making prosciutto piles and shingling melon slices to created dimension. Cut everything into bite-size pieces. Use small dishes for crunchy finishers like toasted nuts. Set out any fancy extras—if you've ever received nice olive oil or salt as a gift, now is the time to break out the good stuff.

Get a head start. The day before, prep vegetables and/or fruit, toast nuts, and make the toppings. You could even toast the bread and wrap it tightly in plastic.

Garnish your board practically. Decorate with things that are compatible on your board. Using a bunch of basil to make a flower in the center not only looks pretty, it's also there for people to put on their bruschetta.

Get people inspired. Have some bruschettas made so your guests can re-create them or use them as inspiration. Or, write suggestions on cards (see the next page for ideas).

Think seasonally. Customize your board based on the time of year (tomatoes, basil, and mozzarella in the summertime, roasted vegetables and pungent cheeses when it gets a little colder).

Toasted Bread for Bruschetta

Serves 4 to 6

Larger than crostini, these garlicky toasts give a flavorful foundation to whatever toppings you choose to pile on. One problem that consistently plagues bruschetta is soggy bread, especially once you add toppings. So any hearty bread will work here, just make sure it's got a tight crumb and is sliced thick enough to give substantial support (flimsy sandwich bread is a no-go); halve larger slices crosswise before arranging on baking sheet. This recipe can easily be doubled.

- 1 (12 by 5-inch) loaf country bread with thick crust, ends discarded, sliced crosswise into ¾-inch-thick pieces
- 1 garlic clove, peeled

  Extra-virgin olive oil

Adjust oven rack 4 inches from broiler element and heat broiler. Arrange bread in single layer on aluminum foil–lined baking sheet. Broil until bread is deep golden and toasted on both sides, 1 to 2 minutes per side. Lightly rub 1 side of each toast with garlic (you will not use all of garlic). Brush with oil and season with kosher or flake sea salt to taste.

Tomato-Basil Topping

Makes about 2 cups

- 12 ounces cherry or grape tomatoes, quartered
- ½ teaspoon table salt
- ¼ teaspoon sugar
- 3 tablespoons extra-virgin olive oil
- 1 tablespoon red wine vinegar
- ¼ teaspoon pepper
- 3 tablespoons chopped fresh basil

Combine tomatoes, salt, and sugar in bowl and let sit for 30 minutes. Transfer tomatoes to salad spinner and spin until excess liquid has been removed, 45 to 60 seconds, redistributing tomatoes several times during spinning. Return tomatoes to bowl along with oil, vinegar, and pepper and toss to combine. (Tomato mixture can be refrigerated for up to 24 hours; bring to room temperature before serving.) Stir in basil and season with salt and pepper to taste.

GET YOUR BRUSCHETTA ON:

Whether you're setting out the components for your guests to build their own or going straight cater and making them all in advance, here are some flavor ideas to get your creative juices flowing.

- Ricotta cheese + caramelized onions + artichoke hearts + olive oil drizzle
- Pesto + cherry tomatoes + balsamic drizzle
- Boursin + roast beef + parsley
- Avocado + flaked salmon + capers + olive oil drizzle
- Ricotta cheese + peaches + balsamic drizzle
- Tapenade + roasted tomatoes + flake sea salt
- Pesto + sautéed summer squash + toasted pine nuts
- Goat cheese + crispy kale + toasted walnuts
- Blue cheese + thinly sliced steak + arugula + olive oil drizzle
- Brie + fresh figs + honey drizzle

LEVEL UP YOUR BOARD

Port-Caramelized Onions

Makes about 1 cup

These onions are especially great when paired with crumbled blue cheese and walnuts, or ricotta and prosciutto-wrapped melon.

- 1½ teaspoons unsalted butter
- 1½ teaspoons vegetable oil
- 1 pound onions, sliced ¼ inch thick
- ½ teaspoon light brown sugar
- ¼ teaspoon table salt
- 1 cup port, preferably ruby

1. Heat butter and oil in 10-inch nonstick skillet over high heat. When foaming subsides, add onions, sugar, and salt and stir to coat. Cook, stirring occasionally, until onions soften and begin to release some moisture, about 5 minutes. Reduce heat to medium and cook, stirring frequently, until onions are deeply browned and sticky, about 35 minutes (if onions are sizzling or scorching, reduce heat; if onions are not browning after 15 minutes, increase heat).

2. Stir in port and continue to cook until port reduces to glaze consistency, 4 to 6 minutes. Let cool to room temperature. (Onion topping can be refrigerated for up to 24 hours; bring to room temperature before serving.)

Smashed Peas with Lemon and Mint

Makes about 2 cups

Pair this spread with crispy pancetta and shaved Parmesan for a springtime delight.

- 8 ounces frozen peas
- ¼ cup water
- 1 cup baby spinach
- 2 tablespoons chopped fresh mint
- 2 tablespoons extra-virgin olive oil
- 1 teaspoon grated lemon zest
- ¼ teaspoon red pepper flakes, divided
- ¼ teaspoon table salt
- ¼ teaspoon pepper

Bring peas and water to simmer in medium saucepan over medium heat. Cover, reduce heat to medium-low, and cook until peas are tender, 8 to 10 minutes. Transfer peas (and any remaining water) to food processor. Add spinach, mint, oil, lemon zest, pepper flakes, salt, and pepper and pulse until coarsely ground, 8 to 10 pulses, scraping down sides of bowl as needed. (Pea topping can be refrigerated for up to 24 hours; bring to room temperature and stir to recombine before serving.) Season with salt and pepper to taste.

THE BRUSCHETTA EQUATION:

There aren't many rules when it comes to bruschetta. But for an organized board, it's helpful to think in categories. Make sure each category is represented at least once on your board so your guests can mix and match.

Spreads: Something to slather on toast and hold all the other toppings in place. To branch out, try pâté (see page 123) or hummus (see page 79).

Toppings: These bulk things up, and can be as hearty or as simple as you'd like. Try any leftovers you have on hand, like salmon (see page 213) or roast beef.

Drizzles: Brings a bit of moisture and adds flavor and richness. Extra-virgin olive oil does the trick, or try a balsamic reduction (see page 148).

Crunchy finishers: Gives textural contrast to make the perfect bite. Toasted nuts are easy, or try crispy shallots (see page 189) or frico (see page 177).

WINGS

Serves 4 to 6

START WITH:

Fried Chicken Wings (page 92)

Wing Sauces (page 93)

Dipping sauces (blue cheese and/or ranch, store-bought or homemade on page 95)

Crunchy vegetables (carrots, cucumbers, radishes, celery)

IF YOU WANT, ADD:

Cauliflower Bites (page 95)

→

WINGS

With the perfect skin-to-meat ratio and crispy crunchy exterior, chicken wings are a disappears-in-seconds kind of party food. Make sure you have a balance of drummies and flats, they both have staunch supporters (I'm a flats fan, myself). As far as sauces are concerned, classic buffalo is always essential, but I like giving the people options, like zingy mango chutney and crowd-pleasing barbecue. But whatever you do, keep plenty of napkins well within reach. This isn't meant to be a tidy situation.

ELLE'S STRATEGY:

Set up shop. Pile the wings (and cauliflower bites, if using) in the center of a large platter according to flavor. Put remaining wing sauce in little bowls and place each next to their respective flavor so people know what's what. Put small dishes of blue cheese dressing and ranch dressing (both have loyal fan bases!) in the center. Fan out the vegetables on either side of the wings. Set out small plates with lots of napkins and moist towelettes.

Get a head start. The blue cheese and ranch can be made up to 4 days ahead of time, and the wing sauces (except for buffalo) up to 3 days. Prep the carrots and celery 2 days in advance. Refrigerate the sticks standing upright in a glass with a few ice cubes in the bottom.

Wings on the fly. No need to be hovering over hot, bubbling oil when your guests arrive (hungry for wings, no doubt). Instead fry chicken wings up to 1 to 2 hours in advance and keep them warm in a 200-degree oven. Toss them with the sauce when you're ready to serve.

I dip, you dip. I always set out a little extra wing sauce for dipping, but you could take it all the way and serve the wings plain with the sauce for dipping.

Keep it simple. Pressed for time? No problem. Order plain wings from your favorite spot and toss with one or more homemade sauces. The blue cheese and ranch dressing can be store-bought, too.

Fried Chicken Wings

Serves 4 to 6

Toss wings with 1 recipe wing sauce just before serving. Use a Dutch oven that holds 6 quarts or more for this recipe. If you buy chicken wings that are already split, with the tips removed, you will need only 2½ pounds. Plan on about ½ pound (roughly 5 wings) per person.

2	quarts peanut or vegetable oil for frying
1½	cups water
1	cup all-purpose flour
3	tablespoons cornstarch
1	teaspoon table salt
1	teaspoon pepper
1	teaspoon cayenne pepper
3	pounds chicken wings, cut at joints, wingtips discarded
¾	cup wing sauce (recipes follow), divided

1. Add oil to large Dutch oven until it measures about 1½ inches deep and heat over medium-high heat to 350 degrees. Set wire rack in rimmed baking sheet.

2. Whisk water, flour, cornstarch, salt, pepper, and cayenne together in large bowl until smooth. Place half of wings in batter and stir to coat. Using tongs, remove wings from batter one at a time, allowing any excess batter to drip back into bowl, and add to hot oil. (Oil temperature will drop sharply after adding wings.) Increase heat to high and cook, stirring occasionally to prevent wings from sticking, until coating is light golden and beginning to crisp, about 7 minutes.

3. Transfer wings to prepared rack. Return oil to 350 degrees and repeat with remaining wings. Reduce heat to medium and let second batch of wings rest for 5 minutes.

4. Heat oil to 375 degrees. Carefully return all wings to oil and cook, stirring occasionally, until deep golden brown and very crispy, about 7 minutes. Return wings to rack and let stand for 2 minutes. (Wings can be kept warm in a 200-degree oven for up to 2 hours.)

5. Pour ½ cup sauce into clean large bowl, add chicken wings, and toss until wings are uniformly coated. Serve immediately, with remaining sauce on the side.

LEFTOVERS? DON'T PANIC.

Depending on how many sauces you want to offer, you may end up with sauce to spare. Here are some ideas for how to use it up.

- **Buffalo:** Swirl into mac and cheese (see page 202) and top with crumbled blue cheese.

- **Barbecue:** Toss with shredded rotisserie chicken and serve on a bun with cole slaw.

- **Mango Chutney:** Add to sautéed tofu and serve over rice with more cilantro, fresh lime wedges, and a sprinkle of chopped peanuts.

Wing Sauces

Each sauce makes about ¾ cup (enough to coat 1 recipe Fried Chicken Wings or Cauliflower Bites, plus extra for serving). But half the fun of the board is trying out different flavors, so go ahead and make more than one—you'll find plenty of ways to use up the extra sauce (see "Leftovers? Don't Panic." for ideas). All sauces, except for buffalo, can be refrigerated for up to 3 days. Bring to room temperature before using.

Buffalo Wing Sauce

Classic buffalo sauce is made with Frank's RedHot Original Cayenne Pepper Sauce.

- ½ cup hot sauce
- 4 tablespoons unsalted butter, melted
- 1 tablespoon molasses

Whisk all ingredients together in bowl.

Smoky Barbecue Wing Sauce

- ¼ cup chicken broth
- ¼ cup ketchup
- 1 tablespoon molasses
- 1 tablespoon cider vinegar
- 1 tablespoon minced canned chipotle chile in adobo sauce
- ¼ teaspoon liquid smoke

Whisk all ingredients together in bowl.

Mango Chutney Wing Sauce

- ¾ cup mango chutney
- 1 shallot, minced
- 3 tablespoons water
- 1 tablespoon minced fresh cilantro
- 1 teaspoon grated lime zest

Whisk all ingredients together in bowl.

CUTTING CAULIFLOWER WITHOUT MAKING A MESS:

1. Pull off any leaves, then cut out core of cauliflower using paring knife.

2. Separate florets from inner stem using tip of knife and then cut larger florets into smaller pieces by slicing through stem end.

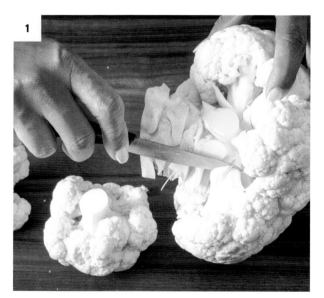

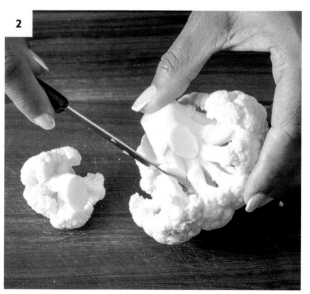

LEVEL UP YOUR BOARD

Cauliflower Bites

Serves 4 to 6

If you've already heated up oil for chicken wings, why not keep that oil bubbling and fry a batch of cauliflower bites to keep your veggie friends happy? Use a Dutch oven that holds 6 quarts or more for this recipe.

- 2 quarts peanut or vegetable oil
- ¾ cup cornstarch
- ¼ cup cornmeal
- ½ teaspoon table salt
- ¼ teaspoon pepper
- 1 pound cauliflower florets, cut into 1½-inch pieces
- ⅔ cup canned coconut milk
- ¾ cup wing sauce (see page 93), divided

1. Preheat oven to 200 degrees. Line baking sheet with triple layer of paper towels. Add oil to large Dutch oven until it measures about 1½ inches deep and heat over medium-high heat to 400 degrees.

2. Meanwhile, combine cornstarch, cornmeal, salt, and pepper in small bowl. Add cauliflower and coconut milk to a large bowl; toss to coat well. Sprinkle cornstarch mixture over cauliflower and fold with rubber spatula until thoroughly coated. Fry half of cauliflower, adding 1 or 2 pieces to oil at a time, until golden and crisp, gently stirring as needed to prevent pieces from sticking together, about 3 minutes. Adjust burner, if necessary, to maintain oil temperature between 375 and 400 degrees.

3. Using slotted spoon, transfer fried cauliflower to prepared sheet and place in oven to keep warm. Return oil to 400 degrees and repeat with remaining cauliflower.

4. Pour ½ cup sauce into clean large bowl, add cauliflower, and gently fold with spatula until uniformly coated. Serve immediately, with remaining sauce on the side.

Creamy Blue Cheese Dressing

Makes about 1 cup

- 2½ ounces blue cheese, crumbled (about ½ cup)
- 3 tablespoons buttermilk
- 3 tablespoons sour cream
- 2 tablespoons mayonnaise
- 2 teaspoons white wine vinegar

Mash blue cheese and buttermilk in small bowl with fork until mixture resembles cottage cheese with small curds. Stir in sour cream, mayonnaise, and vinegar. Season with salt and pepper to taste, cover, and refrigerate until ready to serve. (Dressing can be refrigerated for up to 4 days.)

Ranch Dressing

Makes about 1 cup

You could obviously reach for a bottle here, but once you make your own you may find yourself doing it again.

- ⅔ cup sour cream
- ¼ cup buttermilk
- 2 tablespoons minced fresh cilantro, dill, tarragon, and/or parsley
- 1 tablespoon minced shallot
- 2 teaspoons white wine vinegar
- ½ teaspoon granulated garlic
- ¼ teaspoon table salt
- ¼ teaspoon pepper

Whisk all ingredients together in bowl. Season with salt and pepper to taste, cover, and refrigerate until ready to serve. (Dressing can be refrigerated for up to 4 days.)

NACHOS

Serves 4 to 6

START WITH:

Cheesy Nachos with Refried Beans
(page 99)

Salsa (store-bought, or homemade
on page 99)

Guacamole (store-bought, or
homemade on page 99)

Fresh garnishes (sliced jalapeños,
scallions, lime wedges, cilantro)

Sour cream, or crema (see page 101)

IF YOU WANT, ADD:

Spicy Beef Topping (see page 99)

Escabeche (page 100)

Micheladas (page 100)

→

NACHOS

I'll eat nachos any given day of the week. They're cheesy, crunchy, salty, and satisfying. They're also endlessly customizable depending on who you have stopping by—swap in (or add) chorizo, shredded rotisserie chicken, sautéed poblano peppers (see page 66), or even plant-based meat instead of beef. Layer it all on, or keep the toppings separate and let your guests go to town. Serve everything with micheladas or keep it simple with ice-cold beers. The best part is, in my house, guac never costs extra.

ELLE'S STRATEGY:

Set up shop. The sheet pan is the board here, so set it on a dish towel both to protect your surface and make people aware it's hot. Include serving utensils. There are no rules when it comes to garnishing these nachos, so surround them with bowls of toppings so your guests know they can do it in any order they like. Set out a dish of rim salt and a michelada station off to the side of the nachos. Offer lots of lime wedges for adding some acidic kick to both the nachos and micheladas.

Get a head start. Guacamole and salsa can be made a day or two in advance, and escabeche can be made a week ahead. Have everything else on hand in your pantry or fridge so you're ready to nacho.

Layer up. Too often, a towering pile of nachos looks decadent, but once you get past the top layer, it's bare. And what's sadder than a cheeseless chip? To avoid this all-too-common heartbreak, layer on your toppings and cheese in stages before baking. This not only evenly distributes the goodies, but also allows the cheese to act like glue and make the toppings stick to the chips. Because when the meat starts rolling off my nachos, I'm bummed.

Guac and roll. Push pitted avocado halves (leave the skins on) through a wire cooling rack to dice them in a flash.

Cheesy Nachos with Refried Beans

Serves 4 to 6

To ensure that the tortilla chips are cheesy and spicy, layer them with a whole lotta cheese and sliced jalapeños. Your choice: Keep it veg with the refried beans (check the label to make sure, though!), or sub in the spicy beef topping. You also could cook the beef and serve it on the side. That way, vegetarians and carnivores are happy.

12 ounces tortilla chips

1 (14.5-ounce) can refried beans (optional)

1 pound Monterey Jack cheese, shredded (4 cups)

8 ounces sharp cheddar cheese, shredded (2 cups)

2 large jalapeños, stemmed and sliced thin

1. Adjust oven rack to middle position and heat oven to 400 degrees. Spread half of tortilla chips in even layer in rimmed baking sheet. Dollop twelve 1 tablespoon-size spoonfuls of refried beans over chips, if using. Sprinkle with 2 cups Monterey Jack, 1 cup cheddar, and half of jalapeños. Repeat with remaining tortilla chips, refried beans, 2 cups Monterey Jack, 1 cup cheddar, and jalapeños. Bake until cheese is melted, 7 to 10 minutes.

2. Remove nachos from oven and let cool for 2 minutes. Garnish as desired and serve.

VARIATION

Cheesy Nachos with Spicy Beef Topping

Heat 2 teaspoons vegetable oil in 12-inch skillet over medium heat until shimmering. Add 1 finely chopped small onion and cook until softened, about 3 minutes. Stir in 1 tablespoon chili powder, 1 minced garlic clove, ¼ teaspoon dried oregano, ½ teaspoon ground cumin, ½ teaspoon ground coriander, ¼ teaspoon cayenne pepper, and ⅛ teaspoon table salt and cook until fragrant, about 30 seconds. Add 8 ounces 90 percent lean ground beef and cook, breaking up meat with wooden spoon, until firm crumbles form, about 5 minutes. Substitute beef topping for refried beans.

One-Minute Salsa

Makes 3 cups

½ small red onion, cut into 1-inch pieces

½ cup fresh cilantro leaves

¼ cup jarred sliced jalapeños

2 tablespoons lime juice

2 garlic cloves, chopped

½ teaspoon table salt

1 (28-ounce) can diced tomatoes, drained

Pulse onion, cilantro, jalapeños, lime juice, garlic, and salt in food processor until coarsely chopped, about 5 pulses, scraping down sides of bowl as needed. Add tomatoes and pulse until combined, about 3 pulses. Drain salsa briefly in fine-mesh strainer, then transfer to bowl and season with salt and pepper to taste. (Salsa can be refrigerated for up to 2 days.)

Guacamole

Makes about 2 cups

2 tablespoons finely chopped onion

1 serrano chile, stemmed, seeded, and chopped fine

¼ teaspoon grated lime zest plus 1½ tablespoons juice

1 teaspoon kosher salt

3 ripe avocados, halved, pitted, and cut into ½-inch pieces

1 plum tomato, cored, seeded, and minced

2 tablespoons chopped fresh cilantro

With chef's knife, chop and mash onion, chile, and lime zest with salt until very finely minced and homogeneous. Transfer to medium serving bowl and stir in lime juice. Add avocados and, using sturdy whisk, mash and stir mixture until well combined with some ¼- to ½-inch pieces remaining. Fold in tomato and cilantro and season with salt to taste. Serve. (Guacamole can be refrigerated for up to 24 hours with plastic wrap pressed directly against its surface. To serve, bring to room temperature and season with lime juice and salt to taste.)

LEVEL UP YOUR BOARD

Escabeche

Makes about 2 cups

I love a pickled element on nachos, whether it's pickled red onion (see page 58) or jarred jalapeños. These quick-pickled vegetables add brininess and heat, and are a step up from the jarred stuff.

½ teaspoon coriander seeds

¼ teaspoon cumin seeds

1 cup cider vinegar

½ cup water

1½ teaspoons sugar

¼ teaspoon table salt

1 red onion, halved and sliced thin

2 carrots, peeled and sliced thin

1 jalapeño chile, stemmed and sliced thin

Toast coriander seeds and cumin seeds in medium saucepan over medium heat, stirring frequently, until fragrant, about 2 minutes. Add vinegar, water, sugar, and salt and bring to boil, stirring to dissolve sugar and salt. Remove saucepan from heat and add onion, carrots, and jalapeño, pressing to submerge vegetables. Cover and let cool completely, 30 minutes. (Cooled vegetables can be refrigerated for up to 1 week.)

Micheladas

Makes 4 cocktails

Originating in Mexico, the michelada has lots of variations there, depending on the region. But it's always the perfect refreshing foil to cheesy nachos. Use a well-chilled Mexican lager—Tecate, Corona Extra, and Modelo are all great options. Cholula and Tapatío hot sauces are best for their flavor and thicker consistencies. If using a thinner, vinegary hot sauce such as Tabasco, which is spicier, start with half the amount called for and adjust to your taste after mixing. Do not use bottled lime juice here. This recipe can be easily doubled.

1 cup lime juice (8 limes), plus lime wedges for serving

1 recipe Rim Salt (page 72)

2½ tablespoons hot sauce, plus extra for serving

2 tablespoons Worcestershire sauce

¼ teaspoon table salt

4 (12-ounce) Mexican beers, chilled

Rub rims of 4 pint glasses with 1 lime wedge to moisten, then dip rims into rim salt to coat; set aside. Combine lime juice, hot sauce, Worcestershire, and table salt in 2-cup liquid measuring cup, stirring to dissolve salt. Divide lime juice mixture evenly among prepared glasses. Fill glasses with beer. Serve with lime wedges, extra hot sauce, and remaining beer, topping off glasses as needed.

MAKING CREMA:

Falling somewhere between French crème fraîche and American sour cream, Mexican crema is the tangy, creamy, drizzle-able addition your nachos didn't know they needed. Here's how to make it:

Stir together 1 cup pasteurized cream and 2 tablespoons buttermilk in a container. Cover and place in a warm location (75 to 80 degrees is ideal; lower temperatures will lengthen fermentation time) until the mixture is thickened but still pourable, 12 to 24 hours. Dissolve ⅛ teaspoon salt in 2 teaspoons lime juice and add to mixture. Drizzle over nachos, breakfast tacos (see page 61), or even sliced fruit. Refrigerate for up to 2 months.

MOVIE NIGHT

Serves 4 to 6

START WITH:

Buttered Popcorn (page 105)

DIY Soda Bar (page 107)

IF YOU WANT, ADD:

Candy (a mix of fruity and chocolaty)

More snacks (party mix, chips, pretzels)

→

MOVIE NIGHT

Movie night always feels more like a *thing* than just binge-watching a show. So why not go all out and commemorate that subtle-yet-crucial distinction with a snackpalooza? Salty, buttery, no-kernel-left-unpopped popcorn; all the candy you could dream about; and a customized, fizzy thirst-quencher from a generous soda bar. Skip the concession stand, you've got all you need at home. The only hard part is agreeing on what to watch (I can't help you there).

ELLE'S STRATEGY:

Set up shop. Set out big bowls of popcorn and any other snacks. Get a few mini scoops (or use big spoons if you don't have any) for easy serving. Open up some of the candy and put it on a tray in case people want to make their own mix, and leave some full boxes too. Brown paper bags are perfect for individual servings. For the sodas, corral all of the syrups and seltzers on a tray with a lip for easy cleanup (no sticky countertop spills), along with straws and a mixing spoon.

Get a head start. Soda syrups can be made up to 1 month in advance, and keeping your pantry stocked with snacks at all times is just best practice anyway.

Personal popcorn bags. You can set out brown paper bags for your guests to shake up their own popcorn flavors (see page 105), but you can also pre-roll them. Cut about one-fourth of the top off a bag and then roll it down to the desired size. Don't worry if it tears a little bit, the roll will cover any imperfections.

Lean into the theme. It's movie night—have fun with it! Hit up a party supply store for big boxes of candy and little snack caddies to get your snack on in style.

When in doubt, give it a zap. This popcorn is so good it's best to pop it yourself, but there's no shame in the microwave game in a pinch.

Buttered Popcorn

Makes 14 cups

This popcorn will blow your mind, and leave no kernel stragglers behind. The key is heating three test kernels in a saucepan until the kernels pop (that's how you know the oil's hot enough). Adding the rest of the kernels off the burner and letting it sit for 30 seconds ensures all of the kernels heat up evenly. That way, they all pop at the same rate—no shaking required.

- 3 tablespoons vegetable oil
- ½ cup popcorn kernels
- 2 tablespoons unsalted butter, melted
- ¼ teaspoon table salt

1. Heat oil and 3 kernels in large saucepan over medium-high heat until kernels pop. Remove pan from heat, add remaining kernels, cover, and let sit for 30 seconds.

2. Return saucepan to medium-high heat. Continue to cook with lid slightly ajar until popping slows to about 2 seconds between pops. Transfer popcorn to large bowl. Add melted butter and toss to coat popcorn. Add salt and toss to combine. Serve.

VARIATIONS

Parmesan-Pepper Popcorn

Add ½ teaspoon pepper to butter before melting. Add ½ cup grated Parmesan to popcorn when tossing with butter.

Garlic and Herb Popcorn

Add 2 minced garlic cloves and 1 tablespoon minced fresh or 1 teaspoon dried rosemary, thyme, or dill to butter before melting.

Hot and Sweet Popcorn

Add 2 tablespoons sugar, 1 teaspoon ground cinnamon, and ½ teaspoon chili powder to butter before melting.

Cajun-Spiced Popcorn

Add 1 teaspoon red pepper flakes, 1 teaspoon minced fresh thyme, ¾ teaspoon hot sauce, ½ teaspoon garlic powder, ½ teaspoon paprika, and ¼ teaspoon onion powder to butter before melting.

SHAKE IT UP:

You could make a large batch of already-flavored popcorn, but it's also fun to set out lots of seasoning options for your fellow movie-watchers to make their own creations. Just fill a bag halfway with popcorn, sprinkle on the seasonings, and shake the bag to evenly distribute the flavor. Try these outside-the-box ideas for seasoning:

- Ramen seasoning packet
- Shichimi togarashi
- Nori powder
- Garlic salt
- Onion powder
- Hot sauce
- Spicy honey (see page 148)
- Grated cheese
- MSG
- Nutritional yeast
- Cocoa powder
- Everything bagel seasoning (see page 58)
- Smoked paprika
- Sumac

DIY Soda Bar

Any salty movie snack needs a fizzy drink on the side. Bring the soda fountain home with these supereasy syrups that transform plain seltzer into the ultimate sippable popcorn companion. Keep it simple with a single flavor, or mix them together for a next-level refresher. It's best to buy cans of seltzer (plan on about 1 can per person) instead of large bottles so any extra doesn't go flat.

Citrus Soda Syrup

Makes about 1 cup (enough for about 12 drinks)

- ⅔ cup sugar
- ⅔ cup water
- 1 teaspoon grated lemon or lime zest plus 1 tablespoon juice

1. Combine sugar, water, and zest and juice in 2- or 4-cup jar. Cover jar with lid and shake vigorously until sugar dissolves, about 2 minutes. Let syrup sit for 30 minutes to infuse flavor.

2. Strain syrup through fine-mesh strainer into bowl, pressing on solids to extract as much syrup as possible; discard solids. Return flavored syrup to jar. (Syrup can be refrigerated for up to 1 month.)

To make flavored soda: Place ice in tall glass. Pour 1 cup seltzer water over ice. Add 1 to 2 tablespoons syrup and stir gently to combine. Serve.

VARIATIONS

Berry Soda Syrup

Instead of citrus zest and juice, use 1 cup fresh or frozen raspberries or 1 cup hulled and quartered strawberries.

Pineapple Soda Syrup

Instead of citrus zest and juice, use ½ cup fresh or frozen pineapple chunks.

Watermelon Soda Syrup

Instead of citrus zest and juice, use 1 cup watermelon chunks.

Herb Soda Syrup

Instead of citrus zest and juice, use 1 cup fresh mint, basil, or tarragon leaves, or ¼ cup chopped fresh thyme or rosemary.

Ginger Soda Syrup

Instead of citrus zest and juice, use ½ cup chopped fresh ginger.

GET FANCY WITH IT:

Mix up any of these combos with seltzer for a spirit-free drink that will quench your thirst like nobody's business. (But listen, if you want to add booze, I'm not going to tell you no.)

- **Cosmopolitan:** Citrus Soda Syrup (with lime) + cranberry juice + orange juice
- **Margarita:** Citrus Soda Syrup (with lime) + orange juice
- **Mojito:** Herb Soda Syrup (with mint) + a squeeze of lime
- **Moscow Mule:** Ginger Soda Syrup + a squeeze of lime
- **Piña Colada:** Pineapple Soda Syrup + coconut water

- **Raspberry Lime Rickey:** Berry Soda Syrup (with raspberries) + a squeeze of lime
- **Shirley Temple:** Ginger Soda Syrup + grenadine
- **Strawberry Daiquiri:** Berry Soda Syrup (with strawberries) + a squeeze of lime
- **Watermelon Agua Fresca:** Watermelon Soda Syrup + a squeeze of lime

TAPAS

Serves 6 to 8

START WITH:

Tortilla Española (page 111)

Mixed olives

Spanish cheeses (Manchego, Garrotxa, Murcia al Vino)

Spanish cured meats (chorizo, jamón ibérico, jamón serrano)

Bread and/or crackers

Marcona almonds (or any nuts)

IF YOU WANT, ADD:

Aioli (page 111)

Albóndigas en Salsa de Almendras (page 112)

Sangria for a Crowd (page 113)

Tinned fish (mussels, sardines)

Quince paste

→

TAPAS

Tapas—small, shareable dishes meant to be snacked on with a drink in hand—are the epitome of grazing food. They can be as simple as a dish of olives or as extravagant as stewed octopus—the beauty is that anything goes. I like to focus on one cooked element (like a Tortilla Española with plenty of potatoes and garlicky aioli) and then surround it with Spanish meats and cheeses. It might look impressive, but it's mostly about arranging. See pages 18–31 for more cheese and charcuterie tips.

ELLE'S STRATEGY:

Set up shop. Make larger elements (like the tortilla and meatballs) accessible around the perimeter so it forces guests to move around the board. Place the bread and crackers next to spreadable things (soft cheeses, tinned fish, and quince paste). Sprinkle the nuts and olives over the board. Set the tinned fish on small plates to catch oil drips, and use the smallest forks you can find in your house (too big and they'll tear the delicate fish).

Get a head start. Sliced cheeses and meats are good in your fridge for up to 1 week. Aioli can be made up to 3 days in advance, and the tortilla up to 4 hours ahead. If making meatballs, you can start them up to 24 hours ahead of time and finish them day-of.

It's all about balance. Be intentional about having a lively mix of flavors on your board. Include sweet (like quince paste), salty (Marcona almonds, tinned fish, and some cheeses), and even spicy elements (some cured meats have a kick). Go for soft, hard, mild, and funky cheeses.

Think outside the kitchen. When styling a board with a regional theme, incorporate items from your travels that you may have on display in other rooms in your house. Here I've used some pottery I found on a trip to Spain.

Ask questions. Ask your cheesemonger and people working in specialty shops for recommendations for Spanish cheeses, meats, and other accoutrements.

Tortilla Española

Serves 6 to 8

This egg-and-potato-based anytime snack is just as good (if not better!) served at room temp with aioli. You will need a 10-inch nonstick skillet with a tight-fitting lid for this recipe.

- 1½ pounds Yukon Gold potatoes, peeled, quartered, and sliced ⅛ inch thick
- 1 small onion, halved and sliced thin
- 6 tablespoons plus 1 teaspoon extra-virgin olive oil, divided
- 1 teaspoon table salt, divided
- ¼ teaspoon pepper
- 8 large eggs
- ½ cup jarred roasted red peppers, rinsed, patted dry, and cut into ½-inch pieces
- ½ cup frozen peas, thawed

1. Toss potatoes, onion, ¼ cup oil, ½ teaspoon salt, and pepper together in large bowl. Heat 2 tablespoons oil in 10-inch nonstick skillet over medium-high heat until shimmering. Add potato mixture to skillet and reduce heat to medium-low. Cover and cook, stirring every 5 minutes, until potatoes are tender, about 25 minutes.

2. Whisk eggs and remaining ½ teaspoon salt together in now-empty bowl, then gently fold in red peppers, peas, and potato mixture. Make sure to scrape all of potato mixture out of skillet.

3. Heat remaining 1 teaspoon oil in now-empty skillet over medium-high heat until just smoking. Add egg mixture and cook, shaking skillet and folding mixture constantly, for 15 seconds. Smooth top of egg mixture, reduce heat to medium, cover, and cook, gently shaking skillet every 30 seconds, until bottom is golden brown and top is lightly set, about 2 minutes.

4. Off heat, run heatproof rubber spatula around edge of skillet and shake skillet gently to loosen tortilla; it should slide around freely in skillet. Slide tortilla onto large plate, then invert onto second large plate and slide back into skillet, browned side up. Tuck edges of tortilla into skillet with rubber spatula. Continue to cook over medium heat, gently shaking skillet every 30 seconds, until second side is golden brown, about 2 minutes longer. Slide tortilla onto cutting board and let cool slightly. Serve warm or at room temperature.

Aioli

Makes about ¾ cup

The egg yolks in this recipe are not cooked. If you prefer, ¼ cup Egg Beaters may be substituted.

- 2 large egg yolks
- 2 garlic cloves, peeled and smashed
- 4 teaspoons lemon juice
- 1 tablespoon water, plus extra as needed
- ¼ teaspoon Dijon mustard
- ¼ teaspoon table salt
- ⅛ teaspoon sugar
- ¾ cup vegetable oil

Process egg yolks, garlic, lemon juice, water, mustard, salt, and sugar in blender until combined, about 10 seconds, scraping down sides of blender jar as needed. With blender running, slowly add oil and process until mayonnaise is emulsified, about 2 minutes. Adjust consistency with extra water as needed. Season with salt and pepper to taste. (Mayonnaise can be refrigerated for up to 3 days.)

VARIATIONS

Smoky Aioli

Add 1½ teaspoons smoked paprika to blender with egg yolks.

Herbed Aioli

Add 2 tablespoons chopped fresh basil, 1 tablespoon chopped fresh parsley, and 1 tablespoon minced fresh chives to mayonnaise and pulse until combined but not smooth, about 10 pulses.

LEVEL UP YOUR BOARD

Albóndigas en Salsa de Almendras

Serves 6 to 8

Adding another cooked component such as these meatballs in an almond sauce takes this board from snack time to mealtime. In true tapas fashion, keep the small plates comin'.

PICADA

- ¼ cup slivered almonds
- 1 slice hearty white sandwich bread, torn into 1-inch pieces
- 2 tablespoons extra-virgin olive oil
- 3 tablespoons minced fresh parsley
- 2 garlic cloves, minced

MEATBALLS

- 1 slice hearty white sandwich bread, torn into 1-inch pieces
- 1 large egg
- 2 tablespoons water
- 2 tablespoons chopped fresh parsley, divided
- 2 garlic cloves, minced
- 1 teaspoon table salt
- ½ teaspoon pepper
- 1 pound ground pork
- 1 tablespoon extra-virgin olive oil
- ½ cup finely chopped onion
- ½ teaspoon paprika
- 1 cup chicken broth
- ½ cup dry white wine
- ¼ teaspoon saffron threads, crumbled
- 1 teaspoon sherry vinegar

1. For the picada: Process almonds in food processor until finely ground, about 20 seconds. Add bread and process until bread is finely ground, about 15 seconds. Transfer almond-bread mixture to 12-inch nonstick skillet. Add oil and cook over medium heat, stirring often, until mixture is golden brown, 3 to 5 minutes. Transfer to bowl and let cool slightly. Stir in parsley and garlic and set aside. (Picada can be refrigerated for up to 24 hours.)

2. For the meatballs: Process bread in now-empty processor until finely ground, about 15 seconds. Add egg, water, 1 tablespoon parsley, garlic, salt, and pepper and process until smooth paste forms, about 20 seconds, scraping down sides of bowl as necessary. Add pork and pulse until combined, about 5 pulses.

3. Remove processor blade. Using your moistened hands, form generous 1 tablespoon pork mixture into 1-inch round meatball and transfer to plate; repeat with remaining pork mixture to form about 24 meatballs. (Meatballs can be refrigerated for up to 24 hours.)

4. Wipe skillet clean with paper towels. Heat oil in now-empty skillet over medium heat until shimmering. Add onion and cook, stirring occasionally, until softened, 4 to 6 minutes. Add paprika and cook until fragrant, about 30 seconds. Add broth and wine and bring to simmer. Stir in saffron. Add meatballs and adjust heat to maintain simmer. Cover and cook until meatballs register 160 degrees, 6 to 8 minutes, flipping meatballs once.

5. Stir in picada and continue to cook, uncovered, until sauce has thickened slightly, 1 to 2 minutes longer. Off heat, stir in vinegar. Season with salt and pepper to taste. Transfer to serving dish, sprinkle with remaining 1 tablespoon parsley, and serve.

Sangria for a Crowd

Makes 12 cocktails

This amped-up chilled wine cocktail is the thirst-quenching accompaniment your tapas spread is craving. And not only is it make-ahead friendly, it actually gets smoother and mellower the longer it sits. The classic never-fail red wine version is perfect for this board, but I love whipping up a white wine or even a rosé version on a hot summer day.

- 2 (750-ml) bottles fruity red wine, such as Merlot
- 4 ounces orange liqueur
- 4 ounces Citrus Soda Syrup with lemon (page 107)
- 3 oranges (2 sliced thin, 1 juiced to yield 4 ounces)
- 2 lemons, sliced thin

1. Combine all ingredients in serving pitcher or large container. Cover and refrigerate until flavors meld and mixture is well chilled, at least 2 hours or up to 8 hours.

2. Stir sangria to recombine, then serve in chilled wine glasses (over ice, if desired), garnishing individual portions with macerated fruit.

VARIATIONS

White Wine Sangria

Substitute a fruity white wine, such as Riesling, for the red wine, brandy for the orange liqueur, 8 ounces of apple juice for the orange juice, and 2 apples or pears, sliced thin, for the orange and lemon slices.

Rosé Sangria

Substitute a rosé for the red wine, elderflower liqueur for the orange liqueur, 8 ounces of pomegranate juice for the orange juice, and 2 cups of mixed berries for the orange and lemon slices.

RAW BAR

Serves 6 to 8

START WITH:

Poached Shrimp (page 117)

Raw Bar Sauces (page 119)

Oysters

Lemon wedges

Hot sauce

Crushed ice (see page 117)

IF YOU WANT, ADD:

Crudo (page 121)

Fish roe (salmon, trout, and/or sturgeon)

Accompaniments for roe or caviar (crackers, cucumber slices, crème fraîche)

→

RAW BAR

One New Year's Eve, my friend Stacy hosted a Paris-themed party at her apartment in Chicago. We drank champagne and slurped oysters as a pre-dinner situation, and it felt so celebratory. Oysters always bring that special occasion–vibe, but serving them is simpler than you'd think. Once you've got the shucking down, you're golden. Serve them with shrimp, plenty of sauces, crudo if you're feeling fancy, and ice-cold champagne or martinis (see page 139). It's time to make any party oyster-worthy.

ELLE'S STRATEGY:

Set up shop. Keep all of your serving plates and platters in the fridge until you're ready to set up so they're nice and cold. Fill the chilled platters with crushed ice and, once you're ready to serve, place them on an easily wipeable surface (the ice will cause condensation, so avoid your favorite wooden table). Leaving space for oysters, place shrimp, cucumber slices, roe, and lemon wedges directly on the ice, and nestle small containers of sauces into the ice. Save the oysters for last: Once they're shucked, place them either on chilled oyster plates or directly on the ice.

Get a head start. Shrimp and sauces can be made a day in advance. You can fill several platters with crushed ice and store in the freezer so once you start shucking they're ready.

Successful shucking. You'll need an oyster knife (ATK's favorite is R. Murphy's New Haven–style knife); a few dish towels; trays or lipped platters (or rimmed baking sheets) to fill with ice; a bowl or garbage can for discarding shells; and lots and lots of crushed ice. Plan on 2 or 3 oysters per person (4 to 6 if you skip the shrimp).

Shopping and storing smarts. Make sure the oysters are shut tight, or that they close up when you touch them. Once purchased, oysters can be refrigerated for up to a week in a bowl covered with a damp towel, remoistening as needed to prevent drying out. Do not store oysters directly on or underneath ice; they will die in fresh water. (It's OK to place them on ice for serving.)

Poached Shrimp

Makes 2 pounds shrimp

I always like to add a cooked option to a raw bar—it's good for guests who might be raw fish–averse. But in all honesty, who doesn't love a classic shrimp cocktail? And while many shrimp poaching methods call for plunging them into hot water, this is a far gentler method: Start the shrimp in cold water, bring to just under a simmer, then allow them to finish cooking off heat. This means the insides and outsides of the shrimp cook more evenly, yielding plump, juicy, far-from-rubbery shrimp. Extra-large shrimp (21 to 25 per pound) can be substituted for the jumbo shrimp; reduce covered cooking time to 2 to 4 minutes.

2	pounds shell-on jumbo shrimp (16 to 20 per pound)
2½	tablespoons table salt
10	sprigs fresh thyme
2	teaspoons peppercorns
3	bay leaves
½	teaspoon celery seeds
8	(2-inch) strips lemon zest plus ¼ cup juice, spent halves reserved (2 lemons)
8	cups ice

1. Using kitchen shears, cut through top shell of each shrimp along vein line. Leave shell on and remove and discard vein. Combine shrimp, 4 cups cold water, salt, thyme, peppercorns, bay leaves, and celery seeds in Dutch oven. Set pot over medium-high heat and cook, stirring occasionally, until water registers 170 degrees and shrimp are just beginning to turn pink, 5 to 7 minutes.

2. Remove from heat and add lemon zest and juice and spent halves. Cover and let sit until shrimp are completely pink and firm, 5 to 7 minutes. Stir ice into pot and let shrimp cool completely, about 5 minutes. Drain shrimp in colander and peel, leaving tails intact. Refrigerate shrimp until thoroughly chilled, at least 1 hour or up to 24 hours.

ICE ICE BABY:

To keep your raw bar ice cold, you'll need . . . ice. And plenty of it. Crushed ice is ideal (it keeps the seafood stabilized even as it melts), but even refrigerators with ice makers often have limited capacities. The best way to crush it is by hand. Here's how: Fill a heavy-duty 1-gallon zipper-lock freezer bag about three-quarters full with ice cubes and press out as much air as possible before sealing. Wrap the bag tightly with a large dish towel. Then simply strike the wrapped bag with a mallet, skillet, or rolling pin to break the ice to the desired size.

You'll need about 5 pounds ice to create a 1½-inch-thick layer of ice in a large platter or rimmed baking sheet. This will keep everything cold for about 30 minutes. If you're using a smaller platter, store extra ice in a colander set in a bowl in the fridge. Use this stash to refresh your platter as needed.

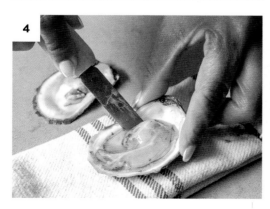

Raw Bar Sauces

Oysters are perfectly delicious on their own. In fact, just a simple squeeze of lemon and maybe a dash of hot sauce and you're good to go. But to add some interest to your board, include one or more of these sauces—a traditional mignonette and/or a gingery one for a little unexpected twist. And of course, what's shrimp cocktail without its eponymous sauce? (The mignonette recipes can easily be halved if you choose to serve more than one.)

Mignonette Sauce

Makes about 1 cup

Bright and clean, mignonette sauce brings out the best in briny, fresh shellfish. One warning: Use this tangy sauce sparingly. A little goes a long way.

- ½ cup red wine vinegar
- 2 medium shallots, chopped fine, or ¼ cup minced red onion
- 2 tablespoons juice from 1 lemon
- 1½ tablespoons minced fresh parsley leaves

Mix everything together in a small bowl. (Sauce can be refrigerated for up to 24 hours.)

Ginger Mignonette

Makes about 1 cup

This gingery take on mignonette adds an unexpected element to your raw bar.

- ⅔ cup rice vinegar
- 1 shallot, minced
- 2 scallions, minced
- 1 teaspoon grated fresh ginger
- 1 teaspoon grated orange zest plus ⅓ cup juice
- ½ teaspoon pepper
- ½ teaspoon sugar

Mix everything together in a small bowl. (Sauce can be refrigerated for up to 24 hours.)

Cocktail Sauce

Makes 1¼ cups

- 1 cup ketchup
- ¼ cup prepared horseradish
- 1 teaspoon Worcestershire sauce
- 1 teaspoon lemon juice
- ½ teaspoon Old Bay seasoning
- ⅛ teaspoon cayenne pepper

Whisk all ingredients together in bowl until combined. (Sauce can be refrigerated for up to 4 days; bring to room temperature before serving.)

HOW TO SHUCK AN OYSTER:

1. Fold dish towel several times into thin, tight roll. Grip towel in fist of hand that will be holding oyster, wrapping 1 end over your thumb and tucking it between your thumb and forefinger.

2. Using your towel-protected thumb, hold oyster in place with hinge facing away from thumb. Insert tip of oyster knife into hinge of oyster.

3. Work tip of knife into hinge using twisting motion. When shells begin to separate, twist knife to pop hinge.

4. Run knife along top shell, scraping abductor muscle from shell to release oyster. Slide knife under oyster to scrape abductor muscle from bottom shell.

Tip: If you're a slow shucker, instead of placing shucked oysters directly on the ice as they're ready (where the ice will likely melt before you're finished), make a foil landing zone. Crumple up aluminum foil so there are hills and valleys, then place shucked oyster on top and press firmly until the foil flattens and the oyster stays full of liquid. Once you've shucked all oysters, put them on ice.

LEVEL UP YOUR BOARD

Crudo

Serves 4 to 6

Once you have the fresh seafood, it's just about contrasting the raw fish with the right garnish. Fruity olive oil, bright lemon juice, and a sprinkle of sea salt are a great start, but other options are endless. Freshness is key when serving fish raw. Try using tuna, sea bass, fluke, and/or scallops. Inspect the fillets for bones and remove before slicing. Freeze the fish for about 15 minutes to make slicing easier.

- 12 ounces skinless sushi-grade fish fillets
- 1½ tablespoons extra-virgin olive oil
- 1   tablespoon lemon juice
     Coarse sea salt

Using sharp knife, cut fillets lengthwise into 2- to 3-inch-wide strips. Working with 1 strip at a time, slice fish crosswise on bias into ⅛-inch-thick slices. Arrange fish attractively on chilled plate. Drizzle with oil and lemon juice and sprinkle with sea salt to taste. Serve immediately.

Furikake

Makes about ½ cup

This briny nori-studded spice blend just tastes at home sprinkled atop crudo.

- 2   nori sheets, torn into 1-inch pieces
- 3   tablespoons sesame seeds, toasted
- 1½ tablespoons bonito flakes
- 1½ teaspoons sugar
- 1½ teaspoons flake sea salt, such as Maldon

Process nori in spice grinder until coarsely ground and pieces are no larger than ½ inch, about 15 seconds. Add sesame seeds, bonito flakes, and sugar and pulse until coarsely ground and pieces of nori are no larger than ¼ inch, about 2 pulses. Transfer to small bowl and stir in salt. (Furikake can be stored in airtight container for up to 3 months.)

BUYING SUSHI GRADE:

What makes fish appropriate for eating raw? Unfortunately, there are no official standards for the label "sushi-grade," although it is assumed that the fish is suitable for raw applications. If a fish that's prone to parasites (salmon, wild cod, mackerel, and freshwater fish) is given this label, it means it was frozen to ensure these parasites were killed before the fish was sold. It is unlikely that farmed fish will have parasites because they are given parasite-free feed. Be sure to talk with your fishmonger to get the freshest, best fish for serving raw.

OTHER SUGGESTED SEASONINGS:

Don't limit yourself to EVOO, lemon juice, and coarse sea salt. Even if sticking to the main categories below, the sky's the limit. (My favorite leveled-up finisher is furikake, but feel free to get creative.)

- **An oil:** Sesame, nut, chili, or herb oil
- **Something acidic:** Citrus juice, ponzu, vinegar
- **Final finisher:** Citrus zest, minced herbs, toasted seeds, spice blends, cracked black pepper

PÂTÉ

Serves 6 to 8

START WITH:

Chicken Liver Mousse (page 125)

Store-bought country-style pâté
(see "A Pâté Primer" on page 127)

Sliced baguettes (toasted if
desired) and crackers

Mustards (Dijon and/or
whole-grain)

Pickles (cornichons, pearl onions)

IF YOU WANT, ADD:

Bistro Salad (page 126)

Smoked Trout Pâté (page 126)

Cheese (blue cheese, Comté,
or other cheese)

Pickled Red Onion (page 58)

Butter

Coarse sea salt

→

PÂTÉ

A pâté board represents top-notch entertaining, but it's also the kind of food my partner and I might have for dinner on a night when I don't want to cook. A nibble of pâté, a swipe of mustard, a briny thing, a piece of cheese . . . we'll nosh until it's gone. I love that you can buy *everything* if you want. It's a fun way to eat because you get to assemble every bite, and can make each bite a little different. And since everything on the board goes well together, you literally can't go wrong.

ELLE'S STRATEGY:

Set up shop. This board requires a lot of schmearing and smudging so leave space around food for people to cut, spread, and assemble (you don't want mustard running into the cheese). Cut up harder cheeses. Arrange pâtés and cheeses in different places and lay trails of crackers and bread slices in between. Fill the spaces with pickles, dollops of mustard, and a dab of softened butter.

Make it ahead. Almost everything can be done ahead, but let the food come to room temperature before serving. Pâtés can be made 3 days ahead. Pickled onions can be made 1 week ahead. Salad greens can be washed several hours ahead; I like to store the washed greens right in the salad spinner in the fridge if there's space available.

Choose the pâtés. If serving more than one pâté, I like to pair a smooth and spreadable version with something rustic and sliceable (see page 127). If I'm adding a third, I might include a fish or veggie pâté or luscious rillettes.

Choose the accompaniments. Pâtés are helped by other strong flavors. For cheese, think aged cheese and blue cheese. Tangy and briny pickles and sharp mustard cut through the richness. Smooth pâtés are great spread onto crusty baguette or lightly toasted bread. Coarse-textured pâtés pair especially well with crackers.

Salt your butter. Sprinkle coarse sea salt on butter to add crunchy texture and pops of brininess.

Chicken Liver Mousse

Makes 1½ cups

I love almost anything in the pâté family, but this rich and silky mousse (also called mousseline) is especially nice. The best part? While some pâtés can be a bit of a project, this one's relatively simple. And if anybody's on the fence about chicken liver, this mousse will sell them: While liver pâtés can be dense, here you fold in whipped cream, which adds lightness and balances the liver-y flavor. The result is so easy to spread and even easier to eat. You will need two 6-ounce ramekins for this recipe.

> 12 ounces chicken livers, rinsed, patted dry, trimmed, and halved if large
>
> ¼ teaspoon table salt
>
> ¼ teaspoon pepper
>
> 2 tablespoons unsalted butter, plus 4 tablespoons cut into 4 pieces and chilled
>
> 2 sprigs fresh thyme, plus ¼ teaspoon minced
>
> 1 shallot, minced
>
> 3 tablespoons brandy
>
> ¼ cup heavy cream

1. Pat chicken livers dry with paper towels and sprinkle with salt and pepper. Melt 2 tablespoons butter in 12-inch nonstick skillet over medium-high heat. Add livers and thyme sprigs to skillet and cook, without stirring, until livers are lightly browned, about 2 minutes. Flip livers, add shallot, and cook until livers are lightly browned on second side and shallot is just beginning to soften, about 2 minutes. Off heat, add brandy and allow residual heat in skillet to reduce brandy to 1 tablespoon, about 1 minute. Discard thyme sprigs.

2. Process liver mixture in food processor until smooth, about 30 seconds, scraping down sides of bowl as needed. With processor running, add remaining 4 tablespoons chilled butter, 1 piece at a time, until incorporated, about 1 minute. Strain liver mixture through fine-mesh strainer into large bowl, pressing on solids to extract as much liver mixture as possible; discard solids.

3. Whip heavy cream in separate large bowl until stiff peaks form. Fold whipped cream and minced thyme into strained liver mixture until fully incorporated. Season with salt and pepper to taste.

4. Spoon mousse into two 6-ounce ramekins and smooth tops. Press plastic wrap against surface of mousse and refrigerate until completely chilled and set, at least 1 hour or up to 3 days. Bring to room temperature before serving.

LEVEL UP YOUR BOARD

Bistro Salad

Serves 6 to 8

This salad works like a palate cleanser. If you're trying different pâtés, a taste of the crisp, slightly bitter leaves in between bites will refresh your palate and prepare you for the next pâté so the flavors don't blend together. It also does a great job of cutting through the richness, and helps the board to serve as a light meal. A combination of frisée and romaine provides plenty of crunchy texture and just enough bitterness.

- 1 tablespoon red wine vinegar
- 1½ teaspoons minced shallot
- ½ teaspoon mayonnaise
- ½ teaspoon Dijon mustard
- ⅛ teaspoon table salt
- ⅛ teaspoon pepper
- 3 tablespoons extra-virgin olive oil
- 1 large head frisée (8 ounces), trimmed and cut into 1-inch pieces
- 1 romaine lettuce heart (6 ounces), trimmed and cut into 1-inch pieces

Whisk vinegar, shallot, mayonnaise, mustard, salt, and pepper together in large bowl. While whisking constantly, slowly drizzle in oil until combined. Add frisée and romaine and toss to coat. Season with salt and pepper to taste. Serve.

Smoked Trout Pâté

Makes about 1½ cups

This creamy, beautiful pâté allows the flavor of smoked trout to shine because it uses just a little cream cheese and sour cream. Minced chives add more flavor, and lemon juice contributes brightness. To soften cream cheese quickly, microwave it for 20 to 30 seconds.

- ⅓ cup sour cream
- 2 ounces cream cheese, softened
- 2 teaspoons fresh lemon juice
- 8 ounces smoked trout, skin removed, broken into 1-inch pieces
- 3 tablespoons minced fresh chives

Process sour cream, cream cheese, and lemon juice in food processor until smooth, about 30 seconds, scraping down sides of bowl as needed. Add trout and pulse until finely chopped and incorporated, about 6 pulses. Transfer pâté to serving bowl, fold in chives, and season with salt and pepper to taste. (The pâté can be refrigerated, wrapped tightly in plastic wrap, for up to 3 days. Season with additional fresh lemon juice, salt, and pepper to taste before serving.)

LEFTOVERS? DON'T PANIC.

Make use of every rich morsel, even if you have to save some for another day.

- **Bistro burger:** Spread a burger bun with a layer of chicken liver mousse for a luxurious topping.

- **Banh mi:** Use extra chicken liver mousse as the pâté layer in a homemade banh mi sandwich, or spread it on the crust of a classic store-bought banh mi.

- **Bagels:** Spread any leftover smoked trout pâté on toasted bagels (with or without cream cheese).

- **Grilled cheese:** All the same ingredients as in the board, now in melty handheld form: Add a layer of pâté (and a slick of mustard) before assembling and griddling.

A PÂTÉ PRIMER:

Country-style pâté: Rustic textured, sliceable pâté, often make from pork ground with lard or bacon (pâté de campagne). Duck can also be done country-style, as can other animals such as rabbit.

Smooth pâté: Often this is duck or goose liver, such as foie gras, or chicken liver. But smooth pâté can also be made from ingredients such as seafood and vegetables. A close cousin, mousseline, incorporates whipped cream to add lightness.

Terrine: Named after the loaf-shaped mold in which it's cooked. Any pâté that is cooked in a terrine can be called a terrine. These are sliceable, and can be rustic or smooth.

Pâté en croûte: Any pâté baked in a pastry crust.

Rillettes: A potted meat (similar to confit) made by braising meat or fish until the meat is tender and easily shreddable, then beating it with fat to create a spread.

AFTERNOON TEA

Serves 6 to 8

START WITH:

British-Style Currant Scones (page 132)

Spreads (marmalade, jam, butter, clotted cream, lemon curd)

Tea

Tea additions (honey, sugar cubes, milk or cream, lemon wedges)

Cookies (madeleines, shortbread, macarons)

Berries

IF YOU WANT, ADD:

Ham and Cheese Palmiers (page 135)

Finger sandwiches (see page 135)

→

AFTERNOON TEA

Traditional afternoon tea has three courses: tea sandwiches and savories, then scones, and finally sweets. Still hungry? I got you. Add in other snacks like mini frittatas (see page 50), Prosciutto-Wrapped Asparagus (page 37), or Lemon Cookie Bars (page 163). You'll need tea cups, but don't worry about breaking out the fine china. Instead, hit up a thrift store for a mismatched look. Then, send your guests home with them as party favors.

ELLE'S STRATEGY:

Set up shop. Set out tea, teacups, saucers, and all the additions. The only utensils needed are spoons and butter knives; otherwise it's all finger food. Group each course together. Stack your tea sandwiches on a platter, and separate the types with the palmiers. No tiered stand? Use a cake stand instead, or even place a plate on an upside-down bowl to add some height.

Get a head start. You can start the palmiers (if making) up to 2 days ahead and assemble the tea sandwiches the night before. And though they are best eaten fresh, you could even make the scones ahead of time: Store them in your freezer and reheat in a 300-degree oven for 15 minutes before serving.

Finger sandwich success. Use the softest bread you can find, slice fillings superthin, and cut the crusts off to make eating easier. You can assemble the sandwiches the night before and refrigerate them on a tray covered loosely with plastic wrap. Bring them to room temperature before serving, and wait to cut the crusts off until just before your guests arrive to avoid dried-out bread.

Give options. If you wanted, you could fill the teapot with hot water and set out a tray of individual tea bags instead of brewing a big pot of tea.

Hot water in a flash. You know what they say: A watched pot never boils. Invest in an electric tea kettle (OXO has a great model) to speed things up.

British-Style Currant Scones

Makes 12 scones

Compared to American scones, scones from across the pond use far less butter, far more baking powder, and are brushed with a light milk-and-egg wash to aid browning. They're also more cake-like, and are not as sweet or as rich as American scones (which means they're perfect for eating with butter and jam). Whole milk is best here, but low-fat milk can be used in a pinch. The dough will be quite soft and wet; dust your work surface and your hands liberally with flour. For a tall, even rise, use a sharp-edged biscuit cutter and push straight down; do not twist the cutter.

- 3   cups (15 ounces) all-purpose flour
- ⅓   cup (2⅓ ounces) sugar
- 2   tablespoons baking powder
- ½   teaspoon table salt
- 8   tablespoons unsalted butter, cut into ½-inch pieces and softened
- ¾   cup dried currants
- 1   cup whole milk
- 2   large eggs

1. Adjust oven rack to upper-middle position and heat oven to 500 degrees. Line rimmed baking sheet with parchment paper. Pulse flour, sugar, baking powder, and salt in food processor until combined, about 5 pulses. Add butter and pulse until fully incorporated and mixture looks like very fine crumbs with no visible butter, about 20 pulses. Transfer mixture to large bowl and stir in currants.

2. Whisk milk and eggs together in second bowl. Set aside 2 tablespoons milk mixture. Add remaining milk mixture to flour mixture and, using rubber spatula, fold together until almost no dry bits of flour remain.

3. Transfer dough to well-floured counter and gather into ball. With floured hands, knead until surface is smooth and free of cracks, 25 to 30 times. Press gently to form disk.

Using floured rolling pin, roll disk into 9-inch round, about 1 inch thick. Using floured 2½-inch round cutter, stamp out 8 rounds, recoating cutter with flour if it begins to stick. Arrange scones on prepared sheet. Gather dough scraps, form into ball, and knead gently until surface is smooth. Roll dough to 1-inch thickness and stamp out 4 rounds. Discard remaining dough.

4. Brush tops of scones with reserved milk mixture. Reduce oven temperature to 425 degrees and bake scones until risen and golden brown, 10 to 12 minutes, rotating sheet halfway through baking. Transfer scones to wire rack and let cool for at least 10 minutes. Serve scones warm or at room temperature.

BREWING THE PERFECT CUPPA:

Start with good water. If your tap water is hard—that is, it has a high mineral content, which can compromise the tea's flavor—run it through a filter, or use bottled water instead.

Back down from boiling. Many tea companies will indicate the appropriate temperature on the packaging. But in general, white and green teas should be made with water that is well under boiling—typically 160 to 180 degrees—and black and herbal teas with water that's just under a boil, about 210 degrees.

Steep with caution. You don't want to oversteep your tea: The longer you steep, the more tannins will leach out of the leaves, making your infusion bitter and overwhelming the tea's more delicate flavors. To avoid this, steep your tea for 1 minute, taste it, and then let it steep longer, tasting as you go, until it meets your approval.

GET THE (TEA) PARTY STARTED:

Why stop at tea? Kick things up a notch with an on-theme cocktail.

Make a tea liqueur. Combine 1 tablespoon dried black or green tea and 14 ounces vodka in pint-size glass jar. Cover tightly and shake. Store jar in cool, dark place for 1 day, shaking mixture occasionally. Set fine-mesh strainer in medium bowl and line with triple layer of cheesecloth. Strain vodka mixture through prepared strainer, pressing on solids to extract as much liquid as possible; discard solids. Return infused vodka to clean jar and add 2 ounces simple syrup (see page 107; skip the citrus zest). Cover and gently shake to combine. (Tea liqueur can be stored in cool, dark place for up to 1 year. Shake gently before using.)

Turn it into a teatini. Add 2 ounces vodka and 2 ounces tea liqueur to mixing glass, then fill three-quarters full with ice. Stir until mixture is fully combined and well chilled, about 30 seconds. Strain cocktail into glass, garnish with lemon slice, and serve.

1

2

3

LEVEL UP YOUR BOARD

Ham and Cheese Palmiers

Makes 34 palmiers

Palmiers are typically sweet cookies made from puff pastry that is sprinkled with sugar before being rolled up and sliced into thin pieces. The baked treats are said to resemble elephant ears (which they are sometimes called), palm leaves, or butterflies. For this savory version, brush a sheet of store-bought puff pastry with Dijon mustard and sprinkle with fresh thyme, then layer on thinly sliced ham and Parmesan cheese and roll the sheet up into the signature double log. The result is a crispy, cheesy, savory cookie you don't need to wait until the end of the meal to indulge in. To thaw frozen puff pastry, let it sit either in the refrigerator for 24 hours or on the counter for 30 minutes to 1 hour.

    1 (9½ by 9-inch) sheet puff pastry, thawed

    2 tablespoons Dijon mustard

    2 teaspoons minced fresh thyme

    4 ounces thinly sliced deli ham

    2 ounces Parmesan cheese, grated (1 cup)

1. Dust counter lightly with flour. Unfold puff pastry and roll into 12-inch square. Brush evenly with mustard, sprinkle with thyme, lay ham evenly over top (to edges of pastry), and sprinkle with Parmesan. Roll up both sides of pastry until they meet in middle. Wrap pastry log in plastic wrap and refrigerate until firm, about 1 hour. (Rolled pastry log can be refrigerated for up to 2 days before slicing and baking.)

2. Adjust oven rack to middle position and heat oven to 400 degrees. Line rimmed baking sheet with parchment paper. Using sharp serrated or slicing knife, trim ends of log, then slice into ⅓-inch-thick pieces (you should have 34 pieces). Space them about 1 inch apart on prepared sheet.

3. Bake until golden brown and crispy, about 25 minutes, rotating sheet halfway through baking. Transfer palmiers to wire rack and let cool for 5 minutes. Serve warm or at room temperature.

MAKING FINGER SANDWICHES:

1. Spread 2 slices of bread with whatever spread you're using (try mayo, cream cheese, Dijon mustard, or butter). This ensures the bread won't dry out, and also keeps the toppings properly anchored. Then add your toppings (make sure they're sliced superthin and blotted dry) to one slice.

2. Put the other slice of bread (spread-side down) on top. Using a very sharp knife, slice the crusts off.

3. Cut sandwich into triangles, squares, or rectangles. Or, use a cookie cutter to cut sandwich into desired shapes. Sandwiches should be small enough to finish in a few bites.

SANDWICH SUGGESTIONS:

What you choose to put in your finger sandwiches is up to you (and whatever you happen to have on hand) but here are some ideas to get you started. Plan on 3 or 4 sandwiches per person.

- Cream cheese + cucumbers + smoked salmon + dill
- Horseradish mayo + roast beef
- Pâté (see page 125) + arugula
- Egg or chicken salad
- Butter + radishes + flake sea salt
- Goat cheese + prosciutto
- Brie + fig jam
- Pesto + fresh mozzarella
- Honey mustard + deli ham

MARTINIS

Serves 4 to 6

START WITH:

Big Batch Martinis (page 139)

Additional dry vermouth, and gin or vodka

Ice

Cocktail onions

Olives (pimento-, garlic-, and/or blue cheese–stuffed)

Olive brine

Lemon twists (see page 141)

Simple snacks (kettle chips, mixed nuts)

IF YOU WANT, ADD:

Easy Cheese Straws (page 140)

Prosciutto-Wrapped Stuffed Dates (page 140)

→

MARTINIS

Martinis are one of my favorite drinks, and they're the main reason I keep olives in my fridge. I'm not a huge fan of olives in food, but if they're soaking in martini juice, I'm in. I love mixing up martinis for friends, but who wants to play bartender all night? The big batch takes the pressure off, and everyone can slightly adjust their drink to meet their particular specifications (I'm dirty, up, and with extra olives, thank you for asking). It's a fancy-seeming drink made casual—tuxedo not required.

ELLE'S STRATEGY:

Set up shop. Set out bottles of gin (or vodka) and vermouth; small dishes for the garnishes; olive juice in a pourable container; and bar equipment—a jigger or shot glass (for customizing the big batch or making your own); a mixing glass with a strainer and a bar spoon (to make an individual martini); and a bucket of ice (to chill an individual martini or serve the big batch on the rocks). Organize the snacks on a separate tray, and put the cheese straws in a tall glass for some height. Keep your martinis in the fridge until just before your guests arrive.

Get a head start. Mix up your martinis up to one month ahead of time. Cheese straws can be made up to 3 days ahead, and prosciutto-wrapped dates up to 8 hours.

Keep it simple. No bar equipment? Use a mason jar as a mixing glass, a measuring spoon as a jigger, and a chopstick as a bar spoon. Or, skip the make-it-your-way altogether—just make the big batch and leave the customization to the garnishes. And no need to stick to traditional glasses, just use whatever you have.

Do the twist. If you want to make the citrus twists ahead of time, store them in ice water to preserve the spiral. Put them in a small dish before your guests arrive.

Perfect pairing. Serve the martinis along with a Raw Bar (page 115), Pâté (page 123), or as a precursor to Steak Frites (page 205) for classic steakhouse vibes.

Big Batch Martinis

Makes 8 cocktails

A classic martini has two main components: Gin and dry vermouth. But the proper balance of these elements is a subject of much discussion. Every martini drinker is different, but a good rule of thumb is 4 parts gin to 1 part vermouth. A measured amount of water adds the perfect amount of dilution so you can serve it straight from the fridge. London dry gin is best here, with its juniper-forward, citrus-tinged flavor profile. This recipe can easily be doubled.

16 ounces London dry gin or vodka

8 ounces water

4 ounces dry vermouth

1. Combine gin, water, and vermouth in serving pitcher or large container. Cover and refrigerate until well chilled, at least 2 hours. (Martinis may be refrigerated for up to 1 month.)

2. Stir cocktail to recombine, then serve in chilled cocktail glasses.

Individual Classic Martini

Makes 1 cocktail

It's good to have this recipe in your back pocket in case you run out of big batch martinis or some unexpected guests show up. That's also why I like to set out bottles of gin (or vodka) and vermouth, so people can make their own if they prefer. Because this martini isn't diluted like the big batch, it's important to stir with ice.

2 ounces London dry gin or vodka

½ ounce dry vermouth

Add gin and vermouth to mixing glass, then fill three-quarters full with ice. Stir until mixture is fully combined and well chilled, about 30 seconds. Strain cocktail into chilled cocktail glass. Garnish as desired and serve.

MAKE-IT-YOUR-WAY MARTINI:

Making a martini to your liking means tinkering with the ratio of gin to dry vermouth and choosing your garnishes. All of these adjustments can happen right in your cocktail glass, or in a mixing glass if you prefer.

- **Dry martini:** Add up to an additional ½ ounce gin or vodka to cocktail glass.

- **Wet martini:** Add up to an additional ½ ounce vermouth to cocktail glass.

- **Dirty martini:** Add ¼ ounce olive brine to cocktail glass.

- **Gibson:** Make a dry martini and garnish with cocktail onions.

- **With a twist:** This one's simple, just garnish with a lemon twist (see page 141).

- **Up:** Serve in a martini glass or coupe (if you have it) without any ice.

- **On the rocks:** Serve in a shorter glass over ice.

LEVEL UP YOUR BOARD

Easy Cheese Straws
Makes 14

To thaw frozen puff pastry, let it sit either in the refrigerator for 24 hours or on the counter for 30 minutes to 1 hour.

- 2 ounces Parmesan cheese, grated (1 cup)
- ¼ teaspoon table salt
- ¼ teaspoon pepper
- 1 (9½ by 9-inch) sheet puff pastry, thawed

1. Adjust oven racks to upper-middle and lower-middle positions and heat oven to 425 degrees. Combine Parmesan, salt, and pepper in bowl. Roll pastry into 10½-inch square on lightly floured counter. Sprinkle pastry with half of Parmesan mixture and press to adhere. Flip pastry and repeat with remaining Parmesan mixture.

2. Using sharp knife or pizza cutter, cut dough into fourteen ¾-inch-wide strips. Gently twist strips in opposite direction and transfer to two parchment paper–lined baking sheets.

3. Bake until fully puffed and golden brown, about 10 minutes, switching and rotating sheets halfway through baking. Let cool completely before serving. (Straws can be stored in an air-tight container for up to 3 days.)

VARIATIONS

Sweet and Spicy Straws
Combine 1 tablespoon sugar, 2 teaspoons chili powder, and ⅛ teaspoon ground cinnamon in bowl. Substitute sugar mixture for Parmesan mixture.

Italian Straws
Combine ¼ cup minced sun-dried tomatoes, 2 tablespoons minced capers, 1 tablespoon minced fresh basil, and 2 minced garlic cloves, salt, and pepper in bowl. Substitute tomato mixture for Parmesan mixture.

Everything Straws
Substitute 1 tablespoon everything bagel seasoning (see page 58) for the Parmesan mixture.

Prosciutto-Wrapped Stuffed Dates
Makes 24

Sweet-salty and irresistible, these snacks are the perfect companion to a briny martini. High-quality, thinly sliced prosciutto is essential here. Look for Medjool dates (as they are particularly sweet) with a dense yet plump texture.

- ⅔ cup walnuts, toasted and chopped fine
- ½ cup minced fresh parsley
- 2 tablespoons extra-virgin olive oil
- ½ teaspoon grated orange zest
- 12 large pitted dates, halved lengthwise
- 12 thin slices prosciutto, halved lengthwise

Combine walnuts, parsley, oil, and orange zest in bowl; season with salt and pepper to taste. Mound 1 generous teaspoon filling into center of each date half. Wrap prosciutto securely around dates. Serve. (Dates can be refrigerated for up to 8 hours; bring to room temperature before serving.)

MORE SIMPLE BAR SNACKS:

- Stuffed olives: Make them yourself with blue cheese, feta, goat cheese, or roasted garlic.

- Spicy whipped feta dip: Blitz together feta, a drizzle of EVOO, a little water, a squeeze of lemon, and a sprinkle of paprika and cayenne in a food processor until smooth. Serve with pita chips (see page 81).

- Cashews tossed with curry powder.

- A bowl of seasoned popcorn (see page 105).

- Cubes of olive oil–soaked focaccia.

- Shards of frico (see page 177).

- Caprese salad skewers with cherry tomatoes, mini fresh mozzarella balls, and fresh basil drizzled with balsamic reduction (see page 148).

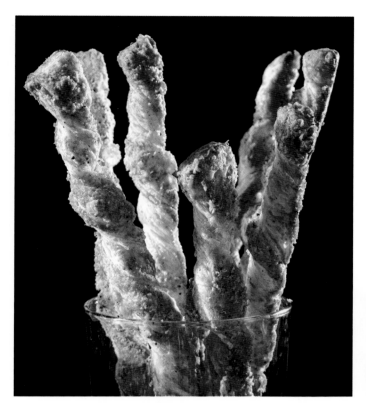

HOW TO MAKE A CITRUS TWIST:

1. Use channel knife to remove 3- to 4-inch strand, working around circumference of citrus in spiral pattern to ensure continuous piece. (If you don't have a channel knife, remove 3- to 4-inch strip zest with vegetable peeler, then slice zest lengthwise into slender strips.)

2. Curl strand tightly to establish uniform twist, then place in cocktail or on edge of glass.

BRING YOUR APPETITE

Dinner-Sized Boards to Fill You Up

145 **Pizza Parlor**

151 **Ballpark**

159 **Picnic**

165 **Oktoberfest**

171 **Chopped Salad**

179 **Grilled Vegetable Platter**

185 **Baked Potatoes**

191 **Shawarma**

197 **Pulled Pork**

205 **Steak Frites**

211 **Salmon Platter**

217 **Clambake**

PIZZA
PARLOR

Serves 4 to 6

START WITH:

French Bread Pizzas (page 147)

Classic pizza toppers (Parmesan, red pepper flakes, dried oregano, granulated garlic)

IF YOU WANT, ADD:

Greek Salad (page 148)

Dipping and drizzling sauces (see page 148)

→

PIZZA PARLOR

French bread pizza takes me back to childhood. My Uncle Pierre loved frozen pizzas. He would wait until I got off the school bus and make them, except he'd jazz them up with other toppings like peppers and onions. This is my homage to the latchkey kid's snack, and to the beginning of my learning that you can step outside of the literal box and elevate your food. If you're overwhelmed by the idea of DIY pizza night, this board is low-lift, but you'll be amazed at how engaged people get, kids and adults alike.

ELLE'S STRATEGY:

Set up shop. Create a pizza parlor vibe with checkered paper napkins and paper plates for quick cleanup. Fill glass cheese and spice shakers with grated Parmesan and red pepper flakes, and little bowls with other seasonings like granulated garlic and oregano. If you're serving dipping or drizzling sauces, pour them into bowls and arrange on and around your board. Just before serving, dress the salad and set out the pizzas on your board, sliced if desired.

Get a head start. The salad can be prepped and dressing made and stored separately up to 24 hours ahead. Pizza sauce can also be made up to 24 hours ahead. If people are building their own pizzas, you can prep the toppings in advance and even toast the bread through step 2.

Make it interactive. Involve everyone in the process by starting out with a build-your-own pizza board: Place sauce and cheeses in bowls, arrange toppings on a board, and let everyone customize their toasted breads before baking.

Any way you slice it. Cutting the pizzas into finger food–size strips allows people to try more topping and sauce combos without having to commit, and it extends the eating time. I also like to cut different-size pieces to offer variety, so everyone can eat at their own pace.

Get adventurous with quirky sauces. Ranch dressing is classic. Why not discover a new favorite? See some ideas on page 148.

French Bread Pizzas

Serves 4 to 6

A 24 by 4-inch loaf of supermarket French bread, which has a soft, thin crust and fine crumb, works best here, but you can substitute one-and-a-half 18-inch baguettes (cut baguettes into six equal pieces, and distribute the toppings evenly).

PIZZA

1	(24 by 4-inch) loaf soft French bread
1	tablespoon extra-virgin olive oil
8	tablespoons unsalted butter, melted
2	teaspoons granulated garlic
¼	teaspoon red pepper flakes
12	ounces mozzarella cheese, shredded (3 cups)
1	ounce Parmesan cheese, grated (½ cup)

SAUCE

1½	cups canned crushed tomatoes
1	tablespoon extra-virgin olive oil
1½	teaspoons Italian seasoning
½	teaspoon sugar
½	teaspoon table salt

1. For the pizza: Adjust oven rack to upper-middle position and heat oven to 450 degrees. Line rimmed baking sheet with aluminum foil. Cut bread in half crosswise, then halve each piece horizontally to create 4 equal pieces. Arrange pieces cut side down on prepared sheet. Brush crust with oil.

2. Combine melted butter, granulated garlic, and pepper flakes in bowl. Flip bread cut side up and brush cut side evenly with melted butter mixture. Bake, cut side up, until browned around edges, about 5 minutes.

3. For the sauce: Meanwhile, combine all sauce ingredients in bowl. (Sauce can be refrigerated for up to 24 hours.)

4. Spread sauce evenly over toasted bread, then top with mozzarella, followed by Parmesan. Bake until cheese is melted and spotty brown, about 15 minutes. Let pizzas cool for 5 minutes. Slice and serve.

BUILD-YOUR-OWN-PIZZA TOPPINGS:

Keep it simple or go wild, but use only up to ½ cup toppings per pizza to avoid overloading. Here are a few guidelines for optimal results:

Onions, peppers, and mushrooms: Thinly slice and cut into 2-inch lengths. Add to pizzas after the Parmesan.

Spinach and basil: Place beneath the cheese to protect them, or add to fully cooked pizza.

Canned vegetables (sliced black olives, baby artichoke hearts, pineapple tidbits): Drain and pat dry with paper towels. Add to pizzas after the Parmesan.

Meat (pepperoni, bacon, sausage, ground beef): Precook and crumble bacon. Brown raw sausage (pinched into ½-inch pieces) or ground beef in skillet for 4 to 5 minutes to render fat and keep meat moist. Add to pizzas after the Parmesan.

LEVEL UP YOUR BOARD

Greek Salad

Serves 4 to 6

The Greek salad at many pizza parlors shows up limp on arrival, but this version keeps things crisp. Seeding the cucumber and using fleshy cherry tomatoes rather than the larger (and juicier) tomatoes some Greek salads call for eliminates that dreaded pool of dressing at the bottom of the bowl, and blending in a little bit of yogurt produces a creamy dressing that clings nicely. Since feta cheese is the star of any Greek salad, some of it gets mixed into the dressing for tangy flavor in every bite. Raw onion can evoke strong opinions, so to please everyone the onion in this salad marinates in the dressing for 20 minutes to tame its harshness. Whole-milk yogurt makes for a richer dressing, but low-fat and nonfat plain yogurt are acceptable. To get a head start, chop the vegetables and make the dressing the day before and store them separately in the fridge.

- 4 ounces feta cheese, crumbled (1 cup), divided
- 3 tablespoons plain whole-milk yogurt
- 1 teaspoon dried oregano
- 1 garlic clove, minced
- 3 tablespoons red wine vinegar
- 6 tablespoons extra-virgin olive oil
- ½ red onion, sliced thin
- 1 English cucumber, halved lengthwise, seeded, and sliced thin
- 12 ounces cherry tomatoes, halved
- ¾ cup pitted kalamata olives
- 2 romaine lettuce hearts (12 ounces), torn into bite-size pieces

1. Process ½ cup feta, yogurt, oregano, garlic, vinegar, and oil in blender until smooth, about 30 seconds. Combine dressing and onion in large bowl and let sit 20 minutes.

2. Add remaining ½ cup feta, cucumber, tomatoes, olives, and romaine to bowl with dressing mixture and toss to combine. Season with salt and pepper. Serve.

SAUCES FOR DIPPING AND DRIZZLING

I didn't grow up dipping, but I definitely grew up with the ranch dressing drizzle. Marinara, ranch (see page 95), blue cheese dressing (see page 95), and barbecue sauce (see page 201) are all fun options, or try out some of these.

Garlic Butter Dipping Sauce

Makes about ½ cup

- 8 tablespoons unsalted butter
- 3 garlic cloves, minced
- ¼ teaspoon table salt

Melt butter in small saucepan over medium heat. Add garlic and salt and cook until just fragrant, about 1 minute. Let cool slightly before serving.

Spicy Honey Drizzle

Makes about ½ cup

Vinegary Frank's RedHot Original Cayenne Pepper Sauce is best here.

- ⅓ cup honey
- 2 tablespoons hot sauce

Bring honey and hot sauce to simmer in small saucepan over medium heat. Let cool slightly before serving.

Balsamic Drizzle

Makes about ½ cup

- ⅔ cup packed dark brown sugar
- ½ cup balsamic vinegar
- ¼ teaspoon table salt

Bring all ingredients to simmer in small saucepan over medium heat and cook until reduced to about ½ cup, 3 to 5 minutes. Let cool slightly before serving. (Drizzle can be refrigerated for up to 1 week; gently warm in microwave before using.)

BALLPARK

Serves 6 to 8

START WITH:

Hot dogs

Buns

Pitch-Perfect Lemonade (page 153)

Basic hot dog condiments (ketchup; yellow, spicy, and/or honey mustard; relish; diced onions)

IF YOU WANT, ADD:

Ballpark Pretzels (page 154)

More hot dog condiments (Chicago-style relish, sauerkraut, chili, grilled peppers and onions, sliced pickles, tomatoes, sport peppers, dill pickle spears)

Shell-on peanuts

Cracker Jack

→

BALLPARK

People always have strong opinions about hot dogs (the ketchup vs. mustard debate can get particularly heated). This board keeps everyone happy— they can make signature ballpark concoctions or just have what they like. As for me? I'm a Coney Dog chick all day long—give me all the meat sauce, onions, and mustard my snappy little frank can handle. Otherwise, I'm a purist: just ketchup, mustard, and some relish. Perfect harmony.

ELLE'S STRATEGY:

Set up shop. Find the longest tray you have in your house and dedicate the first quarter of it to the pretzels and mustard, and the rest to the hot dogs. Place the buns on the board, and scatter condiments (in the smallest containers you have) across the board and on the table for ultimate mix-and-matchability. Put out bowls of baseball-themed snacks. Just before you're ready to eat, put the cooked hot dogs in the buns and fill a pitcher with lemonade and plenty of ice.

Get a head start. Lemonade concentrate can be made up to 2 weeks ahead, and pretzels can be made up to 2 days ahead (or 1 month if you freeze them). Take stock of your pantry and make sure you have enough condiments.

Pick a theme. Re-create what I did here, or make your own spread using toppings from your favorite ballpark or city, or tailor it to teams in the World Series.

Have fun with it. Transport people to a baseball game with tiny plastic baseball helmets, boxes of Cracker Jack, and fast food baskets. (Check out party supply stores or online.) Change up the colors based on your favorite team.

Do the dogs. How you cook your hot dogs is up to you— I like to either boil them or grill them (much easier than pan-frying for a crowd). Make sure you have everything set up before you start cooking, though, so when the hot dogs are ready people can go straight in for it. Plan on about 2 hot dogs per person.

Pitch-Perfect Lemonade

Makes 8 cups lemonade or 4 cups lemonade concentrate

A larger-than-life-size lemonade is a baseball game staple. On a hot day in the stands, nothing quenches your thirst quite like it. This concentrate is perfect to keep on hand because you can make a big batch for a crowd or mix up a glass for yourself. And it can take on a life beyond lemonade, too—shandy or lemon drop, anyone? It's a good idea to have 10 lemons on hand, but you may not need all of them. Use a vegetable peeler, not a paring knife, to remove the zest. To make limeade concentrate, substitute 14 limes for the lemons and wash and zest 6 limes. (Because lime zest has less moisture than lemon zest, the sugar mixture will be less clumpy in step 1 but should still be very fragrant.)

10	lemons, divided
1½	cups (10½ ounces) sugar
¼	teaspoon table salt
2	cups hot water

1. To make concentrate: Select 4 lemons with fewest blemishes and scrub well. Rinse and dry thoroughly. Using vegetable peeler, remove zest of washed lemons in strips. Transfer zest to bowl and add sugar and salt. Toss to combine. Using potato masher, mash zest, sugar, and salt vigorously until mixture is damp, clumpy, and very fragrant, about 2 minutes. Add hot water and stir until sugar is dissolved, about 1 minute. Set aside until cool, about 30 minutes. While mixture cools, juice enough lemons to yield 1½ cups juice.

2. Stir juice into zest mixture until combined. Strain through fine-mesh strainer set over 4-cup liquid measuring cup; discard zest. Refrigerate until chilled, at least 1 hour. (If not using concentrate right away, transfer to airtight container and refrigerate for up to 2 weeks.)

3. To make lemonade: Fill pitcher with ice, add 4 cups cold water and concentrate, and stir to combine; if necessary, dilute with additional water to taste. For sparkling lemonade, substitute plain seltzer for cold water.

WHEN LIFE GIVES YOU LEMONADE, MAKE . . .

- **An Arnold Palmer:** Fill ice-filled glass with half lemonade and half iced tea (see page 202); stir to combine.

- **A shandy:** Fill chilled pint glass ¼ full with lemonade and top with 12 oz. beer (preferably a light lager such as Budweiser or Pabst Blue Ribbon). For best results, make sure all ingredients are cold before combining them.

- **A simple lemon drop:** Fill ice-filled glass with 2 oz. vodka and 8 oz. lemonade; stir to combine. For an optional but excellent touch, start by adding a sugar rim to the glass—run a lemon wedge around the edge of the glass and roll it in sugar. (See page 73 for how to rim a glass.)

LEVEL UP YOUR BOARD

Ballpark Pretzels
Makes 12 pretzels

These pretzels are a well-worth-it project if you've got the time. Warm, soft, and chewy with a shiny, salty exterior—these certainly pass muster. (Speaking of: Pass the mustard, and plenty of it.) Boiling the pretzels in a solution of baking soda and water before they hit the oven promotes browning and shininess and helps set the exterior crust to ensure a dense, chewy interior. Coarse pretzel salt may be substituted for the kosher salt on the exterior of the pretzels. However, be sure to still use kosher salt in the dough. Keep in mind that the dough needs to rise for 60 minutes, and then the shaped pretzels require a 20-minute rise before boiling and baking. These pretzels are best served warm, with mustard. See pages 156–157 for shaping tips.

1½ cups warm water (110 degrees)

3 tablespoons vegetable oil, divided

2 tablespoons packed dark brown sugar

2 teaspoons instant or rapid-rise yeast

3¾ cups (20⅔ ounces) bread flour

2 tablespoons kosher salt, divided

¼ cup baking soda

1. Lightly grease large bowl. In bowl of stand mixer, combine warm water, 2 tablespoons oil, sugar, and yeast and let sit until foamy, about 3 minutes. Combine flour and 4 teaspoons salt in separate bowl. Add flour mixture to yeast mixture. Fit stand mixer with dough hook and knead on low speed until dough comes together and clears sides of bowl, 4 to 6 minutes.

2. Turn out dough onto lightly floured counter and knead by hand until smooth, about 1 minute. Transfer dough to greased bowl and cover with plastic wrap. Let dough rise at room temperature until almost doubled in size, about 60 minutes.

3. Gently press center of dough to deflate. Transfer dough to lightly greased counter, divide into 12 equal pieces, and cover with plastic.

4. Lightly flour 2 rimmed baking sheets. Working with 1 piece of dough at a time, roll into 22-inch-long rope. Shape rope into U with 2-inch-wide bottom curve and ends facing away from you. Crisscross ropes in middle of U, then cross them again. Fold ends toward bottom of U. Firmly press ends into bottom curve of U, 1 inch apart, to form pretzel shape. Transfer pretzels to prepared sheets, knot side up, 6 pretzels per sheet. Cover pretzels loosely with plastic and let rise at room temperature until slightly puffy, about 20 minutes.

5. Adjust oven racks to upper-middle and lower-middle positions and heat oven to 425 degrees. Dissolve baking soda in 4 cups water in Dutch oven and bring to boil over medium-high heat. Using slotted spatula, transfer 4 pretzels, knot side down, to boiling water and cook for 30 seconds, flipping halfway through cooking. Transfer pretzels to wire rack, knot side up, and repeat with remaining 8 pretzels in 2 additional batches. Let pretzels rest for 5 minutes.

6. Wipe flour from sheets and grease with remaining 1 tablespoon oil. Sprinkle each sheet with ½ teaspoon salt. Transfer pretzels to prepared sheets, knot side up, 6 pretzels per sheet. Sprinkle 1 teaspoon salt evenly over pretzels.

7. Bake pretzels until they are mahogany brown and any yellowish color around seams has faded, 15 to 20 minutes, switching and rotating sheets halfway through baking. Transfer pretzels to wire rack and let cool for 10 minutes. Serve.

To Make Ahead: The pretzels are best eaten the day they are baked but will keep at room temperature in airtight container for up to 2 days. Freeze pretzels, wrapped well in plastic wrap, for up to 1 month. To reheat room-temperature pretzels, brush tops lightly with water, sprinkle with salt, and toast on baking sheet at 300 degrees for 5 minutes. Let frozen pretzels thaw before reheating.

BALLPARK ROAD TRIP:

Here are the greatest hot-dog-topper hits from just some of the places I've lived.

- **Boston (Fenway Frank):** Relish, spicy brown mustard, and chopped white onions on a New England–style bun

- **Chicago:** Yellow mustard, chopped white onions, Chicago-style relish, a dill pickle spear, tomato slices or wedges, pickled sport peppers, and a dash of celery salt on a poppy seed bun

- **New York:** Spicy brown mustard, warm sauerkraut and/or "onion sauce" (sautéed onions in a sweet, ketchupy sauce)

- **Detroit (Coney Dog):** Meat chili, chopped white onions, yellow mustard

- **Maryland:** Mac and cheese (see page 202) and crab meat, sprinkled with Old Bay

Shaping Ballpark Pretzels:

1. Divide the dough into quarters.

2. Separate each quarter into thirds.

3. Roll each third into a 22-inch rope.

4. Shape the rope into a U-shape with the ends facing away from you.

5. Cross the rope ends in the middle of the U, then cross them again.

6. Fold the ends toward the bottom of the U.

7. Press the ends firmly into the bottom of the curve, about 1 inch apart.

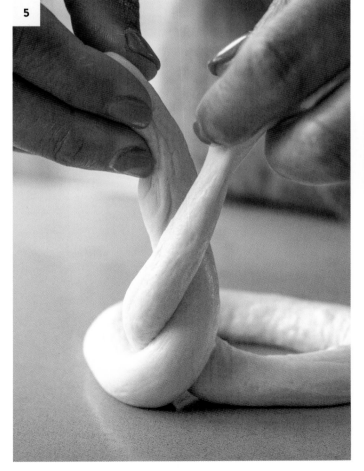

PICNIC

Serves 4 to 6

START WITH:

**Just-Gets-Better Sandwiches
(page 161)**

Chips

**Drinks (sparkling water, lemonade
on page 153, iced tea on page 202,
wine, and/or beer)**

IF YOU WANT, ADD:

Peach and Tomato Salad (page 162)

Lemon Cookie Bars (page 163)

→

PICNIC

Picnics capture the casual, serve-yourself vibe that boards are all about. Plus, eating outside with your faves is always guaranteed to be a good time. You know what isn't guaranteed? Good weather. But that's no reason to cancel the fun; just plan accordingly—bring umbrellas, raincoats, and things to weigh down your blanket if it's extra gusty (big rocks do the trick just fine). And you can never have too many garbage bags. You'll need more than you think for cleanup, and they can double as a raincoat in a pinch.

ELLE'S STRATEGY:

Set up shop. Find a spot that's on level ground and not in direct sunlight (or at least has a little shade). Make sure the ground is dry before you lay out your blanket. Keep everything in the cooler until you're ready to eat, and then bring things out but leave them in their containers for easier cleanup. Wrap the fresh mint in paper towels and add it to the salad just before you serve it so it doesn't get wilty.

Get a head start. Lemon cookie bars can be made 3 days in advance, and sandwiches can be made the day before. Gather your supplies ahead of time, make a list, and check it twice (see page 162). Once you're picnicking there's no running out to a store; you'll just have to improvise with what you have (a scary thought).

Sturdy supplies. Make sure your storage containers are leakproof (they're not all created equal!). Bring reusable plates instead of paper—it's better for the environment, but they also stand up to second helpings of salad.

Perfect packing. Pack your basket(s) in reverse order you need to take things out. Start with snacks (that don't need to be on ice) then plates, cutlery, and napkins; end with the picnic blanket so you can access that right away.

Keep critters at bay. Remember: You're eating in nature. Bring bug spray, drink out of mason jars or other lidded options, and cover the food when done serving (hotel shower caps work great for covering bowls!).

Just-Gets-Better Sandwiches

This oversize sandwich serves 8 and not only can be made in advance, it actually gets more delicious as it sits. Squishing the sandwich beneath a heavy Dutch oven fuses the layers together, making it sturdy enough for travel and easier to bite through. Look for a loaf with a soft crust. If you don't have a Dutch oven to press the sandwich, you can use a baking sheet or skillet loaded with hefty canned goods.

Turkey Picnic Sandwich with Sun-Dried Tomato Spread
Makes 8 sandwiches

SPREAD

- ¾ cup oil-packed sun-dried tomatoes, drained and patted dry
- ¼ cup sliced almonds, toasted
- ¼ cup capers, rinsed
- 1 teaspoon lemon juice
- 1 small garlic clove, minced
- ¼ teaspoon table salt
- ¼ teaspoon red pepper flakes
- 6 tablespoons extra-virgin olive oil

SANDWICH

- 1 large round loaf Italian bread or French bread (about 9-inch diameter)
- 4 ounces sliced Muenster cheese
- 8 ounces thinly sliced deli turkey
- ½ cup fresh parsley leaves
- 1¼ cups jarred roasted red peppers, drained and patted dry

1. For the spread: Process tomatoes, almonds, capers, lemon juice, garlic, salt, and pepper flakes in food processor until finely chopped, about 20 seconds, scraping down sides of bowl as needed. Transfer to bowl and stir in oil. (Spread can be refrigerated for up to 3 says.)

2. For the sandwich: Slice bread in half horizontally. Spread tomato spread evenly on cut sides of bread (use all of it). Layer Muenster, turkey, parsley, and red peppers on bread bottom. Cap with bread top and wrap sandwich tightly in double layer of plastic.

3. Place Dutch oven on top of sandwich and let sit at room temperature for at least 1 hour, or up to 2 hours. (Pressed sandwich can be refrigerated for up to 24 hours; bring to room temperature before serving.) Unwrap sandwich, cut into 8 wedges, and serve.

VARIATION

Roasted Zucchini Picnic Sandwich with Olive Spread
For spread, substitute pitted kalamata olives for sun-dried tomatoes and ½ cup fresh parsley leaves for almonds. For the sandwich, adjust oven rack to middle position and heat oven to 425 degrees. Toss 2 zucchini, cut in half crosswise and sliced lengthwise into ¼-inch-thick planks, with 2 tablespoons oil then arrange in single layer on rimmed baking sheet. Roast until zucchini is spotty brown on both sides, about 15 minutes, flipping halfway through baking; let cool to room temperature. Substitute fresh mozzarella for Muenster, zucchini for turkey, and 1 cup shredded carrots for red peppers. Omit parsley.

LEVEL UP YOUR BOARD

Peach and Tomato Salad

Serves 4 to 6

It might sound like a wild combo, but this salad brings together the two reigning champs of summer produce. It's the salad you didn't know you needed, and the key is choosing the very best peaches and tomatoes; there's no substitute for ripe, sweet in-season fruit (yes, tomatoes are fruit!). Keep mint separate until serving.

1 pound ripe tomatoes, cored, cut into ½-inch-thick wedges, and wedges halved crosswise

1 teaspoon table salt, divided

3 tablespoons extra-virgin olive oil

2 tablespoons cider vinegar

½ teaspoon grated lemon zest plus 1 tablespoon juice

½ teaspoon pepper

1 pound ripe peaches, halved, pitted, cut into ½-inch-thick wedges, and wedges halved crosswise

1 shallot, sliced into thin rings

⅓ cup fresh mint leaves, torn

1. Combine tomatoes and ½ teaspoon salt in bowl and toss to coat; transfer to colander and let drain in sink for 30 minutes.

2. Whisk oil, vinegar, lemon zest and juice, pepper, and remaining ½ teaspoon salt together in large bowl. Add peaches, shallot, and drained tomatoes to dressing and toss gently to coat. Season with salt and pepper to taste. Sprinkle with mint before serving.

10 THINGS YOU'LL BE GLAD YOU BROUGHT:

You've got the food part down, and you already know to bring plenty of ice, but picnics are about so much more than just what you eat. Here are 10 unexpected items to pack in your bag.

- Small cutting board
- Paring knife (with sheath!)
- Dish towels
- Insulated tumblers (to keep drinks cold)
- Garbage bags (bring extras!)
- Bug spray
- Wipes/hand sanitizer
- Portable speaker
- Portable table
- Solar-powered lights (to keep the party going into the evening)

Lemon Cookie Bars

Makes 24 bars

These chewy, zingy bars are like a cross between sugar cookies and lemon bars. They're the perfect end to a summery meal, and are more unexpected than a typical cookie (but travel just as well). Between the bars and the glaze, you will need three lemons for this recipe. To ensure that the glaze has the proper consistency, it's best to weigh the confectioners' sugar. The glaze will feel thick—and that's okay. It should sit atop the bars and not soak in.

BARS

2¼ cups (11¼ ounces) all-purpose flour

½ teaspoon baking soda

½ teaspoon table salt

2 cups (14 ounces) granulated sugar

6 tablespoons unsalted butter, melted

⅓ cup vegetable oil

2 ounces cream cheese, cut into 8 pieces and softened

1 large egg plus 1 large yolk

5 teaspoons grated lemon zest plus 3 tablespoons juice (2 lemons)

2 teaspoons vanilla extract

GLAZE

1½ tablespoons lemon juice

1 tablespoon cream cheese, softened

1 cup (4 ounces) confectioners' sugar

3 tablespoons yellow sprinkles (optional)

1. For the bars: Adjust oven rack to middle position and heat oven to 325 degrees. Make foil sling for 13 by 9-inch baking pan by folding 2 long sheets of aluminum foil; first sheet should be 13 inches wide and second sheet should be 9 inches wide. Lay sheets of foil in pan perpendicular to each other, with extra foil hanging over edges of pan. Push foil into corners and up sides of pan, smoothing foil flush to pan. Spray foil with vegetable oil spray.

2. Whisk flour, baking soda, and salt together in bowl. Whisk granulated sugar, melted butter, oil, and cream cheese together in second bowl (some lumps of cheese will remain but will smooth out later). Add egg and yolk, lemon zest and juice, and vanilla to sugar mixture and whisk until smooth. Add flour mixture and mix with rubber spatula until just combined.

3. Transfer batter to prepared pan, smoothing top with spatula. Bake until light golden brown and toothpick inserted in center comes out clean, 33 to 38 minutes. Let bars cool completely in pan on wire rack, about 2 hours.

4. For the glaze: Once bars are cooled, whisk lemon juice and cream cheese in bowl until combined. Add confectioners' sugar and whisk until smooth. Spread evenly over bars. Scatter sprinkles, if using, over top. Let glaze set fully, about 1 hour.

5. Using foil overhang, lift bars out of pan and transfer to cutting board. Cut into 24 pieces and serve. (Bars can be stored in airtight container at room temperature for up to 3 days.)

OKTOBERFEST

Serves 4 to 6

START WITH:

Beer Brats with Onion and Mustard (page 167)
and/or other German sausages

Hard pretzels, seeded crackers, and/or rye bread

Pickles

Cheese (Gouda or a German cheese like butterkäse)

Sauerkraut

Mustards (whole-grain, spicy brown,
and/or sweet brown)

IF YOU WANT, ADD:

German Potato Salad (page 168)

Apple-Fennel Rémoulade (page 168)
and/or sliced apples

→

OKTOBERFEST

It seems to me that the 1810 wedding of the crown prince of Bavaria should be one of the most famous royal weddings in modern history, since that was the very first Oktoberfest. I wonder what the prince and princess would think of today's Oktoberfest, where something like 2 million gallons of beer is imbibed? And that's just in Munich—never mind every other corner of the world where this folk festival has taken root. This uber-hearty board brings the festivities home year-round, to a manageable crowd.

ELLE'S STRATEGY:

Set up shop. Put the brats in a shallow bowl. Arrange sliced sausages, cheese, and accompaniments on the board around the bowl. Dollop the mustards right onto the board or put into little bowls. Your board ideally will be groaning with food, so the bread basket can live nearby. Set out plates, napkins, and beer mugs (or steins if you've got 'em), plus plenty of toothpicks for spearing.

Get a head start. The potato salad and rémoulade can both be made up to 1 day ahead of time. You can cook the beer brats earlier in the day and keep them warm in a slow cooker.

Bavarian style. A rustic wooden surface lends the effect of an Oktoberfest picnic table or beer barrel. Source blue-and-white decor online. Cue up some oompah music to get the festivities started. To take your fest over the top, make a batch of Ballpark Pretzels (page 154). And since there's always room for dessert, set out some gingerbread cookies. Extra points if they're heart-shaped.

Ein Prosit! German drinking etiquette demands a toast before drinking with friends, no matter what round it is. The traditional beer is Märzen, an amber lager. Nowadays a lighter lager called festbier is served. The traditional nonalcoholic drink is apfelschorle, a delicious blend of apple juice and sparkling water.

Beer Brats with Onion and Mustard

Serves 4 to 6

Perfectly browned and juicy brats alongside a cold beer:
How can you beat that on a crisp fall day? Bratwurst is made
from ground pork (sometimes with veal or beef) that's seasoned
with caraway, coriander, ginger, and nutmeg. Fresh, uncooked
bratwurst is the way to go here; it has a nice coarse texture
that's much more interesting than that of partially cooked
bratwurst. After searing the brats to brown them, you'll make
a flavorful braising liquid from onions, beer, mustard, honey,
vinegar, and caraway seeds and finish cooking the brats in that.
Then, after cooking the braising mixture down to concentrate
the flavors, it becomes a topping.

3	tablespoons vegetable oil, divided
1½	pounds bratwurst (6 sausages)
2	large onions, halved and sliced thin
¼	teaspoon table salt
¼	teaspoon pepper
2	garlic cloves, minced
1	teaspoon caraway seeds
1½	cups mild lager
¼	cup whole-grain mustard
1	tablespoon honey
2	teaspoons cider vinegar

1. Heat 1 tablespoon oil in Dutch oven over medium heat until
shimmering. Add bratwursts and cook until well browned all
over, about 8 minutes. Transfer bratwursts to plate.

2. Heat remaining 2 tablespoons oil in now-empty pot
over medium heat until shimmering. Add onions, salt, and
pepper and cook, covered, until softened, about 5 minutes.
Uncover and continue to cook, stirring occasionally, until
onion is browned, about 4 minutes. Add garlic and caraway
seeds and cook until fragrant, about 30 seconds.

3. Stir in beer, mustard, honey, vinegar, and bratwursts. Cover
and cook until bratwursts are cooked through, 5 to 7 minutes.
Transfer bratwursts to platter. Increase heat to medium-high
and cook until onion mixture is thickened, about 5 minutes.
Serve bratwursts topped with onion mixture.

THE BEST OF THE WURST:

German butchers are justifiably famous for their
hundreds of sausage varieties, so I like to offer a
selection, in their honor. Here are some faves.

Knackwurst: This is a plumper, more sophisticated
version of the American hot dog that is made from
beef or a beef-pork combo.

Liverwurst: Any guesses what liverwurst
contains? It's available in sausages that are firm
enough to slice as well as spreadable versions.

Bockwurst: White pepper, paprika, and herbs
season this veal and pork sausage.

Weisswurst: This beloved Bavarian sausage
made with veal, parsley, and spices is eaten
as a midmorning snack (you bet!) with sweet
mustard, fresh pretzels, and, yes, beer.

LEVEL UP YOUR BOARD

German Potato Salad
Serves 4 to 6

German cooks really know their potatoes and serve them in too many delicious incarnations to count. Kartoffelsalat, aka German potato salad, is a southern German specialty that's like a big warm potato hug. Slices of low-starch small red potatoes, cooked in salted water, keep their shape. For bold flavor, you'll fry up plenty of bacon, then use some of the rendered fat in the dressing, along with cider vinegar, whole-grain mustard, and a little sugar. Including the potato cooking liquid in the salad adds body, and a handful of scallions and parsley finish it off. Use small red potatoes 1 to 2 inches in diameter.

- 8 slices bacon, cut into ½-inch pieces
- 2 pounds small red potatoes, unpeeled, sliced ¼ inch thick
- 3 cups water
- 2 tablespoons plus 1 teaspoon sugar, divided
- 1 teaspoon celery seeds
- 1¼ teaspoons table salt, divided
- 3 tablespoons cider vinegar
- 2 tablespoons whole-grain mustard
- ¼ teaspoon pepper
- 4 scallions, sliced thin
- 3 tablespoons chopped fresh parsley
- 3 tablespoons finely chopped sweet green vinegar peppers (optional)

1. Cook bacon in 12-inch nonstick skillet over medium heat until crispy, 5 to 7 minutes. Using slotted spoon, transfer bacon to paper towel–lined plate. Measure out and reserve ¼ cup fat in medium bowl (if needed, add vegetable oil to fat as needed to equal ¼ cup). Discard remaining fat.

2. Bring potatoes, water, 2 tablespoons sugar, celery seeds, and 1 teaspoon salt to boil in now-empty skillet over high heat. Cook, stirring occasionally, until potatoes are tender, about 15 minutes. Continue to cook until liquid is syrupy and just coats bottom of skillet, 3 to 5 minutes longer. Transfer potatoes and cooking liquid to large bowl.

3. Stir vinegar, mustard, pepper, remaining 1 teaspoon sugar, and remaining ¼ teaspoon salt into reserved bacon fat until combined. Add dressing to potato mixture and stir to thoroughly combine. Let sit for 15 minutes.

4. Add bacon, scallions, parsley, and peppers, if using, to potato mixture. Using rubber spatula, firmly stir to partially break up potatoes and give salad creamy texture. Serve warm. (Potato salad can be refrigerated for up to 1 day; bring to warm room temperature before serving.)

Apple-Fennel Rémoulade
Serves 4 to 6

Just like Germans know their potatoes, so do they love their local apples. Markets all over Germany overflow with dozens of different varieties in the fall, and the fruits make their way into sweet and savory dishes alike. This tangy, creamy salad isn't a traditional Oktoberfest dish, but it has a bright, refreshing crunch that makes it a really nice counterpoint to the rich sausages. Plus, it all comes together in 15 minutes. You can use any variety of apple, but crisp-sweet varieties, including Fuji, Gala, and Honeycrisp, work especially well.

- ¼ cup mayonnaise
- 2 tablespoons whole-grain mustard
- 2 tablespoons lemon juice
- 2 tablespoons capers, rinsed, plus 1 tablespoon brine
- 4 celery ribs, sliced thin on bias
- 1 fennel bulb, 1 tablespoon fronds minced, stalks discarded, bulb halved, cored, and sliced thin crosswise
- 1 apple, cored and cut into 2-inch-long matchsticks

Whisk mayonnaise, mustard, lemon juice, and caper brine together in large bowl. Add capers, celery, fennel bulb, and apple and toss to combine. Season with salt and pepper to taste. Top with fennel fronds and serve. (Rémoulade can be refrigerated up to 1 day; stir to recombine before serving.)

CHOPPED SALAD

Serves 4 to 6

START WITH:

Salad Bar (page 174)

Vinaigrette (see page 175)

IF YOU WANT, ADD:

Easy-Peel Hard-Cooked Eggs (page 176)

Frico Crumble (page 177)

→

CHOPPED SALAD

You're just as likely to find chopped salads at a diner as you are to see them at a fancy al fresco luncheon spot. (Not to mention that quick-casual takeaway chopped salads are *crazy* popular.) Partly that's because chopped salads are universally satisfying, but another reason is that they're endlessly customizable. I love creating a salad bar–style board at home, offering up different ingredient combos that let my guests toss together the creation of their lunch-break dreams.

ELLE'S STRATEGY:

Set up shop. Set out all the ingredients in bowls, or you can even buy salad bar–style containers online if you really want to get in the spirit. Make sure there are plenty of serving spoons and tongs (isn't it the worst when a salad bar is missing those?). Put the dressings in mason jars for easy serving, and arrange them together in one spot to signal the end of the salad-building experience.

Get a head start. Wash produce (including the lettuce) as soon as you get it home; dry it well before storing. Chop sturdy veggies ahead, make the vinaigrette in advance, and cook any proteins like eggs or bacon ahead. Store chopped apples or pears in water with lemon or lime juice squeezed in to keep them from turning brown.

Make it seasonal. Chopped salad deserves to be loved year-round. Include roasted root veggies on your board in the fall, fresh fennel or navel oranges in the winter, and blanched asparagus or fresh raw peas in the spring.

Make it fancy dancy. Dress up your board with Black Pepper Candied Bacon (page 72), Poached Shrimp (page 117), store-bought smoked trout or salmon, or Microwave-Fried Shallots (page 189).

Knives out. The goal with chopped salads is that every component is a uniform size (that ensures no one ingredient takes center stage). Aim for ½-inch pieces, and see page 98 for a mind-blowing avocado-cubing trick.

Salad Bar

Here are some of my fave ingredients to set out—but add or subtract depending on what you like. Step 1 is selecting your greens; aim for roughly 18 ounces cut into ½-inch pieces. I like the crunch of romaine or iceberg lettuce (they're classic with chopped salads) but feel free to add others, such as radicchio as I did with this board, or endive, frisée, or chicory. Even though the end goal is to toss everything together with dressing for totally integrated bites, you should still think about what to add to your greens base in terms of layers: layers of texture and layers of flavor. Make sure you have crispy/juicy, chewy, creamy, and crunchy textures; I include at least two items from each category. Include flavors ranging from mild to bold, even spicy or sweet. You can offer larger quantities of staples like tomatoes and cukes and smaller portions of things like olives and nuts. And a word to the wise: You can never have too much cheese or bacon.

	Ingredient	Preparation
CRISPY/JUICY	1 English cucumber	Cut into ½-inch pieces
	12 ounces grape or cherry tomatoes	Halved
	2 apples and/or pears	Cored and cut into ½-inch pieces or thin slices
	1 small red onion	Chopped
	1 cup frozen corn and/or peas	Thawed
	1 cup pepperoncini	Chopped
CHEWY	4 ounces deli ham, turkey, and/or salami	Cut into ½-inch pieces (1 cup)
	1 pound bacon	Cooked and crumbled (1 cup)
	1 cup kalamata olives	Pitted and halved
	1 cup dried cranberries, currants, and/or raisins	
CREAMY	2 avocados	Halved, pitted, and cut into ½-inch pieces
	4 ounces feta, goat, or blue cheese	Crumbled (1 cup)
	4 ounces cheddar, Monterey Jack, and/or sharp provolone cheese	Cut into ½-inch pieces (1 cup)
	4 hard-cooked large eggs (see page 176)	Cut into ½-inch pieces
	1 (15-ounce) can black beans, cannellini beans, and/or chickpeas	Rinsed
CRUNCHY	1 cup toasted almonds, pecans, and/or walnuts	Coarsely chopped
	Store-bought crispy chickpeas	
	Croutons (see page 177)	

Dressings

Making your own dressing lets you offer something more special and creative (and more cost effective) than the typical salt-bomb supermarket choices. It's fast and it's make-ahead, so there's no excuse. I like to include two versions to add options. If you crave something creamy for your board, a Ranch Dressing recipe is on page 95.

Basic Vinaigrette
Makes about ½ cup

- 2 tablespoons cider vinegar
- 2 teaspoons minced shallot
- ½ teaspoon salt
- ½ teaspoon pepper
- 2 teaspoons honey
- 1 teaspoon mayonnaise
- 1 teaspoon Dijon mustard
- 6 tablespoons extra-virgin olive oil

Combine vinegar, shallot, salt, and pepper in 2-cup jar with tight-fitting lid; let sit for 5 minutes. Add honey, mayonnaise, and mustard and stir with fork until mixture is milky in appearance and no lumps remain. Add oil, seal jar, and shake vigorously until emulsified, about 30 seconds. Season with salt and pepper to taste. (Vinaigrette can be refrigerated for up to 2 days; whisk to recombine before using.)

VARIATIONS
Lemon-Herb Vinaigrette
Substitute lemon juice for cider vinegar. Add 1 tablespoon minced fresh thyme, 2 teaspoons chopped fresh mint, and ½ teaspoon lemon zest with honey.

Tarragon-Caper Vinaigrette
Substitute red wine vinegar for cider vinegar. Add 1 tablespoon minced fresh parsley, 1 tablespoon minced fresh tarragon, and 1 teaspoon minced rinsed capers with honey.

Cilantro-Chili Vinaigrette
Substitute lime juice for cider vinegar. Add 2 tablespoons minced fresh cilantro and 1 tablespoon chili powder with honey.

Easy-Peel Hard-Cooked Eggs

Makes 2 to 6 eggs

With this cooking method, the shells practically fly off. Use large eggs that have no cracks and are cold from the refrigerator.

2–6   large eggs

1. Bring 1 inch water to rolling boil in medium saucepan over high heat. Place eggs in steamer basket. Transfer basket to saucepan. Cover, reduce heat to medium-low, and cook eggs for 13 minutes.

2. When eggs are almost finished cooking, combine 2 cups ice cubes and 2 cups cold water in medium bowl. Using tongs or spoon, transfer eggs to ice bath; let sit for 15 minutes. Peel before serving. (Eggs can be refrigerated in their shells in airtight container for up to 5 days.)

LEVEL UP YOUR BOARD

Frico Crumble

Makes 1½ cups

Cheese usually lends a soft or creamy element to a chopped salad, but when you turn it into frico, it brings the crunch. This crispy, crumbly topping adds a blast of flavor and texture. Aged Asiago is great here, but aged Manchego or cheddar cheese is also a good option. Use a rasp-style grater to grate the cheese.

4 ounces aged Asiago cheese, finely grated (2 cups), divided

1. Sprinkle half of cheese evenly over bottom of cold 10-inch nonstick skillet. Cook over medium heat until edges are lacy and light golden, 2 to 3 minutes. Remove skillet from heat and let sit for 1 minute.

2. Using 2 spatulas, carefully flip frico. Return to medium heat and cook until second side is golden, about 1 minute. Carefully slide frico onto plate and set aside until cooled, about 10 minutes.

3. Wipe skillet clean with paper towels and repeat with remaining cheese. Let cool to room temperature, then crumble into bite-size pieces. (Frico can be stored in airtight container at room temperature for up to 5 days.)

SOME FAVORITE COMBOS:

When creating a chopped salad, the sky's the limit combination-wise, but here are some ideas to get you started:

- **Southwestern Spice:** Cilantro + corn + black beans + avocado + Monterey Jack + Cilantro-Chili Vinaigrette

- **The Cobb:** Red onion + bacon + eggs + avocado + blue cheese + Lemon-Herb Vinaigrette

- **Antipasto:** Basil + salami + provolone + pepperoncini + olives + Tarragon-Caper Vinaigrette

- **Fall Classic:** Radicchio + apple + goat cheese + dried cranberries + walnuts + Basic Vinaigrette

---

CROUTON CREATIVITY:

I'm not knocking the store-bought box, but think outside that too, depending on your other ingredients. You can turn practically anything into a crouton, including tortilla or corn chips, bagel chips, pita chips (see page 81 for homemade), cheese straws (see page 140 for homemade), or sturdy crackers. To make simple from-scratch croutons, toss 1½ cups (½-inch) bread cubes with 1½ tablespoons olive oil and seasonings of your choice, then spread on rimmed baking sheet and bake at 400 degrees for 8 to 10 minutes. After cooling, store in airtight container or plastic bag for up to 3 days.

GRILLED VEGETABLE PLATTER

Serves 4 to 6

START WITH:

Grilled Vegetables (page 183)

Lemon-Herb Vinaigrette (page 175)

Cheese (burrata, fresh mozzarella, or shaved Parmesan)

Baby greens

Fresh basil

Good olive oil for drizzling

IF YOU WANT, ADD:

Marinated White Beans with Garlic and Capers (page 182)

Grilled crusty bread

Grilled lemon halves

Olives (including blue cheese stuffed)

Canned tuna packed in oil

→

GRILLED VEGETABLE PLATTER

On sultry summer evenings, when it's almost too hot to eat and I just want to relax with friends and sip cold rosé, I bring the board outside with grilled vegetables, which have amazing charry flavor and are even better at room temperature than they are hot. You can add hearty accessories, but they're plenty satisfying on their own. My favorite way to serve this is al fresco, but if you're one of those brave souls who grills outside anytime, more power to you: This is just as irresistible in January as it is in July.

ELLE'S STRATEGY:

Set up shop. Put cheese in a bowl in the center and then scatter a bed of baby greens across the board. Fan out the vegetables on top of the greens, separating types into 2 or 3 sections. Fill in empty spaces with olives and basil sprigs. Place the bread around the edges of the board to keep it crisp, as well as the dressing so that it doesn't drip all over the rest of the food. Add the beans and tuna in separate bowls. Have tongs on hand for serving.

Get a head start. You can make the marinated white beans up to 3 days ahead and the vinaigrette up to 2 days ahead. Otherwise, one of the beauties of this board is that it comes together so fast: Just trim and slice the veggies, fire up the grill, and pop open that bottle of rosé.

Punch up flavor. I love this with the Lemon-Herb Vinaigrette (it's so summery), but any of the choices on page 175 would be delish, as would the Quick Salsa Verde (page 220) or the Aioli (page 111). Or just halve a couple of lemons to char on the grill alongside the veggies, then squeeze them over the top, drizzle on a little more olive oil, and you're good to go.

Make it hearty. The bread adds crisp-chewy substance and keeps all the cooking on the grill. Or buy a tube of cooked polenta, slice it into 1-inch rounds, oil them, then put on the grill. A nice off-the-grill option is a grain salad (see page 215). And this is the perfect time to splash out on high-quality jarred or tinned tuna.

Marinated White Beans with Garlic and Capers

Serves 4 to 6

Turn canned beans into superstars by marinating them briefly in olive oil infused with golden garlic, briny capers, and red pepper flakes.

6	tablespoons extra-virgin olive oil, divided
3	garlic cloves, sliced thin
2	(15-ounce) cans cannellini beans
1	tablespoon capers, rinsed
½	teaspoon dried oregano
½	teaspoon red pepper flakes
¼	teaspoon table salt
1	tablespoon white wine vinegar

Combine ¼ cup oil and garlic in 12-inch nonstick skillet and cook over medium heat until garlic begins to brown lightly at edges, about 3 minutes. Add beans, capers, oregano, pepper flakes, and salt and cook until heated through, about 5 minutes, stirring occasionally. Off heat, stir in vinegar and remaining 2 tablespoons oil. Let sit until flavors meld, about 30 minutes. Serve. (Beans can be refrigerated for up to 3 days; bring to room temperature before serving.)

Grilled Vegetables

Serves 4 to 6

Why heat up your kitchen when you can get crisp-tender veggies with gorgeous char from your grill? Prep is all about two things: maximizing surface area to get the best browning, and cutting shapes that keep them from falling apart—or through the cooking grate. Brushing the vegetables with oil (as well as oiling the grate as usual) prevents sticking. And once these summertime jewels are on the grill, keep them moving to avoid hot spots. Pull them off when they're just tender and streaked with grill marks.

- 2 red bell peppers
- 1 red onion, cut into ½-inch-thick rounds
- 4 plum tomatoes, cored and halved lengthwise
- 2 zucchini, ends trimmed, sliced lengthwise into ¾-inch-thick planks
- 3 tablespoons extra-virgin olive oil
- 1 eggplant, ends trimmed, cut crosswise into ½-inch-thick rounds
- 1 teaspoon kosher salt
- ½ teaspoon pepper

1. Slice ¼ inch off tops and bottoms of bell peppers and remove cores. Make slit down 1 side of each bell pepper, then press flat into 1 long strip, removing ribs and remaining seeds with knife as needed. Cut strips in half crosswise (you should have 4 bell pepper pieces).

2. Push toothpick horizontally through each onion round to keep rings intact while grilling. Brush onion, bell peppers, tomatoes, and zucchini all over with oil, then brush eggplant with remaining oil (it will absorb more oil than other vegetables). Sprinkle vegetables with salt and pepper.

3A. For a charcoal grill: Open bottom vent completely. Light large chimney starter filled with charcoal briquettes (6 quarts). When top coals are partially covered with ash, pour evenly over grill. Set cooking grate in place, cover, and open lid vent completely. Heat grill until hot, about 5 minutes.

3B. For a gas grill: Turn all burners to high, cover, and heat grill until hot, about 15 minutes. Turn all burners to medium-high.

4. Clean and oil cooking grate. Place vegetables on grate and cook until skins of bell peppers and tomatoes are well browned and onions, eggplant, and zucchini are tender, 10 to 16 minutes, flipping and moving vegetables as necessary to ensure even cooking and transferring vegetables to baking sheet as they finish cooking. Place bell peppers in bowl, cover with plastic wrap, and let them steam to loosen skins, about 5 minutes.

5. Remove toothpicks from onion and separate rings. When cool enough to handle, peel bell peppers, discarding skins; slice into 1-inch-thick strips. Serve vegetables warm or at room temperature.

LICENSE TO GRILL:

Change things up with different vegetables, or just add more to increase the garden bounty. (In that case, you're gonna need a bigger board.)

- **Asparagus:** Snap off tough ends; grill for 5 to 7 minutes, turning once.

- **Fennel:** Remove feathery fronds and stalks, trim base of bulb, and slice vertically into ½-inch-thick planks; grill for 8 to 10 minutes, turning as needed.

- **Portobello mushrooms:** Discard stems and wipe caps clean; grill for 8 to 12 minutes, turning as needed.

- **Radicchio:** Quarter 10-ounce head through core; grill for 5 to 7 minutes, until edges are browned and wilted but centers are still slightly firm, turning as needed.

BAKED POTATOES

Serves 6 to 8

START WITH:

Simple Baked Potatoes (page 187)

Fresh toppings (chives, arugula)

Creamy/cheesy toppings (sour cream and/or Garlic and Chive Sour Cream on page 189, goat cheese and/or Herbed Goat Cheese Topping on page 189, cheddar cheese)

Crunchy toppings (bacon, Savory Seed Brittle on page 256)

Classic toppings (butter, salt and pepper, hot sauce)

IF YOU WANT, ADD:

Compound butter (see page 189)

Spicy Honey Drizzle (page 148)

Microwave-Fried Shallots (page 189)

Something unexpected (dried fruit)

→

BAKED POTATOES

What's a more crowd-pleasing meal than a baked potato? This spread kicks things up a notch, with perfectly cooked sweet or russet potatoes (dealer's choice!) and enough toppings to turn this side dish into a full-blown meal. And you don't have to buy everything, either. I've included some recipes, but you can keep it simple—this is a great empty-out-your-refrigerator situation. Raid the condiment section of your fridge, pop open a couple of jars, and you're in business.

ELLE'S STRATEGY:

Set up shop. To give some order to the endless options, set out two different trays with toppings that go together nicely—this subtly gives your guests a starting point with suggestions. Place your baked potatoes on a wooden board in case people want to cut theirs in half, and preslice pats of butter to make things easier (keep them chilled so they don't melt together).

Get a head start. Creamy toppings can be made up to 4 days in advance, and fried shallots a month ahead of time. If you want to bake your potatoes ahead of time, you can keep them warm in a low oven (just don't cut them until you're ready to serve).

Tip-top toppings. Anything goes on a baked potato (see Creative Combinations, right, for some ideas), but for a balanced spread, I like to make sure there's something creamy, something crunchy, something fresh, and something unexpected, along with the crowd-pleasing classics.

Go in with a plan. I like to think about what I want my potato goals to be. It's easy to end up with lots of toppings but no sense of cohesion, so I imagine a couple of different themes and include toppings to fit those themes. Here, I went with the classic toppings and some healthy-ish autumnal options. People can stick to one tray or mix and match to make their own creations.

Simple Baked Potatoes

Serves 6 to 8

Including some sweet potatoes on your baked potato board brings an unexpected element (and a little color) and keeps things interesting. Sweet potatoes take longer than russets to bake, so microwaving them before baking them yields the creamiest interiors. No need to microwave the russets, which are done in about an hour. Any variety of orange- or red-skinned, orange-fleshed sweet potato can be used in this recipe, but I highly recommend using Garnet or Diane. Be sure to avoid varieties with tan or purple skin, which are starchier and less sweet than varieties with orange and red skins.

6–8 sweet potatoes and/or russet potatoes (8 ounces each), unpeeled, each lightly pricked with fork in 3 places

1. Adjust oven rack to middle position and heat oven to 450 degrees. Place sweet potatoes, if using, on large plate and microwave until potatoes yield to gentle pressure and centers register 200 degrees, 6 to 9 minutes, flipping potatoes every 3 minutes.

2. Set wire rack in aluminum foil–lined rimmed baking sheet and spray rack with vegetable oil spray. Arrange sweet potatoes and russet potatoes on prepared rack and bake until sweet potatoes feel very soft when squeezed and russets register at least 205 degrees, about 1 hour.

CREATIVE COMBINATIONS:

Baked potatoes offer a blank canvas for a variety of toppings. I have yet to run into a topping that didn't work on a potato—let your imagination go wild! Here are some suggestions to get you started:

- Black beans + cotija + pickled jalapeños
- Broccoli + cheddar cheese
- Bacon + sour cream + chives
- Chili + cheddar cheese + cilantro
- Soft-boiled egg + arugula

- Shredded chicken + buffalo sauce (see page 93)
- Pulled pork + barbecue sauce (see page 93)
- Mozzarella cheese + pepperoni + marinara
- Smoked salmon + chives

FLUFFY POTATO CLOUD:

1. Using a paring knife, make 2 slits, forming an X, in each baked potato.

2. Using a clean dish towel, hold ends and squeeze slightly to push flesh up and out.

The Ultimate Toppers

I like to whip up a couple of simple toppings to add a homemade touch among store-bought items. Whether it's a creamy dollop or a crunchy finisher, these toppers take your board to new heights.

Garlic and Chive Sour Cream

Makes about ½ cup

We all know sour cream is the classic baked potato companion, but spike it with a little garlic and some fresh chives and you've added a whole new dimension.

- ½ cup sour cream
- 1 tablespoon minced fresh chives
- 1 garlic clove, minced
- ⅛ teaspoon table salt

Combine all ingredients in bowl. (Sour cream can be refrigerated for up to 4 days.)

Herbed Goat Cheese Topping

Makes ¾ cup

This tangy, creamy topper is the perfect addition to a sweet potato.

- 4 ounces goat cheese, softened
- 2 tablespoons extra-virgin olive oil
- 2 tablespoons minced fresh parsley
- 1 tablespoon minced shallot
- ½ teaspoon grated lemon zest

Mash goat cheese with fork. Stir in oil, parsley, shallot, and lemon zest. Season with salt and pepper to taste. (Topping can be refrigerated for up to 4 days.)

Microwave-Fried Shallots

Makes about ½ cup

These crunchy little nuggets deliver crunch and savoriness to any baked potato creation. Use the leftover cooking oil in dressings.

- 3 shallots, sliced thin
- ½ cup vegetable oil

Combine shallots and oil in medium bowl. Microwave for 5 minutes. Stir and continue to microwave 2 minutes longer. Repeat stirring and microwaving in 2-minute increments until beginning to brown (4 to 6 minutes). Repeat stirring and microwaving in 30-second increments until deep golden brown (30 seconds to 2 minutes). Using slotted spoon, transfer shallots to paper towel–lined plate; season with salt to taste. Let drain and crisp, about 5 minutes. (Shallots can be stored in an airtight container for up to 1 month.)

EASY COMPOUND BUTTERS:

Straight butter never fails, but for even more *oomph*, mix together 4 tablespoons softened unsalted butter and ¼ teaspoon to 3 tablespoons of any flavorful ingredients you have on hand (try the ideas below!). Make sure ingredients are minced. Dollop compound butter over finished dish, or wrap it in plastic wrap and roll into log; keep it in the fridge for up to 4 days or freeze for up to 2 months.

- White miso paste + scallions
- Shallot + parsley + garlic
- Blue cheese + thyme
- Lime zest + ginger
- Thai red curry paste + cilantro
- Capers + dill

SHAWARMA

Serves 4 to 6

START WITH:

Chicken Shawarma (page 193)

Toppings (shredded lettuce, cucumbers, tomatoes)

IF YOU WANT, ADD:

Sumac Onions (page 194)

Cabbage Slaw (page 194)

More toppings (pickled vegetables, parsley, radishes)

Hot sauce

→

SHAWARMA

This sandwich never fails to quell my cravings for the best street food around, and the build-your-own nature is perfect in board form. The secret to bringing straight-off-the-rotisserie flavor (without constructing an actual at-home vertical rotisserie)? The broiler. It develops a flavorful crust on the chicken, mimicking the deeply savory exterior achieved from a restaurant-style roaster. Surrounded by soft pita, crunchy vegetables, and a creamy yogurt sauce, you're going to want to get to it.

ELLE'S STRATEGY:

Set up shop. I love using parchment for easy cleanup—fold it along the edges to fit whatever board you're using. Try to find the longest board you have in your house so you can lay everything out in the order the sandwich should be built (like a shawarma assembly line), but if all else fails line up the toppings in bowls. Dedicate space off to the side for a wrapping station with pre-cut sheets of tin foil so your guests don't have to wrangle a big roll.

Get a head start. The sumac onions can be made up to a week ahead of time and the yogurt sauce up to 4 days ahead. The cabbage slaw can be made a day in advance.

Round it out. You've already got the broiler on, why not broil some other vegetables to offer alongside the chicken? Try eggplant, mushrooms, or bell peppers. On the side, you can add hummus (see page 79), tabbouleh, or cooked grains (see page 215) for guests to make bowls.

Structurally sound shawarma. Because the pitas in shawarmas are rolled, not stuffed, use flat (not puffy) pitas. To avoid cracking, make sure they're fresh. Layer the sandwich starting with a sturdier item (like sliced radishes) and then shredded lettuce to serve as a buffer between items that could make the pita soggy. Wrap it all up in foil to keep that juiciness where it belongs.

Chicken Shawarma

Serves 4 to 6

YOGURT SAUCE

- 1 cup plain whole-milk yogurt
- 1 teaspoon grated lemon zest plus 2 tablespoons juice
- 1 garlic clove, minced

CHICKEN FILLING

- 2½ pounds boneless, skinless chicken thighs, trimmed
- 2 tablespoons extra-virgin olive oil
- 2 teaspoons paprika
- 2 teaspoons ground cumin
- 1 teaspoon table salt
- ½ teaspoon pepper
- 1 lemon

  Pita bread, warmed

1. For the yogurt sauce: Whisk all ingredients together in bowl and season with salt and pepper to taste. Cover and refrigerate for at least 30 minutes to allow flavors to meld. (Sauce can be refrigerated for up to 4 days.)

2. For the chicken filling: Adjust oven rack 6 inches from broiler element and heat broiler. Line rimmed baking sheet with aluminum foil and set wire rack in sheet. Pat chicken dry with paper towels. Combine oil, paprika, cumin, salt, and pepper in large bowl. Add chicken and toss to coat. Place chicken in single layer on prepared wire rack. Trim ends from lemon, then cut lemon in half. Place lemon halves cut side up on rack. Broil until chicken is well browned and registers at least 175 degrees, 16 to 20 minutes, rotating sheet halfway through broiling. Transfer chicken to cutting board, let cool slightly, then slice into thin strips.

3. Serve chicken filling with lemon halves, yogurt sauce, pita, and extra toppings.

VARIATION
Tofu Shawarma

The tofu slabs are delicate and may break while turning; this will not affect the final dish.

Cut 2 (14-ounce) blocks firm or extra-firm tofu crosswise into ½-inch-thick slabs. Arrange tofu over paper towel–lined baking sheet and let drain for 20 minutes. Gently press tofu dry with paper towels. Substitute tofu slabs for chicken and broil until well browned, 20 to 30 minutes, flipping halfway through broiling. Cut slabs into ½-inch-thick fingers.

LEVEL UP YOUR BOARD

Sumac Onions

Makes about 2 cups

- 1 red onion, halved and sliced thin into ¼-inch pieces
- 2 tablespoons lemon juice
- 2 tablespoons red wine vinegar
- 1 tablespoon extra-virgin olive oil
- 1 tablespoon ground sumac
- ½ teaspoon sugar
- ¼ teaspoon table salt

Combine all ingredients in bowl. Let sit, stirring occasionally, for 1 hour. (Onions can be refrigerated for up to 1 week.)

Cabbage Slaw

Makes about 6 cups

- 1 small head red cabbage (1¼ pounds), cored and sliced very thin (6 cups)
- ½ cup fresh parsley leaves
- ¼ cup extra-virgin olive oil
- ½ teaspoon table salt

Combine all ingredients in bowl. (Slaw can be refrigerated for up to 24 hours; toss to recombine before serving.)

THREE TIPS FOR BROILING SUCCESS:

There's no reason to be scared of your broiler; it's the perfect way to add lots of deep charred flavor to your food. Here are some tips to make your broiling more successful.

When in doubt, go for "high." You don't usually see a broiler setting specified in a recipe, but since the point of most broiling is to expose food to intense heat, turn it up!

Measure up. Because ovens vary, the measurement between the heating element and the oven rack is much more specific than a rack position such as "middle" or "top."

Elevate it. Set your food on a wire rack to prevent the bottom from steaming. It's all about the browning, baby.

FOLDING A POCKETLESS PITA SANDWICH:

Although pocketed pitas are easier to find, the pocketless versions are better shawarma vehicles for their thick, pillowy texture and deeper flavor. When layering ingredients on the pita in step 1, leave a 1-inch border on all sides.

1. Place pita on top of aluminum foil, layer sandwich ingredients on pita, and fold one side of pita over filling. Fold opposite side of pita over filling so it overlaps first side.

2. Fold one side of foil over sandwich.

3. Fold up bottom of foil.

4. Wrap other side of foil over sandwich to fully enclose it.

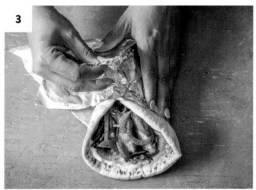

PULLED PORK

Serves 6 to 8

START WITH:

Indoor Pulled Pork (page 199)

Pulled Pork Sauces (page 201)

Pickles and sliced onions

Buns/sliced bread

Cornbread (store-bought)

Sweet Iced Tea (page 202)

Tabasco

IF YOU WANT, ADD:

Simple Stovetop Macaroni and Cheese (page 202)

Dressed-up (store-bought) coleslaw (see page 203)

Foolproof Boiled Corn (page 202) with flavored salt (see page 72)

→

PULLED PORK

This board re-creates the fun of a barbecue joint where you grab your tray, lay out a sheet of butcher paper, and start adding your meat and sides. It's a celebration on a sheet pan, without any need to heat a smoker or grill. I remember when I first had barbecue served this way, thinking how genius it was for home entertaining . . . on pans we already use all the time. And while you could cook up a storm, you can also buy any part of it (or all of it), knowing you'll still come out looking like a rock star.

ELLE'S STRATEGY:

Set up shop. Line a large sheet pan with butcher paper. This is your board. It will corral all the juices so fill it with as many foods as will fit (use a second pan if needed). I like to set smaller dishes within it: a quarter sheet pan for the pork and a small casserole for the mac and cheese. Set out all the barbecue sauces you want in small bowls or jars. Small tongs such as ice tongs work well for handling the pork. Scatter pickles and onions right on the sheet pan and don't forget a bottle of hot sauce.

Get a head start. Everything can be made ahead aside from the mac and cheese and corn. Make the pulled pork up to 2 days ahead. Barbecue sauce up to 4 days. Coleslaw up to 1 day. Sweet iced tea up to 1 week.

Sheet pan plan. I give each person a quarter sheet pan to fill up (sturdy paper plates work, too). The small rimmed baking sheets are worth owning in multiples as they have countless uses, like small-batch roasting and baking (they fit in many toaster ovens) or letting meat rest or grains cool. They can contain your mise en place ingredients, serve as a contained space to season raw meat, and make the ideal tray to hold drippy foods in the fridge. Grab them for cheap at a restaurant supply store or online.

Choosing sides. I went with some of my favorite Southern staples; feel free to swap in yours. Baked beans, collard greens, creamy potato salad, chips, or broccoli salad would all be a great fit here.

Indoor Pulled Pork

Serves 6 to 8

Most oven-cooked pulled pork doesn't hold a candle to pit-smoked barbecue, but this comes pretty darn close. Liquid smoke (naturally derived from smoldering wood chips) infuses the meat with smoky flavor. The meat turns meltingly tender, and the surface develops a bark so good your guests will clamor for the best pieces. Serve the pork with up to three of the barbecue sauces, or use your favorite bottled sauce. If using multiple sauces, I'd refrain from tossing the pork with any one sauce and let guests spoon it on themselves. The sauce is thinned with ½ cup defatted pork juices; if you're making multiple sauces, you can use chicken broth if additional liquid is needed. If the pork is enhanced, do not brine in step 1.

- 1 cup table salt for brining
- ½ cup sugar for brining
- 3 tablespoons plus 2 teaspoons liquid smoke, divided
- 5 pounds boneless pork butt roast, trimmed and cut in half horizontally
- ¼ cup yellow mustard
- 2 tablespoons sugar
- 2 tablespoons smoked paprika
- 2 tablespoons pepper
- 2 teaspoons table salt
- 1 teaspoon cayenne pepper
- 1 recipe Pulled Pork Sauce (page 201)

1. Dissolve 1 cup salt, ½ cup sugar, and 3 tablespoons liquid smoke in 4 quarts cold water in large container. Submerge pork in brine, cover, and refrigerate for 1½ to 2 hours.

2. While pork brines, combine mustard and remaining 2 teaspoons liquid smoke in bowl; set aside. Combine sugar, paprika, pepper, salt, and cayenne in second bowl; set aside.

3. Adjust oven rack to lower-middle position and heat oven to 325 degrees. Set wire rack in aluminum foil–lined rimmed baking sheet. Remove pork from brine and thoroughly pat dry with paper towels. Rub mustard mixture over entire surface of each piece of pork. Sprinkle entire surface of each piece with sugar mixture. Place pork on prepared wire rack.

Place piece of parchment paper over pork, then cover with sheet of foil, sealing edges to prevent moisture from escaping. Roast pork for 3 hours.

4. Remove pork from oven; discard foil and parchment. Carefully pour off liquid in bottom of sheet into fat separator and reserve for sauce. Return pork to oven and roast, uncovered, until well browned and tender and meat registers 200 degrees, about 1½ hours. Transfer pork to dish, tent with foil, and let rest for 20 minutes.

5. Using 2 forks, shred pork into bite-size pieces and season with salt and pepper. Toss pork with 1 cup sauce if desired and serve, passing remaining sauce separately. (Cooled shredded pork can be refrigerated, tightly covered, for up to 2 days; reheat gently before serving.)

Pulled Pork Sauces

It's best to utilize the reserved defatted pork juices from the Indoor Pulled Pork recipe (page 199); if you're making multiple sauces, you can use chicken broth if additional liquid is needed. Sauces can be refrigerated for up to 4 days. Each recipe makes 2½ cups.

Lexington Vinegar Barbecue Sauce

- 1 cup cider vinegar
- ½ cup defatted pork juices
- ½ cup ketchup
- ½ cup water
- 1 tablespoon sugar
- ¾ teaspoon table salt
- ¾ teaspoon red pepper flakes
- ½ teaspoon pepper

Whisk together all ingredients in medium bowl.

South Carolina Mustard Barbecue Sauce

- 1 cup yellow mustard
- ½ cup defatted pork juices
- ½ cup white vinegar
- ¼ cup packed light brown sugar
- ¼ cup Worcestershire sauce
- 2 tablespoons hot sauce
- 1 teaspoon table salt
- 1 teaspoon pepper

Whisk together all ingredients in medium bowl.

Sweet and Tangy Barbecue Sauce

- 1½ cups ketchup
- ½ cup defatted pork juices
- ¼ cup molasses
- 2 tablespoons Worcestershire sauce
- 1 tablespoon hot sauce
- ½ teaspoon table salt
- ½ teaspoon pepper

Whisk together all ingredients in medium bowl.

LEVEL UP YOUR BOARD

Simple Stovetop Macaroni and Cheese

Serves 6 to 8 as a side

This superquick mac and cheese is melty smooth (thanks to American cheese and the emulsifiers in it), yet full of cheesy flavor (thanks to extra-sharp cheddar). The macaroni cooks in a precise amount of liquid, so don't use other pasta shapes. Use a block of American cheese from the deli counter rather than presliced.

- 1½ cups water
- 1 cup milk
- 8 ounces elbow macaroni
- 4 ounces American cheese, shredded (1 cup)
- ½ teaspoon Dijon mustard
  Small pinch cayenne pepper
- 4 ounces extra-sharp cheddar cheese, shredded (1 cup)
- ⅓ cup panko bread crumbs
- 1 tablespoon extra-virgin olive oil
- ⅛ teaspoon table salt
- ⅛ teaspoon pepper
- 2 tablespoons grated Parmesan cheese

1. Bring water and milk to boil in medium saucepan over high heat. Stir in macaroni and reduce heat to medium-low. Cook, stirring frequently, until macaroni is soft (slightly past al dente), 6 to 8 minutes. Add American cheese, mustard, and cayenne and cook, stirring constantly, until cheese is completely melted, about 1 minute. Off heat, stir in cheddar until evenly distributed but not melted. Cover saucepan and let stand for 5 minutes.

2. Meanwhile, combine panko, oil, salt, and pepper in 8-inch nonstick skillet until panko is evenly moistened. Cook over medium heat, stirring frequently, until evenly browned, 3 to 4 minutes. Off heat, sprinkle Parmesan over panko mixture and stir to combine. Transfer panko mixture to small bowl.

3. Stir macaroni until sauce is smooth (sauce may look loose but will thicken as it cools). Season with salt and pepper to taste. Transfer to warm serving dish and sprinkle panko mixture over top. Serve immediately.

Sweet Iced Tea

Serves 6 to 8

If I'm not drinking an Arnold Palmer (page 153), I like an iced tea that's smooth and sweet. This room-temperature steeping method yields a strong tea without any bitter undertones. Since the tea never gets hot, I make a sugar syrup to sweeten the brew. This recipe can easily be doubled.

- 12 black tea bags
- 8 cups water, room temperature, divided
- ¼ cup sugar
- 2 lemons, sliced thin, divided
  Ice

1. Tie strings of tea bags together (for easy removal) and place in large pitcher along with 7 cups water; let steep for 45 minutes.

2. Microwave sugar and remaining 1 cup water in bowl until heated through, about 1 minute. Stir mixture constantly until sugar has dissolved completely. Discard tea bags from pitcher. Add sugar mixture and half of lemon slices to tea and stir to combine. (Tea can be refrigerated for up to 1 week; lemon flavor will intensify over time.) Serve chilled over ice with remaining lemon slices.

FOOLPROOF BOILED CORN:

Here's some kitchen magic: Put fresh ears of corn in water that's between 150 and 170 degrees for 10 minutes and its starches will turn sweet, but the kernels won't break down and become mushy. How? Bring 4 quarts water to boil in a large Dutch oven. Turn off the heat, add 6 to 8 ears corn, cover, and let stand for at least 10 minutes or up to 30 minutes. Serve the corn with butter, salt, and pepper, or sprinkle with a flavored salt (see page 72).

DRESSING UP BAGGED COLESLAW MIX:

Convenient presliced cabbage slaw has a secondary benefit: It requires no salting or draining. Choose your dressing style (below), toss with a 14-ounce bag of slaw, and refrigerate for 20 minutes. Add more salt and pepper to taste. Don't worry if your bag varies by an ounce or two; it won't make a difference.

- **Classic creamy:** ¼ cup mayonnaise + 1 tablespoon white vinegar + ½ teaspoon Dijon mustard + ½ teaspoon sugar + ½ teaspoon toasted caraway seeds + ⅛ teaspoon pepper

- **Sweet and tangy:** ¼ cup cider vinegar + 2 tablespoons honey + 2 tablespoons vegetable oil + 2 teaspoons Dijon mustard + ¼ teaspoon salt + ¼ teaspoon pepper

- **Cajun:** ½ cup mayonnaise + 2 tablespoons white vinegar + 4 teaspoons Cajun seasoning + 2 teaspoons whole-grain mustard + 1 teaspoon sugar + ¼ teaspoon pepper + 1 minced celery rib + 1 thinly sliced scallion

- **Buttermilk:** ½ cup mayonnaise + ½ cup buttermilk + 1 tablespoon cider vinegar + ¼ teaspoon salt + ¼ teaspoon pepper

STEAK FRITES

Serves 4 to 6

START WITH:

Easy Steak Frites with Parsley-Shallot Butter (page 207)

IF YOU WANT, ADD:

Port-Caramelized Onions (page 86)

Dipping sauces (see page 209)

Flake salt

Sliced tomatoes and charred scallions

→

STEAK FRITES

Steak frites was made to be served as a board—the fries soak up the steak's juices for a cohesive flavor-bomb of a meal. It's a simple dish, but it can be tricky to pull off at home (nobody likes cold fries). This game-changing recipe has you start the fries in cold oil, cook the steak as they bubble away, and then tent the steak with foil and let it rest as the fries finish. By the time they're done, the steak will be ready to slice and serve. Then all that's left to do is uncork a bottle of wine or mix up some martinis (see page 139).

ELLE'S STRATEGY:

Set up shop. Spread out the hot fries and nestle the sliced steak among them (you want everything to touch!). Put condiments and sauces in tiny ramekins to really make it feel like a bistro. You could serve this on a carving board (or something with a lip to catch the steak's juices), but because you want it to be served hot, I like to arrange the fries on a roasting pan or griddle and keep them warm in a 200-degree oven while waiting for everyone to get to the table. Don't slice the steak until ready to serve.

Get a head start. Much of this should happen a couple of hours before you eat, but the sauces can be made up to 2 days ahead of time, or a week ahead for the steak sauce.

Save your oil. Don't toss the frying oil once you're finished. Instead, let it come down to room temp, strain, and then transfer to an airtight container and put back in the pantry. You can reuse it up to three times.

Slice smarter. Identify the lines that run parallel to each other on the steak: That's the grain. Slice against (perpendicular to) the grain, creating thin slices that have shorter muscle fibers for a tender, not chewy, bite.

Freshen up. My family from the South serves scallions (quickly charred in a skillet) and tomatoes with everything for a fresh bite that ties a meal together. A nice bistro salad (see page 126) would also be delicious here.

Easy Steak Frites with Parsley-Shallot Butter

Serves 4 to 6

This isn't your average meat and potatoes meal. Bring the bistro home with crispy fries and perfectly cooked steak, all ready at the same time thanks to an easy-to-execute timeline. The secret is having everything prepped and ready to go, and then putting the potatoes in the oil 30 minutes before you want to eat. Use large Yukon Gold potatoes (10 to 12 ounces each) that are similar in size for the most uniform fries. Peanut oil is best for frying because it has a high smoke point and imparts a clean taste to fried foods, but you can use vegetable oil, if desired. Use a Dutch oven that holds 6 quarts or more for this recipe.

- 4 tablespoons unsalted butter, softened
- 1 shallot, minced
- 1 tablespoon minced fresh parsley
- 1 garlic clove, minced
- 2½ pounds large Yukon Gold potatoes, unpeeled
- 6 cups plus 1 tablespoon peanut or vegetable oil
- 2 (1-pound) boneless strip steaks, 1¼ to 1½ inches thick, trimmed and halved crosswise

1. Mash butter, shallot, parsley, garlic, ½ teaspoon salt, and ¼ teaspoon pepper together in bowl; set compound butter aside.

2. Square off potatoes by cutting ¼-inch-thick slice from each of their 4 long sides; discard slices. Cut potatoes lengthwise into ¼-inch-thick planks. Stack 3 or 4 planks and cut into ¼-inch-thick fries. Repeat with remaining planks. (Do not place sliced potatoes in water.)

3. Line rimmed baking sheet with triple layer of paper towels. Combine potatoes and 6 cups oil in large Dutch oven. Cook over high heat until oil is vigorously bubbling, about 5 minutes. Continue to cook, without stirring, until potatoes are limp but exteriors are beginning to firm, about 15 minutes. Using tongs, stir potatoes, gently scraping up any that stick, and continue to cook, stirring occasionally, until golden and crispy, 7 to 10 minutes longer.

4. Meanwhile, pat steaks dry with paper towels and season with salt and pepper. Heat remaining 1 tablespoon oil in 12-inch skillet over medium-high heat until just smoking. Add steaks and cook until well browned and meat registers 125 degrees (for medium-rare), 4 to 7 minutes per side. Transfer steaks to platter, top each with compound butter, tent with aluminum foil, and let rest for 10 minutes.

5. Using spider or slotted spoon, transfer fries to prepared sheet and season with salt. Serve fries with steaks.

CUTTING FRENCH FRIES:

1. Cut ¼-inch-thick slice from each of potatoes' 4 long sides to square off.

2. Cut potatoes lengthwise into ¼-inch-thick planks.

3. Stack 3 or 4 planks and cut into ¼-inch-thick fries. Repeat with remaining planks.

Dipping Sauces

Don't settle for ketchup (the horror!). Elevate your experience with one or more of these primo sauces to dip your fries and steak in. Where would a proper steakhouse meal be without them?

Classic Steak Sauce

Makes about 1 cup

The secret ingredient in this sauce is raisins (trust me!), which add depth and sweetness. For an accurate measurement of boiling water, bring a full kettle of water to a boil and then measure out the desired amount. Be sure to let the raisins rehydrate before pureeing them with the other ingredients.

- ½ cup boiling water
- ⅓ cup raisins
- ¼ cup ketchup
- 3 tablespoons Worcestershire sauce
- 2 tablespoons Dijon mustard
- 2 tablespoons white vinegar

Combine water and raisins in bowl and let sit, covered, until raisins are plump, about 5 minutes. Process raisin mixture, ketchup, Worcestershire, mustard, and vinegar in blender until smooth. Season with salt and pepper to taste. (Sauce can be refrigerated for up to 1 week; bring to room temperature before serving.)

Belgian-Style Dipping Sauce

Makes about ½ cup

- 5 tablespoons mayonnaise
- 3 tablespoons ketchup
- 1 garlic clove, minced
- ½ teaspoon hot sauce
- ¼ teaspoon table salt

Whisk all ingredients together in small bowl. Cover and refrigerate until ready to serve. (Sauce can be refrigerated for up to 2 days.)

Chive and Black Pepper Dipping Sauce

Makes about ½ cup

- 5 tablespoons mayonnaise
- 3 tablespoons sour cream
- 2 tablespoons minced fresh chives
- 1½ teaspoons lemon juice
- ¼ teaspoon table salt
- ¼ teaspoon pepper

Whisk all ingredients together in small bowl. (Sauce can be refrigerated for up to 2 days.)

SALMON PLATTER

Serves 4 to 6

START WITH:

Slow-Roasted Salmon (page 213)

Lemon-Chive Dressing (or another option on page 213)

Skillet-Roasted Green Beans (page 214)

Grain salad (see page 215)

Lemon wedges

$\longrightarrow$

SALMON PLATTER

Fish is easy to cook and translates to an elegant board. Get out your favorite platter, add a grain salad, a vegetable side, and a sauce, and you've got a good-for-you dinner that looks as stellar as it tastes. Plus, it's supremely flexible; the fish is the anchor, and you can build a different meal around it every time, changing up the grain salad, the vegetable, or the sauce. In fact, the board can be reimagined in so many different ways that it reminds me of the loaves and fishes story. It feeds multitudes.

ELLE'S STRATEGY:

Set up shop. Assembly here is simply a matter of laying your cooked fish in the middle of a platter and surrounding it with the grain salad and vegetables. I aim for a snug fit; you want the foods to get to know each other as the sauce works well with everything. Don't forget to include plenty of lemon wedges (or lime wedges, depending on where you take the flavors).

Get a head start. You can precook and refrigerate the grains up to 3 days ahead and make the dressing up to 4 days ahead. With that out of the way, the rest is easy.

Shop your pantry. This board will elevate simple ingredients you've likely already got. I start by asking myself what grains I have and build the outer parts of the dish from there with on-hand vegetables, cheeses like feta, and nuts. I try to use as many pantry items as I can.

Destination dinner. This is also a board I'd prepare for friends when we're staying at a vacation rental, since it feels special but requires very little in the way of kitchen equipment, plus you can tailor the meal to whatever local ingredients you find. Seek out a farmers' market and get exploring!

Slow-Roasted Salmon

Serves 4 to 6

You can substitute granulated sugar for the brown sugar, if desired. If a 2½-pound salmon fillet is unavailable, use six 6- to 8-ounce skinless salmon fillets instead. In step 1, sprinkle both sides of the fillets evenly with the sugar mixture and arrange them side by side in the baking dish so they are touching. The cooking time remains the same. If using wild salmon, reduce the cooking time to 45 to 50 minutes, or until the salmon registers 120 degrees. This recipe uses a glass baking dish. If you use a ceramic baking dish or metal pan, check the temperature of the salmon 10 minutes early. The thickness of the salmon will affect baking time, so try to purchase salmon that's 1½ inches thick.

- 1 tablespoon packed brown sugar
- 1 teaspoon kosher salt
- ½ teaspoon pepper
- 1 (2½-pound) skinless center-cut salmon fillet, about 1½ inches thick
- ½ cup dressing (see right)

1. Adjust oven rack to middle position and heat oven to 250 degrees. Combine sugar, salt, and pepper in small bowl. Sprinkle salmon all over with sugar mixture.

2. Place salmon, flesh side up, in 13 by 9-inch glass baking dish. Roast until center is still translucent when checked with tip of paring knife and registers 125 degrees (for medium-rare), 55 to 60 minutes.

3. Remove dish from oven and immediately pour dressing evenly over salmon. Let rest for 5 minutes. Using 2 spatulas, transfer salmon to serving platter. Stir together any juices left in dish and spoon over salmon. Serve.

A SAUCE FOR EVERYTHING:

Each of these dressings make about 1 cup; pour half on the salmon and save the rest to toss with the grain salad.

Lemon-Chive Dressing
Combine ½ cup extra-virgin olive oil, ¼ cup minced fresh chives (or dill or parsley), 4 teaspoons grated lemon zest plus 3 tablespoons juice, and ½ teaspoon salt in bowl.

Miso-Ginger Dressing
Whisk ⅓ cup mayonnaise, ¼ cup red miso, 3 tablespoons water, 4 teaspoons maple syrup, 4 teaspoons sesame oil, 2 teaspoons sherry vinegar, and 2 teaspoons grated fresh ginger together in bowl until emulsified.

Tahini Dressing
Whisk together 6 tablespoons extra-virgin olive oil, ¼ cup lemon juice (2 lemons), 3 tablespoons tahini, 2 tablespoons water, 1 minced garlic clove, ½ teaspoon table salt, and ⅛ teaspoon pepper together in bowl until emulsified.

Skillet-Roasted Green Beans

Serves 4 to 6

These stay in the skillet long enough to develop some char so they're more deeply flavored than steamed green beans. You will need a 12-inch nonstick skillet with a tight-fitting lid for this recipe.

- 1½ pounds green beans, trimmed
- 3 tablespoons extra-virgin olive oil
- 2 tablespoons water
- 1 teaspoon table salt
- ½ teaspoon pepper

1. Combine green beans, oil, water, salt, and pepper in 12-inch nonstick skillet. Cover and cook over medium-high heat until beans are nearly tender, about 8 minutes, shaking skillet occasionally to redistribute beans.

2. Stir beans and continue to cook, uncovered, until water has evaporated and beans are spotty brown and tender, 5 to 7 minutes. Serve.

Improvising Grain Salad

Cook your grain of choice, then add options from the categories below; a good salad will contrast different textures and flavors. Toss the salad with the remaining dressing you used for the salmon (about ½ cup). Season with salt and pepper before serving.

Ingredient	Quantity
FRUITS AND VEGETABLES (CHOOSE 1 OR 2):	
Cherry tomatoes, halved	½ cup
Fennel or celery, thinly sliced	½ cup
Endive or radicchio, chopped	½ cup
Roasted squash or sweet potato pieces	1 cup
Orange or grapefruit segments	½ cup
Blueberries or sliced strawberries	½ cup
Baby greens	1 cup
CHEESE AND SALTY FOODS (CHOOSE 1):	
Feta or goat cheese, crumbled	½ cup
Parmesan, shaved	½ cup
Olives, halved	¼ cup
Capers, drained	¼ cup
Sun-dried tomatoes, chopped	¼ cup
NUTS/SEEDS AND DRIED FRUIT (CHOOSE 1 OR 2):	
Almonds, walnuts, pecans, or cashews, toasted and chopped	¼ cup
Pepitas or sunflower seeds, toasted	¼ cup
Dried apricots or figs, chopped	½ cup
Dried cranberries, cherries, or raisins	½ cup
AROMATICS (CHOOSE 1 OR 2):	
Scallions, sliced	¼ cup
Red onion, sliced	½ cup
Fresh parsley, cilantro, chives, or dill, chopped	½ cup

COOKING GRAINS (MAKES 4 CUPS):

Bring 4 quarts water to boil in large pot. Stir in 1½ cups grain and 1 teaspoon table salt and cook until tender, following timing below. Drain well. Refrigerate cooled grains for up to 3 days.

GRAIN	COOKING TIME
Pearl barley	20 to 40 minutes
Farro	15 to 30 minutes
Freekeh	30 to 45 minutes
Long-grain white rice	10 to 15 minutes
Long-grain brown rice	25 to 30 minutes
Wild rice	35 to 40 minutes
Wheat berries	60 to 70 minutes

SOME GREAT COMBOS:

- Farro + cherry tomatoes + feta + almonds + raisins + red onions + Lemon-Chive Dressing

- Long-grain brown rice + oranges + green olives + cashews + scallions + Miso-Ginger Dressing

- Barley + fennel + shaved Parmesan + dried apricots + parsley + Lemon-Parsley Dressing

- Freekeh + roasted squash + feta + golden raisins + walnuts + cilantro + Tahini Dressing

- Wheat berries + endive + blueberries + goat cheese + pecans + Lemon-Chive Dressing

CLAMBAKE

Serves 6 to 8

START WITH:

Indoor Clambake for a Crowd (page 219)

IF YOU WANT, ADD:

Rémoulade (page 220)

Quick Salsa Verde (page 220)

Lemons

Crusty bread

→

CLAMBAKE

My family does clambakes on special occasions, but with a recipe this easy any day can be clambake-worthy. The best part about this meal is its casual vibe—you're eating with your hands, getting messy, and making friends really fast. Make sure to let your guests know they're coming to a clambake so they know what they're in for (they don't want to wear their best duds to *this* party). And whatever you do, don't run out of butter.

ELLE'S STRATEGY:

Set up shop. Layer newspaper over the table and create an edible centerpiece with the clambake—no serving dishes or decorations needed here. But do have plates available for people who might want them. If you prefer, you can put the clambake on rimmed baking sheets instead of newspaper. Set out buckets or bowls for spent shells and small bowls of butter and sauces. Make sure everyone has a lobster cracker and a bib, and offer rolls of paper towels and plenty of moist towelettes (it's a messy affair).

Get a head start. Because the success of this recipe relies on the freshest seafood, most of it takes place day-of. Sauces (if you're making them) can be made a few days in advance. Start stockpiling newspaper ahead of time.

Break it down. I sometimes like to help my guests out by removing some of the lobster from their shells (see page 222) so people have something to start with (and they aren't fighting over the tails).

Keep it tidy. For an extra layer of protection, cut a (clean, unscented) garbage bag along the seam and spread it out underneath the newspaper.

Butter up. Make individual melted butters for everyone, so double dipping can be encouraged. Sprinkle some Old Bay or other seasonings into each bowl to jazz things up.

Indoor Clambake for a Crowd

Serves 6 to 8

A clambake is the ultimate seafood meal: clams, mussels, and lobster, nestled with sausage, corn, and potatoes, all steamed together with hot stones in a sand pit by the sea. A real-deal clambake is an all-day affair and, of course, requires a beach. This supereasy recipe brings the clambake indoors (and is ready in under 30 minutes!). Everything cooks in one large pot, without any water needed because the shellfish releases enough liquid to steam everything else. Small littlenecks are best for this recipe; if your market carries larger clams, use 8 pounds. Look for small potatoes that are 1 to 2 inches in diameter. You will need a 20-quart canning pot or stockpot with a tight-fitting lid for this recipe. The recipe can be halved using a 12-quart stockpot.

- 2 pounds kielbasa sausage, cut into 2-inch lengths
- 4 pounds small littleneck clams or small cherrystone clams, scrubbed
- 4 pounds mussels, scrubbed and debearded
- 2 pounds small new potatoes or red potatoes, unpeeled, halved
- 8 ears corn, silk and all but the last layer of husk removed, halved
- 4 (1½-pound) live lobsters
- 1 pound salted butter, melted

1. Layer kielbasa, clams, mussels, potatoes, corn, and lobsters (in that order) in 20-quart canning pot or stockpot. Cover and cook over high heat until potatoes are tender and lobsters are bright red, 17 to 20 minutes.

2. Off heat, set lobsters and corn aside to cool slightly. Using slotted spoon, transfer kielbasa, clams, mussels, and potatoes to large serving platter or newspaper-lined table. Peel husks from corn and arrange on platter with lobsters. Serve immediately with melted butter.

STORING SEAFOOD:

Follow these tips to keep your shellfish in tip-top shape.

Mussels and clams: Place in bowl, cover with layer of wet paper towels or newspaper to keep them moist, and set bowl in second bowl filled with ice. Refrigerate and replenish ice as necessary. Cook mussels within 3 days and clams within 1 week. How to tell if they're still fresh? A live mussel or clam will smell pleasantly briny. If open, its shell should close up when lightly tapped (but give it a moment; some take longer than others to clam up). Discard any mussel or clam that smells unpleasant, has a cracked or broken shell, or a shell that won't close.

Lobsters: Place in a bowl and cover with wet paper towels or newspaper. Or, ask your fishmonger for a breathable seafood bag. Place in refrigerator and cook within 24 hours.

LEVEL UP YOUR BOARD

Rémoulade

Makes about 1 cup

This sauce is classic with crab cakes or grilled seafood, but it's killer with lobster. You can also toss it with poached shrimp or grated or julienned celery root for a cold salad. The egg yolks in this recipe are not cooked. If you prefer, ¼ cup Egg Beaters may be substituted.

2 large egg yolks

2 tablespoons water, plus extra as needed

4 teaspoons lemon juice

1 teaspoon Dijon mustard

1 small garlic clove, minced

¼ teaspoon table salt

¾ cup vegetable oil

1 tablespoon capers, rinsed

1 tablespoon minced fresh parsley

1 tablespoon sweet pickle relish

Process egg yolks, water, lemon juice, mustard, garlic, and salt in blender until combined, about 10 seconds, scraping down sides of blender jar as needed. With blender running, slowly add oil and process until sauce is emulsified, about 2 minutes. Add capers, parsley, and relish and pulse until combined but not smooth, about 10 pulses. Adjust consistency with extra water as needed. Season with salt and pepper to taste. (Rémoulade can be refrigerated for up to 3 days.)

Quick Salsa Verde

Makes 1 cup

This zippy sauce is incredible with every element of this meal, and brings a welcome brightness. And when in doubt, I dunk my bread in it.

1 cup minced fresh parsley

½ cup extra-virgin olive oil

2 tablespoons capers, rinsed and minced

4 teaspoons lemon juice

2 anchovy fillets, rinsed and minced

1 garlic clove, minced

¼ teaspoon table salt

Whisk all ingredients together in bowl. (Salsa verde can be refrigerated for up to 2 days. Bring to room temperature and whisk to recombine before serving.)

> LOBSTER MADE EASY:
>
> Cooking lobster might seem intimidating, but it doesn't have to be. Here are two tips to take the stress out of cooking these crustaceans.
>
> **Keep the bands on.** The rubber bands on lobsters' claws have no impact on the flavor of the lobster, so it's completely fine to save your fingers and leave them in place until after the lobster is cooked.
>
> **Freeze it.** To ensure food safety and firmer flesh, lobsters should be cooked alive. There are a lot of different schools of thought about the most humane way to go about cooking lobster, but the best route is to chill them in the freezer for 30 minutes. This induces a coma-like state that makes it easier and safer to maneuver them into the pot.

DEBEARDING MUSSELS:

Most mussels are cultivated on long ropes suspended from rafts, which leaves them free of sand and grit—and for the most part, beards. In general, all they need is a quick rinse under the tap to clean them. If you do find a few beards, simply use a clean dish towel to grasp the beard and then pull it firmly to remove.

Removing Lobster Meat from the Shell

1. Once cooked lobster is cool enough to handle, set it on cutting board. Grasp tail with your hand and grab body with your other hand and twist to separate.

2. Lay tail on its side on counter and use both your hands to press down on tail until shell cracks.

3. Hold tail, flippers facing you and shell facing down. Pull sides back to open shell and remove meat. Remove green tomalley and dark vein. Slice tail lengthwise if desired for easy sharing.

4. Twist "arms" to remove claws and attached "knuckles." Twist knuckle and claw to separate. Break knuckles at joint using back of chef's knife or lobster-cracking tool. Use handle of teaspoon to push out meat.

5. Wiggle hinged portion of each claw to separate. If meat is stuck inside small part, remove with skewer. Break open claws, cracking 1 side and then flipping to crack other side, and remove meat.

6. Twist legs to remove. Lay flat on counter. Using rolling pin, roll toward open end, pushing out meat. Stop rolling before reaching end of legs; otherwise leg can crack and release pieces of shell.

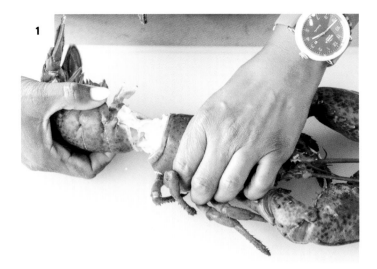

4

6A

5A

5B

6B

5C

SWEET THINGS

Dessert Boards to Satisfy
Your Sweet Tooth

227 **Ice Cream Sundaes**

233 **Pavlovas**

239 **Chocolate Fondue**

245 **Cookie Decorating**

253 **Dessert Cheese Board**

ICE CREAM SUNDAES

Serves 4 to 6

START WITH:

Ice cream

Sprinkles

Candy toppings (M&M's, gummy bears, mini chocolate chips, mini marshmallows, mini peanut butter cups)

Maraschino cherries

Classic Hot Fudge Sauce (page 229)

Whipped Cream (page 229)

IF YOU WANT, ADD:

Salted Butterscotch Sauce (page 231)

Mixed Berry Coulis (page 231)

More toppings (crushed up chocolate and/or plain ice cream cones, crumbled Oreos)

Waffles (store-bought)

Bananas

→

ICE CREAM SUNDAES

Ice cream is a food stylist's worst nightmare: It melts at lightning speed on set, so you've only got a tiny window of time to get that perfect shot. But that doesn't stop me from flexing my sundae skills at home. For flavors, make sure you've got the classics (chocolate and vanilla never fail) but I like to mix in some funky flavors, too, like this beet-chocolate masterpiece from my friend and colleague Jackie Gochenouer's ice cream business. And who could say no to a waffle sundae like they do at Disney?

ELLE'S STRATEGY:

Set up shop. Put your toppings in small bowls and each sauce in something that's easy to pour from. Corral everything on a tray, but don't worry about where the ice cream will go—keeping it separate makes things easier. Set out scoops (owning at least two lets you scoop and fill bowls twice as fast), bowls, and spoons. Save the ice cream for last, and just do a few pints. When they start to get soupy, switch them out for backups from the freezer.

Get a head start. Clear out your freezer to make room for all that ice cream (plan on about ½ pint per person, or more if you want more selection). Make your sauces ahead of time; the hot fudge sauce is good for a month! You can even prep your toppings—just cover the dishes in plastic wrap.

Think outside the box. Don't be afraid to lean into non-sweet toppings. Try cereals, crumbled potato chips, balsamic reduction (see page 148), candied bacon (see page 72), or even flake sea salt (so good with pecan ice cream).

The perfect scoop. Put your scoops in mugs of water. This makes it easier to scoop but also keeps you from double dipping and mixing up the ice cream flavors.

Pints aplenty. If I buy bigger containers of ice cream, I like to repack it into smaller containers to help keep things as cold as possible. You can find empty pints online, but Tupperware works just fine.

Classic Hot Fudge Sauce

Makes about 2 cups

Nothing on earth is better than rich, chocolaty hot fudge sauce, and this recipe is the chocolatiest thanks to the cocoa powder–unsweetened chocolate combo. Using milk, rather than cream, helps preserve that intense chocolate flavor, and incorporating cold butter creates a thick consistency and makes the sauce nice and glossy.

- 1¼ cups (8¾ ounces) sugar
- ⅔ cup whole milk
- ¼ teaspoon table salt
- ⅓ cup (1 ounce) unsweetened cocoa powder, sifted
- 3 ounces unsweetened chocolate, chopped fine
- 4 tablespoons unsalted butter, cut into 8 pieces and chilled
- 1 teaspoon vanilla extract

1. Heat sugar, milk, and salt in medium saucepan over medium-low heat, whisking gently, until sugar has dissolved and liquid starts to bubble around edges of saucepan, about 6 minutes. Reduce heat to low, add cocoa, and whisk until smooth.

2. Off heat, stir in chocolate and let sit for 3 minutes. Whisk sauce until smooth and chocolate is fully melted. Whisk in butter and vanilla until fully incorporated and sauce thickens slightly. (Sauce can be refrigerated for up to 1 month; gently warm in microwave before using, stirring every 10 seconds, until pourable.)

VARIATION

Chocolate-Tahini Sauce

Add ⅓ cup tahini with the butter and vanilla.

Whipped Cream

Makes about 2 cups

A dollop of whipped cream is always the right sundae move. Where else would that cherry perch? This recipe is so much better than the canned stuff, and the flavor variations add a unique twist your guests won't see coming (hello, brown sugar and bourbon).

- 1 cup heavy cream, chilled
- 1 tablespoon sugar
- 1 teaspoon vanilla extract
- Pinch table salt

Using stand mixer fitted with whisk attachment, whip cream, sugar, vanilla, and salt on medium-low speed until foamy, about 1 minute. Increase speed to high and whip until soft peaks form, 1 to 3 minutes. (Whipped cream can be refrigerated in fine-mesh strainer set over small bowl and covered with plastic wrap for up to 8 hours.)

VARIATIONS

Maple Whipped Cream

Substitute 2 tablespoons maple syrup for sugar. Reduce vanilla to ½ teaspoon.

Brown Sugar and Bourbon Whipped Cream

Omit vanilla. Substitute ½ cup packed light brown sugar for granulated sugar. Increase salt to ⅛ teaspoon. Add ½ cup sour cream and 2 teaspoons bourbon. Before whipping, whisk all ingredients together in bowl of stand mixer, cover with plastic wrap, and refrigerate for at least 4 hours, or up to 24 hours. Whisk again to combine before whipping.

Orange Whipped Cream

Substitute 2 tablespoons orange juice for vanilla. Add 1 teaspoon grated orange zest to stand mixer with cream before whipping.

Peanut Butter Whipped Cream

Add ¼ cup creamy peanut butter to stand mixer with cream before whipping. Once mixture is foamy, continue to whip on medium-low speed until soft peaks form, 1 to 3 minutes.

GET EVEN:

Say goodbye to soupy tops and rock-solid centers. For evenly defrosted pints, don't go straight from the freezer to counter. Instead, put the pints in the refrigerator for 30 minutes. Why? The greater the disparity between the temperature of the food and the temperature of the air around it, the more unevenly it warms up. The refrigerator tempers the ice cream, ensuring it defrosts evenly all the way through.

LEVEL UP YOUR BOARD

Salted Butterscotch Sauce

Makes about 1½ cups

This is so much easier than making a caramel sauce, and it's just as delicious—if not more so; the salty-sweet combo is killer. Do yourself a favor and make a little extra to drizzle over pie, bread pudding, or cake.

- 1 cup packed (7 ounces) light brown sugar
- ½ cup heavy cream
- 8 tablespoons unsalted butter, cut into 8 pieces and chilled, divided
- ½ teaspoon table salt
- ½ teaspoon vanilla extract

1. Combine sugar, cream, 4 tablespoons butter, and salt in medium saucepan. Cook over medium-high heat, stirring often with rubber spatula, until large bubbles burst on surface of sauce, about 4 minutes. Remove from heat.

2. Carefully stir in vanilla and remaining 4 tablespoons butter until fully combined, about 1 minute. Carefully transfer sauce to bowl and let cool for 30 minutes (sauce will thicken as it cools). Serve. (Sauce can be refrigerated for up to 1 week. Reheat in microwave before serving.)

Mixed Berry Coulis

Makes about 1½ cups

The type of berries used as well as their ripeness will affect the sweetness of the coulis, so the amount of sugar is variable. Start with 5 tablespoons, then add more to taste in step 2. Additional sugar should be stirred into the warm coulis immediately after straining so that the sugar will readily dissolve.

- 15 ounces (3 cups) fresh or thawed frozen blueberries, blackberries, and/or raspberries
- ¼ cup water
- 5 tablespoons sugar, plus extra for sweetening
- ⅛ teaspoon table salt
- 2 teaspoons lemon juice

1. Bring berries, water, sugar, and salt to gentle simmer in medium saucepan over medium heat and cook, stirring occasionally, until sugar is dissolved and berries are heated through, about 1 minute.

2. Process mixture in blender until smooth, about 20 seconds. Strain through fine-mesh strainer into bowl, pressing on solids to extract as much puree as possible; discard solids. Stir lemon juice into puree and sweeten with extra sugar as needed. Cover and refrigerate until well chilled, about 1 hour. Adjust consistency with extra water as needed. (Sauce can be refrigerated for up to 4 days; stir to recombine before using.)

SPRUCE UP STORE-BOUGHT HOT FUDGE:

Nothing beats homemade, but if you're popping open a jar instead, there are some things you can do to add a little pizzazz.

- Spice it up with a sprinkle of ground cardamom, cinnamon, ginger, or even cayenne or curry powder.

- Add a splash of mint, vanilla, almond, coconut, or anise extract.

- Get boozy with some Grand Marnier, Chambord, or Kahlúa liqueur.

- Catch a buzz by stirring in some instant espresso or matcha powder.

PAVLOVAS

Serves 6 to 8

START WITH:

Individual Pavlovas (page 235)

Fruit toppings (see page 236)

Whipped Cream (page 229)

IF YOU WANT, ADD:

Nuts (walnuts, slivered almonds)

Pomegranate molasses

Mixed berry jam (or any jam)

Passion fruit curd (or any fruit curd)

Powdered sugar

Fresh mint

→

PAVLOVAS

You heard it here first: Pavlovas are the new cupcakes. These marshmallowy, crisp-shelled meringues piled high with lightly whipped cream and fresh fruit are the perfect alternative dessert for a special occasion that might normally call for cake. The best part is, the success of this board lies in its simplicity. Each component is picture-perfect, so you don't need a whole lot of extras for it to impress. (Although if you're feeling it, pile it on, it's your pavlova party, after all.)

ELLE'S STRATEGY:

Set up shop. Set out the meringues and fruit toppings on separate platters—the meringues can get sticky, so you want to keep them dry, and the fruit is a little drippy. Put out a big bowl of whipped cream, small dishes of nuts and other toppings, and put powdered sugar in a strainer set over a plate to keep things tidy(ish).

Get a head start. You can make your meringues up to 1 week ahead of time (just be sure to wrap them tightly in plastic wrap—moisture is their mortal enemy). Whipped cream can be made up to 8 hours before serving. See page 229 for more whipped cream make-ahead tips.

I dip, you dip. The little dip in the center of pavlovas is for more than just aesthetics. It ensures that the pavlova is structurally sound and provides a nice resting spot for the toppings. Spoon some curd or jam into the well first, followed by whipped cream and other toppings.

The perfect blank slate. Because meringues and whipped cream are so simple in flavor, anything goes. You can use any fruit that's in season (in addition to or instead of the leveled-up toppings on page 236), and use whatever "extras" (nuts, candy, sprinkles, curds, and jams) you like.

Practice patience. Letting your assembled pavlova sit for a few minutes softens the meringue and makes it easier to eat.

Individual Pavlovas

Makes 10 meringues

Because eggs can vary in size, measuring the egg whites by weight or volume is essential to ensure that you are working with the correct ratio of egg whites to sugar. Open the oven door as infrequently as possible while the meringues are inside. Don't worry if the meringues crack; it is part of the dessert's charm. The insides of the meringues will remain soft.

1½	cups (10½ ounces) sugar
¾	cup (6 ounces) egg whites (5 to 7 large eggs)
1½	teaspoons distilled white vinegar
1½	teaspoons cornstarch
1	teaspoon vanilla extract

1. Adjust oven racks to upper-middle and lower-middle positions and heat oven to 250 degrees. Combine sugar and egg whites in bowl of stand mixer; place bowl over saucepan filled with 1 inch simmering water, making sure that water does not touch bottom of bowl. Whisking gently but constantly, heat until sugar is dissolved and mixture registers 160 degrees, 5 to 8 minutes.

2. Fit stand mixer with whisk attachment and whip mixture on high speed until meringue forms stiff peaks, is smooth and creamy, and is bright white with sheen, about 4 minutes (bowl may still be slightly warm to touch). Stop mixer and scrape down bowl with spatula. Add vinegar, cornstarch, and vanilla and whip on high speed until combined, about 10 seconds.

3. Spoon about ¼ teaspoon meringue onto each corner of 2 rimmed baking sheets. Line sheets with parchment paper, pressing on corners to secure. Spoon heaping ½ cup meringue into 5 evenly spaced piles on each sheet. Spread each meringue pile with back of spoon to form 3½-inch disk with slight depression in center.

4. Bake meringues until exteriors are dry and crisp and meringues release cleanly from parchment when gently lifted at edges with thin metal spatula, about 50 minutes. Meringues should be quite pale (a hint of creamy color is OK). Turn off oven, prop door open with wooden spoon, and let meringues cool in oven for 1½ hours. Remove from oven and let cool completely before topping, about 15 minutes. (Cooled meringues can be wrapped tightly in plastic wrap and stored at room temperature for up to 1 week.)

A SWEET RIVALRY:

The history of pavlova is storied with an ongoing debate between New Zealand and neighboring Australia: Both countries lay claim to the dessert. As Kiwis have it, a Wellington chef created the dish in honor of the prima ballerina Anna Pavlova, citing her billlowy tutu as inspiration. But Australians insist that it was invented at a hotel in Perth and got its name when a diner declared it to be "light as Pavlova." More recently, it's been asserted that pavlova began life as a German torte and eventually traveled to the United States.

Fruit Toppings

These elegantly simple toppings provide sweetness and necessary juiciness to soften the crispy pavlovas. Choose one (or more!) of these to make for your board. Or in a pinch, just tossing fresh berries or other fruit with sugar and letting it macerate in the fridge until the fruit softens and releases some of its juices is never a bad move. (You could even stir in a little prosecco at the end if you're feeling fancy.) Each topping makes enough for 5 pavlovas (half a recipe). These recipes can easily be doubled.

Orange, Cranberry, and Mint Topping

Makes about 3 cups

You can substitute tangelos or Cara Cara oranges for the navel oranges, if desired. Valencia or blood oranges can also be used, but since they are smaller, increase the number of fruit to six.

- ½ cup (3½ ounces) sugar
- ½ cup water
- 3 ounces (¾ cup) frozen cranberries
- 3 navel oranges
- 3 tablespoons chopped fresh mint

1. Bring sugar and water to boil in medium saucepan over medium heat, stirring to dissolve sugar. Off heat, stir in cranberries. Let cranberries and syrup cool completely, about 30 minutes. (Cranberries in syrup can be refrigerated for up to 24 hours.)

2. Cut away peel and pith from oranges. Cut each orange into quarters from pole to pole, then cut crosswise into ¼-inch-thick pieces. Just before serving, toss oranges and mint with cranberries in bowl until combined.

Mango, Kiwi, and Blueberry Topping

Makes about 3 cups

Do not substitute frozen blueberries for fresh here.

- 1 mango, peeled, pitted, and cut into ½-inch pieces (1½ cups)
- 2 kiwi, peeled, quartered lengthwise, and sliced crosswise ¼ inch thick
- 2½ ounces (½ cup) blueberries
- 1½ teaspoons sugar

Toss all ingredients together in large bowl. Set aside for 30 minutes before serving.

Strawberry, Lime, and Basil Topping

Makes about 3 cups

Do not substitute frozen strawberries for fresh here.

- 18 ounces strawberries, hulled and quartered (3 cups)
- 1½ teaspoons sugar
- ¼ teaspoon grated lime zest plus ½ teaspoon juice
  Pinch table salt
- 2 tablespoons chopped fresh basil

Toss strawberries with sugar, lime zest and juice, and salt in large bowl. Set aside for 30 minutes. Just before serving, stir in basil.

SHAPING PAVLOVAS :

1. Whip mixture on high speed until meringue forms stiff peaks, is smooth and creamy, and is bright white with sheen.

2. Spoon heaping ½ cup meringue into evenly spaced piles on baking sheets. Spread each meringue pile with back of spoon to form 3½-inch disk with slight depression in center.

CHOCOLATE FONDUE

Serves 6 to 8

START WITH:

Chocolate Fondue (page 241)

Fresh fruit (strawberries, bananas)

Cookies (madeleines, mini stroopwafels)

IF YOU WANT, ADD:

Crispy Rice Cereal Treats (page 242)

Marshmallows

Potato chips

Candied orange peel (or other dried fruit)

→

CHOCOLATE FONDUE

When I was young my mom often threw cheese fondue parties, and I would gorge myself on mini sausage links dipped in the molten cheese. This is my sweet version, which I love putting together as a way to keep the evening going when it's dessert time and people aren't ready to get up from the table. The abundance is the attraction—you want guests to feel like they have a lot of dipping options—so pile it on, and mix in some outside-the-box things to keep it interesting (see page 242 for ideas).

ELLE'S STRATEGY:

Set up shop. Place the fondue pot in the center so everyone can reach (if using an electric fondue pot make sure you're near an outlet). Set out small plates of prepped fruit so they're easier to refill as needed. Organize all of the dipping items in long trails (like rays of sun) around the fondue pot. If you don't have a board this size, put everything on plates or in bowls around the fondue and set it out on an easily wipeable surface (or use a tablecloth you don't mind people dripping chocolate on).

Get a head start. Wash your berries in advance (see page 44). Crispy Rice Cereal Treats can be made 3 days ahead of time.

No pot? No problem. If you don't have a fondue pot with a heat source, use a 1½- to 7-quart slow cooker set to the warm setting.

Skewer time. If your fondue pot didn't come with forks, choose sturdy wooden skewers that are about 8 inches long. Avoid toothpicks (too small) and metal skewers (when they get hot, everything slides off).

Dip without fail. Avoid anything too crumbly or that has a powdery coating (like powdered sugar donuts). Cut everything into small pieces that can fit on a fondue fork and be eaten in one bite.

Chocolate Fondue

Serves 6 to 8

Dipping an enormous red strawberry into a pot of warm melted chocolate is guaranteed to make just about anybody happy. But despite its short ingredient list, getting chocolate fondue right can take some finessing. Too much chocolate, and the texture is thick and difficult to dip delicious morsels into. Too much cream, and the texture is drippy and the chocolate's flavor is muted—and I want amped-up chocolatiness, don't you? The perfect proportion is slightly more chocolate than cream, with a little corn syrup (secret ingredient alert!) for that showstopping glossy finish.

12   ounces chocolate, chopped

1⅓ cups heavy cream

    Pinch table salt

1   tablespoon corn syrup

1. Place chocolate in bowl. Bring cream and salt just to simmer in small saucepan over medium heat, then pour hot cream over chocolate. Cover bowl and let chocolate soften for 3 minutes. Whisk chocolate mixture until smooth, then add corn syrup and whisk to incorporate.

2. Transfer chocolate mixture to fondue pot, warm pot over Sterno flame for 5 minutes, and serve immediately.

VARIATIONS

Five-Spice Chocolate Fondue

Add 2 teaspoons ground cinnamon, 5 whole cloves, 1 teaspoon black peppercorns, 2 star anise pods, and two ½-inch pieces fresh ginger to saucepan with cream. Bring mixture to simmer, then cover, remove from heat, and let steep for 10 minutes. Strain mixture through fine-mesh strainer into bowl; discard spices. Return cream to simmer in now-empty saucepan before pouring over chocolate.

Orange Chocolate Fondue

Add 1 tablespoon grated orange zest to saucepan with cream. Bring mixture to simmer, then cover, remove from heat, and let steep for 10 minutes. Strain mixture through fine-mesh strainer into bowl; discard zest. Return cream to simmer in now-empty saucepan before pouring over chocolate. Add 2 tablespoons orange liqueur, such as Grand Marnier or Cointreau, with corn syrup.

CHOOSE YOUR CHOCOLATE WISELY:

Chocolate fondue stays true to the flavor of the chocolate used to make it, so be sure to use a high-quality chocolate you like straight from the package.

Milk chocolate: A mild and sweet fondue

Bittersweet chocolate: A pronounced bitter and even slightly acidic-tasting fondue

For the best of both worlds, use half milk chocolate and half bittersweet chocolate for just a touch of bitterness without being overly sweet.

LEVEL UP YOUR BOARD

Crispy Rice Cereal Treats

Makes 24 bars

These sweet, chewy, crispy treats are a blast from the past, and always make you feel like a kid. You can't go wrong with classic plain, but to make it even more special (with hardly any more work) I like to customize them with mix-ins. Try one of the variations here or create your own concoction using any sorts of candies or snacks you have on hand. Be sure to dampen your hands before pressing the mixture into the pan so you don't get sticky cereal all over you. Do not use mini marshmallows here. For the best results, weigh the cereal.

8	tablespoons unsalted butter
2	(10-ounce) packages large marshmallows
2	teaspoons vanilla extract
¼	teaspoon table salt
10	cups (10 ounces) crisped rice cereal

1. Spray rubber spatula and 13 by 9-inch baking pan with vegetable oil spray. Melt butter in Dutch oven over medium heat. Add marshmallows, vanilla, and salt and cook, stirring often with prepared spatula, until marshmallows are just melted, about 3 minutes (some marshmallows may not be fully melted; this is OK). Off heat, stir in cereal until fully combined.

2. Transfer cereal mixture to prepared pan. Using your damp hands, press cereal mixture into even layer. Let sit for 1 hour to set. Run knife around edge of pan to loosen treats, then turn out onto cutting board. Flip treats right side up and cut into 24 equal-size bars. (Bars can be stored in airtight container for up to 3 days.) Serve.

VARIATIONS

Candy Bar Crispy Rice Cereal Treats

Chop two 2-ounce Snickers bars and combine with ½ cup M&M's Minis in bowl. Add 1 cup candy mixture to Dutch oven with cereal in step 1. Sprinkle remaining heaping ¼ cup candy mixture over cereal mixture in pan before pressing into even layer.

Nutella and Hazelnut Crispy Rice Cereal Treats

Add ½ cup Nutella and ¼ teaspoon instant espresso powder to Dutch oven with marshmallows in step 1. Sprinkle ½ cup hazelnuts, toasted, skinned, and chopped, over cereal mixture in pan before pressing into even layer.

Bacon and Salted Caramel Crispy Rice Cereal Treats

Cook 6 slices bacon in 12-inch nonstick skillet over medium heat until crispy, 7 to 9 minutes. Transfer bacon to paper towel–lined plate, let sit until cool enough to handle, then crumble.

Add two-thirds of bacon to Dutch oven with cereal in step 1. Sprinkle remaining one-third of bacon over cereal mixture in pan before pressing into even layer. After pressing, drizzle with ¼ cup store-bought caramel sauce, then sprinkle with ¼ teaspoon salt.

Peanut Butter and Honey Crispy Rice Cereal Treats

Add ¼ cup creamy peanut butter to Dutch oven with marshmallows in step 1. After pressing into even layer, drizzle with 2 tablespoons honey.

DUNK TANK:

Include at least one thing from each category for a balanced fondue board.

- **Something sweet:** Dried or candied fruit, candy bars, crispy rice cereal treats, cookies, marshmallows, doughnuts, macaroons, stroopwafels, brownies, peanut brittle, animal crackers
- **Something fresh:** Berries, apples, bananas, orange or grapefruit slices, pineapple, mango, grapes, melon
- **Something neutral and bready:** Graham crackers, banana bread, pound cake, baguette, pretzels, granola bars, saltines, madeleines
- **Something unexpected:** Potato chips, beef jerky, pickles, veggie chips, cheese puffs, candied ginger, bacon (see pages 50 and 72)

While you can technically serve fondue in any vessel (a saucepan is a popular choice), a fondue set has a festive feel and saves you from having to constantly rewarm the chocolate. ATK's winning model is the Oster Titanium Infused DuraCeramic 3-Qt Fondue Pot. In addition to a nonstick ceramic coating that's impervious to scratches, this fondue pot has heat-resistant plastic handles for moving the pot while still hot and a clearly labeled temperature dial with both degrees and recommendations for type of fondue printed on the knob.

COOKIE DECORATING

Serves 6 to 8

START WITH:

Roll-and-Cut Sugar Cookies (page 248)

All-Purpose Glaze (page 249)

Decorating Icing (page 249)

IF YOU WANT, ADD:

Decorating sugar (store-bought, or DIY on page 250)

Sprinkles

Small candies (gumdrops, mini M&M's, jelly beans)

→

COOKIE DECORATING

Cookie decorating really takes the DIY nature of boards to a whole new level, and is sure to bring out the kid in everyone. What's more fun than some friendly (and delicious) competition? And sure, this may be the ultimate cold-weather activity, but change up the shapes and icing colors and you could have a cookie decorating–themed bridal shower, birthday party, or even Super Bowl party (and you can even customize your beverage offerings; try hot chocolate, tea, or the mimosas on page 52).

ELLE'S STRATEGY:

Set up shop. Place the undecorated cookies on a tray. Set out the decorating accoutrements (sprinkles, candies, etc.) next to the icing and glazes. Either premix the frosting colors or offer food coloring so your guests can make their own, and fill up some pastry bags for your guests, too. Sometimes I like to set up individual stations around a table (a few cookies on a plate, some frosting, and utensils). Put a rack in a rimmed baking sheet off to the side for finished cookies.

Get a head start. Cookie dough can be made up to 5 days ahead of time, and cookies can be baked 5 days in advance (store them in an airtight container with a slice of bread to keep them fresh).

Stay organized. Turn a muffin tin into a cookie decorating tackle box by decanting sprinkles and small candies into each cup. This will keep your station tidy, and allow for easy sharing among cookie decorators.

Get equipped. You'll need pastry bags fitted with $\frac{1}{16}$-inch round tips for all the icing colors (look for the brand Wilton, or see page 251 for a workaround) as well as small bowls for mixing colors of icing; plenty of spoons and/or offset spatulas (at least a couple per color); a rimmed baking sheet with a rack; toothpicks for detail work; and containers for your guests to take home their creations. To really make it cute, order small boxes online and set out colorful bakery twine to wrap them up.

Roll-and-Cut Sugar Cookies

Makes about 40 cookies

These perfect blank-slate sugar cookies taste as great as they are easy to make. Superfine sugar (made by grinding granulated sugar in the food processor) ensures the cookies are crisp without a hint of graininess. Baking the cookies at a gentle 300 degrees on a rimless baking sheet (to allow for more airflow around the cookies) gives them an even, golden color with minimal browning, along with a crisp, crunchy texture from edge to edge. If you don't have a rimless baking sheet, just flip over your rimmed baking sheet. In step 3, use a rolling pin and a combination of rolling and a pushing or smearing motion to form the soft dough into an oval.

1	large egg
1	teaspoon vanilla extract
¾	teaspoon table salt
¼	teaspoon almond extract
2½	cups (12½ ounces) all-purpose flour
¼	teaspoon baking powder
¼	teaspoon baking soda
1	cup (7 ounces) granulated sugar
16	tablespoons unsalted butter, cut into ½-inch pieces and chilled

1. Whisk egg, vanilla, salt, and almond extract together in small bowl. Whisk flour, baking powder, and baking soda together in second bowl.

2. Process sugar in food processor until finely ground, about 30 seconds. Add butter and process until uniform mass forms and no large pieces of butter are visible, about 30 seconds, scraping down sides of bowl as needed. Add egg mixture and process until mixture is smooth and paste-like, about 10 seconds. Add flour mixture and process until no dry flour remains but mixture remains crumbly, about 30 seconds, scraping down sides of bowl as needed.

3. Turn out dough onto counter and knead gently by hand until smooth, about 10 seconds. Divide dough in half. Place 1 piece of dough in center of large sheet of parchment paper and press into 7 by 9-inch oval. Place second large sheet of parchment over dough and roll dough into 10 by 14-inch oval of even ⅛-inch thickness. Transfer dough with parchment to rimmed baking sheet. Repeat pressing and rolling with second piece of dough, then stack on top of first piece on sheet. Refrigerate until dough is firm, at least 1½ hours (or freeze for 30 minutes). (Rolled dough can be wrapped in plastic wrap and refrigerated for up to 5 days.)

4. Adjust oven rack to lower-middle position and heat oven to 300 degrees. Line rimless cookie sheet with parchment. Working with 1 piece of rolled dough, gently peel off top layer of parchment. Replace parchment, loosely covering dough. (Peeling off parchment and returning it will make cutting and removing cookies easier.) Turn over dough and parchment and gently peel off and discard second piece of parchment. Using cookie cutter, cut dough into shapes. Transfer shapes to prepared cookie sheet, spacing them about ½ inch apart.

5. Bake until cookies are lightly and evenly browned around edges, 14 to 17 minutes, rotating sheet halfway through baking. Let cookies cool on sheet for 5 minutes. Using wide metal spatula, transfer cookies to wire rack; let cool completely. Repeat cutting and baking with remaining dough. (Dough scraps can be patted together, rerolled, and chilled once before cutting and baking.)

All-Purpose Glaze

Makes about 1 cup; enough for 40 cookies

Spread this glaze onto completely cooled cookies using the back of a spoon, or pipe the glaze onto cookies to form a pattern or design. Let the glaze dry completely, about 30 minutes, before eating or packing away.

- 2 cups (8 ounces) confectioners' sugar
- 3 tablespoons milk
- 1 ounce cream cheese, softened
  Food coloring (optional)

Whisk all ingredients in bowl until smooth. (Glaze should be used immediately; if it hardens, remix with a bit of water, whisking well to make glaze smooth.)

VARIATIONS

Citrus Glaze

Substitute lemon, lime, or orange juice for milk.

Coffee Glaze

Add 1¼ teaspoons instant espresso powder or instant coffee to glaze ingredients.

Decorating Icing

Makes 1⅓ cups; enough for 40 cookies

Decorating icing has more structure than glaze, making it ideal for detailed piping work.

- 2 large egg whites
- 2⅔ cups (10⅔ ounces) confectioners' sugar
- 1–2 drops food coloring (optional)

1. Using stand mixer fitted with whisk attachment, whip egg whites, sugar, and food coloring, if using, on medium-low speed until combined, about 1 minute. Increase speed to medium-high and whip until glossy, soft peaks form, 3 to 4 minutes, scraping down bowl as needed. (Icing should be used immediately; if it hardens, remix with a bit of water, whisking well to make icing smooth.)

2. Transfer icing to pastry bag fitted with small round pastry tip. Decorate cookies and let icing harden, about 1½ hours, before serving.

THREE WAYS TO GLAZE:

Spread: Spoon a small amount of glaze in the center of the cookie, then spread it into an even layer. Using the back of a spoon or a small offset spatula, spread the glaze outward from the center to ensure even coverage.

Drag two glazes together: Glaze the entire cookie and then pipe small drops of a second colored glaze in a pattern. While both glazes are still wet, drag a toothpick through the glazes to create a design (try hearts, stars, wiggly lines, and swirls). This idea works best with glazes that are two very different hues.

Fill in piped borders: For glazed cookies with cleaner edges than those made using the spreading technique, carefully pipe the glaze around the border of the cookie, let it dry slightly, then add more glaze to the center of the cookie and spread the extra glaze into an even layer. Note that piping with glaze will be less detailed and neat than piping with decorating icing.

MAKING COLORFUL DECORATING SUGAR:

1. Place ½ cup granulated sugar in bowl. Add about 5 drops food coloring and mix thoroughly.

2. To ensure even color, push sugar through fine-mesh strainer. Spread sugar in pie plate and let it dry completely.

TAKING YOUR COOKIES TO THE NEXT LEVEL:

Pipe: To apply intricate designs, such as dots or fine lines, to cookies, pipe the icing directly onto the cookie. Use a pastry bag fitted with a ⅟₁₆- or ⅛-inch round tip or a zipper-lock bag with a small snip in one corner to pipe the icing.

Layer icing and play with patterns: Create visual interest and a sense of depth by piping layers of icing over one another. Start by coating the cookie with a thin, smooth layer of icing. Let the first layer dry before piping dots, lines, or other patterns in a second layer on top. Play around with combinations of lines, dots, and swirls to make different patterns, from snowflake fractals to free-form loops to orderly rows.

Add embellishments: Small confections, such as shiny silver or gold balls known as dragées, can be used to dress up cookies. While the icing is still soft, place decorations on top and then allow them to dry. Other small candies—gumdrops, mini chocolate morsels, jelly beans—can be used in a similar fashion. Add the candies immediately after applying the icing. As the icing dries, it will affix the candies in place.

NO PASTRY BAG? NO PROBLEM.

Whether you don't own pastry bags or there's not enough to go around, try this easy trick for transforming zipper-lock bags into makeshift pastry bags. This works with or without pastry tips.

1. Measure desired width diagonally across 1 bottom corner of zipper-lock bag. Use pen to mark bag at both ends of line. Fill bag with decorating icing or glaze.

2. Cut from 1 mark to other in slight arc shape to create circular opening.

3. Pipe icing or glaze onto cookie.

DESSERT CHEESE BOARD

Serves 4 to 6

START WITH:

Saint-André cheese or other rich, creamy cheese

Candied tangerines or dried fruit

Honeycomb, honey, or jam

Fresh fruit (grapes, figs, pears, currants)

Dark chocolate

IF YOU WANT, ADD:

Skillet Candied Nuts (page 256)

Savory Seed Brittle (page 256)

Grilled peaches or nectarines

Lillet (or other dessert drink on page 254)

→

DESSERT CHEESE BOARD

After opening with an essential savory cheese board (page 19) and going on an excellent adventure through the world of boards, buffets, and spreads, it's fitting to finish with a dessert-focused cheese board. Not overtly sweet like the other dessert boards, it has wonderful textures, flavors, and colors to end a festive meal. I love to build it around Saint-André, a decadent triple-crème cow's milk cheese from Normandy with a bloomy rind; think of it as a buttery, more intensely flavored take on Brie.

ELLE'S STRATEGY:

Set up shop. Start by selecting your cheese. Anything goes here; I love rich, creamy cheeses like Saint-André, but you can try goat cheese drizzled in honey, a big wedge of blue, or even gouda. Whichever you choose, make the cheese the anchor point (I think just one cheese is best for this board), then arrange sections of fresh and dried fruit around the cheese. Fill in spaces with honey or jam, dark chocolate, and other fancy snacky things. See pages 21–23 for more cheese board styling tips.

Get a head start. Take cheese out of the refrigerator 1 to 2 hours ahead for the fullest flavor and texture. Grill peaches a day ahead and refrigerate. Make the nuts up to 1 week ahead and the seed brittle up to 1 month ahead.

Make it special. To give peaches or nectarines a kiss in a grill pan or on the grill, halve, pit, brush with a little oil, and then grill for about 3 minutes per side. And although you can use any sharp knife for the cheese, a cheese knife will make a cleaner cut, help prevent sticking, and look stylish to boot. The same knife can be used to slice the honeycomb (yes, you can eat the wax!).

Dessert drinks. I love to serve chilled Lillet, an aromatized fortified wine similar to vermouth. The Blanc is classic; it's also available in Rosé and Rouge. Other great choices: On the lighter side, choose an off-dry German Riesling or a frizzante Moscato d'Asti. On the richer side, try ice wine, oloroso sherry, Tokaji, or Sauternes.

LEVEL UP YOUR BOARD

Skillet Candied Nuts

Makes about 1 cup

I keep these in my pantry at all times. Besides adding rich flavor and crunchy texture to the dessert cheese board, candied nuts make a special topping for ice cream (or oatmeal)—or a great little snack all on their own. You can use any variety of nuts, but I'm partial to cashews, pistachios, and almonds. And the recipe is easily customizable with herbs and spices to create different flavor profiles. As the sugar caramelizes toward the end of cooking, it may start to get a little smoky; that's OK.

- 1 **cup coarsely chopped raw, unsalted nuts**
- 2 **tablespoons water**
- 2 **tablespoons sugar**
- ¼ **teaspoon table salt**

1. Toast nuts in 10-inch nonstick skillet over medium heat until fragrant and spotty brown, about 3 minutes. Quickly add water, sugar, and salt and stir with rubber spatula to evenly coat nuts.

2. Cook, stirring often, until sugar mixture caramelizes and nuts begin to clump together, 2 to 3 minutes. Quickly transfer nuts to large plate and spread into even layer. Let cool for 10 minutes. Break nut clusters into small pieces with your hands. (Nuts can be stored in airtight container for up to 1 week.)

VARIATIONS

Skillet Candied Nuts with Fresh Herbs

Just before transferring candied nuts to plate, stir in 1 teaspoon minced fresh rosemary, sage, or thyme.

Spiced Skillet Candied Nuts

Combine ⅛ teaspoon ground coriander, ⅛ teaspoon ground ginger, and pinch ground cinnamon in bowl. Just before transferring candied nuts to plate, stir in spice mixture.

Savory Seed Brittle

Makes about 2 cups

Maple syrup and soy sauce might sound a little unconventional, but they create a sophisticated crunchy seed brittle with a barely sweet, slightly savory flavor. And all those different seeds along with some oats really bring the texture, and pair nicely with the creamy cheese. This is another pantry condiment I try to keep on hand; it also makes an excellent salad topping. Don't substitute quick or instant oats in this recipe.

- 2 **tablespoons maple syrup**
- 1 **large egg white**
- 1 **tablespoon extra-virgin olive oil or vegetable oil**
- 1 **tablespoon soy sauce**
- 1 **tablespoon caraway seeds, crushed**
- ½ **teaspoon table salt**
- ¼ **teaspoon pepper**
- ½ **cup old-fashioned rolled oats**
- ⅓ **cup raw, unsalted sunflower seeds**
- ⅓ **cup raw, unsalted pepitas**
- 2 **tablespoons sesame seeds**
- 2 **tablespoons nigella seeds**

1. Adjust oven rack to upper-middle position and heat oven to 300 degrees. Line 8-inch square baking pan with parchment paper and spray parchment with vegetable oil spray. Whisk maple syrup, egg white, oil, soy sauce, caraway seeds, salt, and pepper together in large bowl. Stir in oats, sunflower seeds, pepitas, sesame seeds, and nigella seeds until well combined.

2. Transfer oat mixture to prepared pan and spread into even layer. Using stiff metal spatula, press oat mixture until very compact. Bake until golden brown and fragrant, 45 to 55 minutes, rotating pan halfway through baking.

3. Transfer pan to wire rack and let brittle cool completely, about 1 hour. Break cooled brittle into pieces of desired size, discarding parchment. (Brittle can be stored in airtight container for up to 1 month.)

NUTRITIONAL INFORMATION FOR OUR RECIPES

To calculate the nutritional values of our recipes per serving, we used The Food Processor SQL by ESHA research. When using this program, we entered all the ingredients, using weights wherever possible. We also used our preferred brands in these analyses. Any ingredient listed as "optional" was excluded from the analyses. If there is a range in the serving size, we used the highest number of servings to calculate nutritional values. We did not include additional salt or pepper for food that's seasoned to taste.

	CALORIES	TOTAL FAT (G)	SAT FAT (G)	CHOL (MG)	SODIUM (MG)	TOTAL CARB (G)	DIETARY FIBER (G)	TOTAL SUGARS (G)	PROTEIN (G)
Get on Board									
CHEESE BOARD (SERVES 6 TO 8)									
Goat Cheese Log with Herbes de Provence	90	8	4.5	20	95	1	0	0	3
Blue Cheese Log with Walnuts and Honey	114	8	5	24	210	6	0	6	4
Cheddar Cheese Log with Chives	130	12	6	29	172	1	0	1	4
Fig-Balsamic Jam (2 tbsp)	90	0	0	0	20	23	1	22	0
Seeded Pumpkin Crackers	230	9	1.5	45	1980	32	3	14	6
CHARCUTERIE BOARD (SERVES 6 TO 8)									
Quick Pickled Fennel	10	0	0	0	15	2	1	1	0
Stuffed Pickled Sweet Peppers (1 pepper)	70	4.5	2	15	480	2	0	0	4
Bacon Jam (2½ tbsp)	280	23	8	35	380	12	0	10	7
CRUDITÉS BOARD (SERVES 6 TO 8)									
Whipped Cashew Dip with Roasted Red Peppers and Olives (⅓ cup)	270	23	3.5	0	100	13	1	3	7
Beet Tzatziki (⅓ cup)	120	9	4	10	230	5	1	4	4
Green Goddess Dip (⅓ cup)	230	25	5	25	240	2	0	1	1
Prosciutto-Wrapped Asparagus	220	16	8	55	1160	7	2	3	16
First Things First									
GRANOLA PARFAITS (SERVES 4 TO 6)									
Almond-Raisin Granola (¼ cup)	190	9	1	0	40	24	3	12	4
Apricot-Orange Granola (¼ cup)	180	7	1	0	45	26	3	14	3
Cherry–Chocolate Chip Granola (¼ cup)	220	11	2	0	40	26	3	12	4
Honey-Pecan Granola (¼ cup)	180	9	1	0	40	23	2	11	3
Salted Caramel–Peanut Granola (¼ cup)	180	10	2	0	120	19	2	5	4
Strawberry Compote	70	0	0	0	25	18	1	14	0
Strawberry-Lime Compote	70	0	0	0	25	18	1	14	0
Strawberry-Vanilla Compote	70	0	0	0	25	18	1	14	0

	CALORIES	TOTAL FAT (G)	SAT FAT (G)	CHOL (MG)	SODIUM (MG)	TOTAL CARB (G)	DIETARY FIBER (G)	TOTAL SUGARS (G)	PROTEIN (G)
LOW-LIFT BRUNCH (SERVES 6 TO 8)									
Muffin Tin Frittatas with Chorizo, Parsley, and Pepper Jack Filling (1 frittata)	220	17	7	155	530	5	0	1	13
Muffin Tin Frittatas with Asparagus, Dill, and Goat Cheese Filling (1 frittata)	140	9	4	130	260	6	0	1	8
Mimosa	135	0	0	0	6	14	0	10	1
Bellini	96	0	0	0	4	8	1	6	1
Orange-Thyme Spritzer	90	0	0	0	25	22	0	20	1
Grapefruit-Rosemary Spritzer	80	0	0	0	25	21	0	9	1
BAGELS AND LOX (SERVES 4 TO 6)									
Garlic and Herb Cream Cheese Spread	99	10	5	31	106	2	0	1	2
Olive and Scallion Cream Cheese Spread	86	8	4	23	146	2	1	1	2
Smoked Salmon and Chive Cream Cheese Spread	106	10	6	33	151	1	0	1	3
Honey-Rosemary Cream Cheese Spread	113	10	5	31	104	6	0	5	2
Cinnamon-Sugar Cream Cheese Spread	111	10	5	31	104	5	0	4	2
Everything Bagel Seasoning	40	3	0	0	560	4	2	0	2
Pickled Red Onion	10	0	0	0	50	2	0	1	0
BREAKFAST TACOS (SERVES 4 TO 6)									
Scrambled Eggs	180	13	5	380	340	1	0	0	13
Migas	260	17	4	255	360	17	1	3	12
Salsa Roja	17	0	0	0	190	4	1	2	1
Sautéed Poblanos, Beans, and Corn	110	3	0	0	240	17	4	2	4
BLOODY MARY BAR (SERVES 6 TO 8)									
Bloody Marys for a Crowd (1 cocktail)	120	0	0	0	357	7	1	4	1
Black Pepper Candied Bacon	70	6	2	10	95	3	0	2	2
Herb Rim Salt	0	0	0	0	3360	0	0	0	0
Sriracha Rim Salt	10	0	0	0	3540	2	0	2	0
Snacks and Sips									
HUMMUS (SERVES 6 TO 8)									
Ultracreamy Hummus (⅓ cup)	218	12	1	0	287	23	7	4	8
Baharat-Spiced Beef Topping	70	5	1	10	100	1	0	0	3
Herb and Olive Salad Topping	35	3.5	0	0	15	1	0	0	1
Olive Oil–Sea Salt Pita Chips	181	14	2	0	102	13	2	0	2
BRUSCHETTA (SERVES 4 TO 6)									
Toasted Bread for Bruschetta	190	1	0	0	270	39	2	1	7
Tomato-Basil Topping	70	7	1	0	200	2	1	2	1
Port-Caramelized Onions	110	2	0.5	0	100	11	1	8	1
Smashed Peas with Lemon and Mint	80	4.5	0.5	0	105	6	2	2	2

	CALORIES	TOTAL FAT (G)	SAT FAT (G)	CHOL (MG)	SODIUM (MG)	TOTAL CARB (G)	DIETARY FIBER (G)	TOTAL SUGARS (G)	PROTEIN (G)
Snacks and Sips (cont.)									
WINGS (SERVES 4 TO 6)									
Fried Chicken Wings	480	32	10	155	1250	20	0	3	24
Buffalo Wing Sauce	80	8	5	20	499	3	0	3	0
Smoky Barbecue Wing Sauce	25	0	0	0	123	6	0	5	0
Mango Chutney Wing Sauce	60	1	0	0	115	12	1	3	1
Cauliflower Bites	390	32	11	20	980	26	2	4	2
Creamy Blue Cheese Dressing (2 tbsp)	90	8	3.5	15	200	1	0	1	3
Ranch Dressing (2 tbsp)	42	4	2	10	69	1	0	1	1
NACHOS (SERVES 4 TO 6)									
Cheesy Nachos with Refried Beans	690	48	23	110	990	40	0	1	30
Cheesy Nachos with Spicy Beef Topping	780	54	25	135	1100	42	1	1	38
One-Minute Salsa (½ cup)	30	0	0	0	570	7	0	3	1
Guacamole (¼ cup)	124	11	2	0	205	7	5	1	2
Escabeche	20	0	0	0	65	4	1	2	0
Micheladas (1 cocktail)	170	0	0	0	979	19	0	2	2
MOVIE NIGHT (SERVES 4 TO 6)									
Buttered Popcorn	150	11	3	10	95	11	2	0	2
Parmesan-Pepper Popcorn	170	12	3.5	15	180	11	2	0	4
Garlic and Herb Popcorn	150	11	3	10	95	11	2	0	2
Hot and Sweet Popcorn	170	11	3	10	105	16	3	5	2
Cajun-Spiced Popcorn	150	11	3	10	115	12	3	0	2
Citrus Soda Syrup (1 drink)	45	0	0	0	0	11	0	11	0
Berry Soda Syrup (1 drink)	50	0	0	0	0	12	1	12	0
Pineapple Soda Syrup (1 drink)	45	0	0	0	0	12	0	12	0
Watermelon Soda Syrup (1 drink)	45	0	0	0	0	12	0	12	0
Herb Soda Syrup (1 drink)	45	0	0	0	0	11	0	11	0
Ginger Soda Syrup (1 drink)	45	0	0	0	0	12	0	11	0
TAPAS (SERVES 6 TO 8)									
Tortilla Española	250	16	3	185	410	18	1	1	9
Aioli	200	22	3.5	45	80	1	0	0	1
Smoky Aioli	200	22	3.5	45	80	1	0	0	1
Herbed Aioli	210	22	3.5	45	80	1	0	0	1
Albóndigas en Salsa de Almendras	280	20	6	65	440	8	1	2	13
Sangria for a Crowd (1 cocktail)	197	0	0	0	6	23	1	19	0
White Wine Sangria (1 cocktail)	150	0	0	0	5	10	1	7	0
Rosé Sangria (1 cocktail)	150	0	0	0	5	9	1	5	0
RAW BAR (SERVES 6 TO 8)									
Poached Shrimp	60	1	0	105	160	1	0	0	12
Mignonette Sauce (1 tbsp)	5	0	0	0	0	1	0	0	0
Ginger Mignonette (1 tbsp)	5	0	0	0	0	1	0	1	0
Cocktail Sauce (1 tbsp)	20	0	0	0	150	4	0	3	0
Crudo	90	4	0.5	20	25	0	0	0	14
Furikake (1 tbsp)	25	1.5	0	0	400	2	1	1	1

	CALORIES	TOTAL FAT (G)	SAT FAT (G)	CHOL (MG)	SODIUM (MG)	TOTAL CARB (G)	DIETARY FIBER (G)	TOTAL SUGARS (G)	PROTEIN (G)
Snacks and Sips (cont.)									
PÂTÉ (SERVES 6 TO 8)									
Chicken Liver Mousse (¼ cup)	130	10	6	140	85	1	0	0	6
Bistro Salad	60	5	1	0	50	2	1	1	1
Smoked Trout Pâté (¼ cup)	160	9	4.5	60	280	2	0	1	15
AFTERNOON TEA (SERVES 6 TO 8)									
British-Style Currant Scones	269	10	6	53	210	41	2	13	6
Ham and Cheese Palmiers	40	2.5	1	5	120	3	0	0	2
MARTINIS (SERVES 4 TO 6)									
Big Batch Martinis (1 cocktail)	160	0	0	0	2	0	0	0	0
Individual Classic Martini	160	0	0	0	2	0	0	0	0
Easy Cheese Straws	90	6	3	7	168	4	0	0	4
Sweet and Spicy Straws	53	3	1	0	33	5	0	1	1
Italian Straws	52	3	1	0	53	5	0	0	1
Everything Straws	50	3	1	0	22	4	0	0	1
Prosciutto-Wrapped Stuffed Dates	80	4	0.5	5	190	10	1	8	3
Bring Your Appetite									
PIZZA PARLOR (SERVES 4 TO 6)									
French Bread Pizzas	610	33	19	85	1300	54	3	7	23
Greek Salad	220	19	5	20	240	8	1	5	5
Garlic Butter Dipping Sauce (1 tbsp)	100	11	7	30	75	0	0	0	0
Spicy Honey Drizzle (1 tbsp)	60	0	0	0	95	17	0	16	0
Balsamic Drizzle (1 tbsp)	80	0	0	0	80	21	0	20	0
BALLPARK (SERVES 6 TO 8)									
Pitch-Perfect Lemonade (1 cup)	150	0	0	0	75	40	0	38	0
Ballpark Pretzels	320	4	0	0	840	57	2	3	10
PICNIC (SERVES 4 TO 6)									
Turkey Picnic Sandwiches with Sun-Dried Tomato Spread	340	20	4.5	25	820	27	3	3	13
Roasted Zucchini Picnic Sandwiches with Olive Spread	270	16	3.5	10	540	25	2	3	7
Peach and Tomato Salad	115	7	1	0	418	13	3	9	2
Lemon Cookie Bars	205	7	3	19	90	34	0	23	2
OKTOBERFEST (SERVES 4 TO 6)									
Beer Brats with Onion and Mustard	520	41	12	85	1260	13	1	5	16
German Potato Salad	305	16	5	26	785	33	4	7	9
Apple-Fennel Rémoulade	100	7	1	5	270	8	2	5	1
CHOPPED SALAD (SERVES 4 TO 6)									
Basic Vinaigrette (2 tbsp)	210	22	3	0	330	3	0	3	0
Lemon-Herb Vinaigrette (2 tbsp)	210	22	3	0	330	3	0	3	0
Tarragon-Caper Vinaigrette (2 tbsp)	210	22	3	0	350	3	0	3	0
Cilantro-Chili Vinaigrette (2 tbsp)	210	22	3	0	340	3	0	3	0
Easy-Peel Hard-Cooked Eggs	70	5	1.5	185	70	0	0	0	6
Frico Crumble (2 tbsp)	35	2.5	1.5	10	115	0	0	0	2

	CALORIES	TOTAL FAT (G)	SAT FAT (G)	CHOL (MG)	SODIUM (MG)	TOTAL CARB (G)	DIETARY FIBER (G)	TOTAL SUGARS (G)	PROTEIN (G)
Bring Your Appetite (cont.)									
GRILLED VEGETABLE PLATTER (SERVES 4 TO 6)									
Marinated White Beans with Garlic and Capers	210	14	2	0	380	15	5	5	6
Grilled Vegetables	120	8	1	0	200	12	4	8	3
BAKED POTATOES (SERVES 6 TO 8)									
Simple Baked Russet Potatoes	180	0	0	0	10	41	3	1	5
Simple Baked Sweet Potatoes	170	0	0	0	120	40	7	12	3
Garlic and Chive Sour Cream (1 tbsp)	30	2.5	1.5	10	60	1	0	0	0
Herbed Goat Cheese Topping (1 tbsp)	45	4.5	1.5	5	45	0	0	0	2
Microwave-Fried Shallots (1 tbsp)	15	1	0	0	0	0	0	0	0
SHAWARMA (SERVES 4 TO 6)									
Chicken Shawarma	490	19	4.5	180	790	38	5	2	42
Tofu Shawarma	370	14	2	5	650	41	6	3	21
Sumac Onions (⅓ cup)	30	2.5	0	0	100	2	0	1	0
Cabbage Slaw (⅓ cup)	110	9	1.5	0	240	6	2	3	1
PULLED PORK (SERVES 6 TO 8)									
Indoor Pulled Pork	530	29	10	170	1600	13	1	9	49
Lexington Vinegar Barbecue Sauce (⅓ cup)	35	0	0	0	420	7	0	6	0
South Carolina Mustard Barbecue Sauce (⅓ cup)	60	1	0	0	840	11	1	8	1
Sweet and Tangy Barbecue Sauce (⅓ cup)	90	0	0	0	760	24	0	20	0
Simple Stovetop Macaroni and Cheese	260	11	6	30	380	27	0	3	13
Sweet Iced Tea	25	0	0	0	0	0	0	6	0
STEAK FRITES (SERVES 4 TO 6)									
Easy Steak Frites with Parsley-Shallot Butter	550	30	9	100	580	32	0	0	39
Classic Steak Sauce (1 tbsp)	25	0	0	0	120	6	0	5	0
Belgian-Style Dipping Sauce (1 tbsp)	30	3	0	0	100	1	0	1	0
Chive and Black Pepper Dipping Sauce (1 tbsp)	35	3.5	1	5	70	0	0	0	0
SALMON PLATTER (SERVES 4 TO 6)									
Slow-Roasted Salmon	570	44	8	105	490	3	0	3	39
Skillet-Roasted Green Beans	90	7	1	0	105	7	3	3	2
CLAMBAKE (SERVES 6 TO 8)									
Indoor Clambake for a Crowd	950	52	23	355	3050	51	4	6	74
Rémoulade (1 tbsp)	100	11	1	25	65	1	0	0	0
Quick Salsa Verde (1 tbsp)	60	7	0.5	0	65	0	0	0	0

	CALORIES	TOTAL FAT (G)	SAT FAT (G)	CHOL (MG)	SODIUM (MG)	TOTAL CARB (G)	DIETARY FIBER (G)	TOTAL SUGARS (G)	PROTEIN (G)
Sweet Things									
ICE CREAM SUNDAES (SERVES 4 TO 6)									
Classic Hot Fudge Sauce (2 tbsp)	130	6	3.5	10	40	19	1	16	1
Chocolate-Tahini Sauce (2 tbsp)	170	10	4	10	45	20	1	16	3
Whipped Cream (⅓ cup)	150	14	9	45	35	3	0	3	1
Maple Whipped Cream (⅓ cup)	160	14	9	45	35	6	0	5	1
Brown Sugar and Bourbon Whipped Cream (⅓ cup)	250	18	12	60	95	21	0	20	2
Orange Whipped Cream (⅓ cup)	150	14	9	45	35	4	0	4	1
Peanut Butter Whipped Cream (⅓ cup)	210	20	10	45	85	5	1	4	3
Salted Butterscotch Sauce (2 tbsp)	160	10	7	30	100	16	0	16	0
Mixed Berry Coulis (2 tbsp)	40	0	0	0	20	10	0	8	0
PAVLOVAS (SERVES 6 TO 8)									
Individual Pavlovas	130	0	0	0	30	30	0	30	2
Orange, Cranberry, and Mint Topping (⅓ cup)	60	0	0	0	0	16	1	14	0
Mango, Kiwi, and Blueberry Topping (⅓ cup)	40	0	0	0	0	9	1	7	1
Strawberry, Lime, and Basil Topping (⅓ cup)	20	0	0	0	30	5	1	4	0
CHOCOLATE FONDUE (SERVES 6 TO 8)									
Chocolate Fondue	350	29	17	50	30	30	0	22	3
Five-Spice Chocolate Fondue	350	29	17	50	30	30	0	22	3
Orange Chocolate Fondue	360	29	17	50	30	32	0	24	3
Crispy Rice Cereal Treats	160	4	2.5	10	110	30	0	15	2
Candy Bar Crispy Rice Cereal Treats	200	6	3.5	10	125	36	0	20	2
Nutella and Hazelnut Crispy Rice Cereal Treats	210	8	3	10	115	34	0	19	2
Bacon and Salted Caramel Crispy Rice Cereal Treats	180	4.5	3	10	160	32	0	16	2
Peanut Butter and Honey Crispy Rice Cereal Treats	180	5	2.5	10	125	32	0	17	2
COOKIE DECORATING (SERVES 6 TO 8)									
Roll-and-Cut Sugar Cookies	90	4.5	3	15	55	11	0	5	1
All-Purpose Glaze (1 tsp)	20	0	0	0	0	5	0	5	0
Citrus Glaze (1 tsp)	20	0	0	0	0	5	0	5	0
Coffee Glaze (1 tsp)	20	0	0	0	0	5	0	5	0
Decorating Icing (1 tsp)	15	0	0	0	0	4	0	4	0
DESSERT CHEESE BOARD (SERVES 4 TO 6)									
Skillet Candied Nuts	114	9	1	0	56	7	2	3	3
Skillet Candied Nuts with Fresh Herbs	114	9	1	0	56	7	2	3	3
Spiced Skillet Candied Nuts	114	9	1	0	56	7	2	3	3
Savory Seed Brittle	80	5	1	0	135	6	1	2	3

CONVERSIONS AND EQUIVALENTS

Some say cooking is a science and an art. We would say that geography has a hand in it, too. Flours and sugars manufactured in the United Kingdom and elsewhere will feel and taste different from those manufactured in the United States. So we cannot promise that the loaf of bread you bake in Canada or England will taste the same as a loaf baked in the States, but we can offer guidelines for converting weights and measures. We also recommend that you rely on your instincts when making our recipes. Refer to the visual cues provided. If the dough hasn't "come together in a ball" as described, you may need to add more flour—even if the recipe doesn't tell you to. You be the judge.

The recipes in this book were developed using standard U.S. measures following U.S. government guidelines. The charts below offer equivalents for U.S. and metric measures. All conversions are approximate and have been rounded up or down to the nearest whole number.

EXAMPLE:

1 teaspoon = 4.9292 milliliters, rounded up to 5 milliliters
1 ounce = 28.3495 grams, rounded down to 28 grams

VOLUME CONVERSIONS:

U.S.	Metric
1 teaspoon	5 milliliters
2 teaspoons	10 milliliters
1 tablespoon	15 milliliters
2 tablespoons	30 milliliters
¼ cup	59 milliliters
⅓ cup	79 milliliters
½ cup	118 milliliters
¾ cup	177 milliliters
1 cup	237 milliliters
1¼ cups	296 milliliters
1½ cups	355 milliliters
2 cups (1 pint)	473 milliliters
2½ cups	591 milliliters
3 cups	710 milliliters
4 cups (1 quart)	0.946 liter
1.06 quarts	1 liter
4 quarts (1 gallon)	3.8 liters

WEIGHT CONVERSIONS:

Ounces	Grams
½	14
¾	21
1	28
1½	43
2	57
2½	71
3	85
3½	99
4	113
4½	128
5	142
6	170
7	198
8	227
9	255
10	283
12	340
16 (1 pound)	454

CONVERSIONS FOR COMMON BAKING INGREDIENTS:

Baking is an exacting science. Because measuring by weight is far more accurate than measuring by volume, and thus more likely to produce reliable results, in our recipes we provide ounce measures in addition to cup measures for many ingredients. Refer to the chart below to convert these measures into grams.

Ingredient	Ounces	Grams
Flour		
1 cup all-purpose flour*	5	142
1 cup cake flour	4	113
1 cup whole-wheat flour	5½	156
Sugar		
1 cup granulated (white) sugar	7	198
1 cup packed brown sugar (light or dark)	7	198
1 cup confectioners' sugar	4	113
Cocoa Powder		
1 cup cocoa powder	3	85
Butter†		
4 tablespoons (½ stick or ¼ cup)	2	57
8 tablespoons (1 stick or ½ cup)	4	113
16 tablespoons (2 sticks or 1 cup)	8	227

* U.S. all-purpose flour, the most frequently used flour in this book, does not contain leaveners, as some European flours do. These leavened flours are called self-rising or self-raising. If you are using self-rising flour, take this into consideration before adding leaveners to a recipe.

† In the United States, butter is sold both salted and unsalted. We generally recommend unsalted butter. If you are using salted butter, take this into consideration before adding salt to a recipe.

OVEN TEMPERATURES:

Fahrenheit	Celsius	Gas Mark
225	105	¼
250	120	½
275	135	1
300	150	2
325	165	3
350	180	4
375	190	5
400	200	6
425	220	7
450	230	8
475	245	9

CONVERTING TEMPERATURES FROM AN INSTANT-READ THERMOMETER:

We include doneness temperatures in many of the recipes in this book. We recommend an instant-read thermometer for the job. Refer to the table above to convert Fahrenheit degrees to Celsius. Or, for temperatures not represented in the chart, use this simple formula:

Subtract 32 degrees from the Fahrenheit reading, then divide the result by 1.8 to find the Celsius reading.

EXAMPLE:
"Roast chicken until thighs register 175 degrees."

To convert:
175°F – 32 = 143°
143° ÷ 1.8 = 79.44°C, rounded down to 79°C

INDEX

Note: Page references in *italics* indicate photographs.

A

Afternoon Tea Board, *128–29,* 129–35
Aioli, 111
   Herbed, 111
   Smoky, 111
**Albóndigas en Salsa de Almendras
   (Meatballs in Almond Sauce),** 112, *113*
All-Purpose Glaze, 249, *249*
Almond(s)
   Cherry–Chocolate Chip Granola, 43
   -Raisin Granola, 43, *43*
   Sauce, Meatballs in (Albóndigas en
      Salsa de Almendras), 112, *113*
Anchovies
   Quick Salsa Verde, 220, *221*
Apple-Fennel Rémoulade, 168, *169*
Apricot(s)
   -Orange Granola, 43
   Seeded Pumpkin Crackers, 25, *25*
Arnold Palmer, 153
Asparagus
   Dill, and Goat Cheese Frittata Filling, 51
   grilling directions, 183
   preparing, for crudités, 34
   Prosciutto-Wrapped, 37, *37*
Avocados
   Guacamole, *97,* 99

B

Bacon
   Black Pepper Candied, *68,* 72
   German Potato Salad, 168, *169*
   Jam, 31, *31*
   oven baking, 50
   and Salted Caramel Crispy Rice
      Cereal Treats, 242
Bagel chips, preparing, 58
Bagels and Lox Board, *54–55,* 55–58

Baharat-Spiced Beef Hummus Topping,
   80, *81*
Baked Potatoes
   Board, *184–85,* 185–89
   Simple, 187–88, *188*
Baked Potato Toppings
   Easy Compound Butters, 189
   Garlic and Chive Sour Cream, 189
   Herbed Goat Cheese, 189
   Microwave-Fried Shallots, 189
   more ideas for, 187
Ballpark Board, *150–51,* 151–57
Ballpark Pretzels, 154–57, *155*
Balsamic
   Drizzle, 148
   -Fig Jam, 24
Barbecue Sauces
   Lexington Vinegar, 201, *201*
   South Carolina Mustard, 201, *201*
   Sweet and Tangy, 201, *201*
Barbecue Wing Sauce, Smoky, 93
Bark, The Ultimate Granola, 43, *43*
Barley, cooking directions, 215
Bars, Lemon Cookie, 163, *163*
Bar snack ideas, 140
Basic Vinaigrette, 175, *175*
Basil
   Garlic and Herb Cream Cheese
      Spread, 57, *59*
   Herbed Aioli, 111
   Italian Straws, 140
   Strawberry, and Lime Pavlova Topping,
      236, *237*
   -Tomato Bruschetta Topping, 85, *87*
Beans
   green, preparing for crudités, 34
   Green, Skillet-Roasted, 214, *214*
   Poblanos, and Corn, Sautéed, 66, *67*
   Refried, Cheesy Nachos with, *96,* 99
   Ultracreamy Hummus, 79, *79*
   White, Marinated with Garlic and
      Capers, 182, *182*
Beef
   Baharat-Spiced, Hummus Topping,
      80, *81*

Beef *(cont.)*
   Easy Steak Frites with Parsley-Shallot
      Butter, 207, *207*
   knackwurst, about, 167
   Topping, Spicy, Cheesy Nachos with, 99
Beer
   Brats with Onion and Mustard, 167, *167*
   Micheladas, 100, *101*
   Shandy, 153
Beet Tzatziki, 36
Belgian-Style Dipping Sauce, 209, *209*
Bellini, 52
Berry(ies)
   Cranberry, Orange, and Mint Pavlova
      Topping, 236, *237*
   Mango, Kiwi, and Blueberry Pavlova
      Topping, 236, *237*
   Mixed, Coulis, *230,* 231
   Soda Syrup, 107
   Strawberry, Lime, and Basil Pavlova
      Topping, 236, *237*
   Strawberry Compote, *40,* 45
   Strawberry-Lime Compote, 45
   Strawberry-Vanilla Compote, 45
   washing and storing, 44
Big Batch Martinis, 139, *139*
Bistro Salad, 126, *127*
Black Pepper
   Candied Bacon, *68,* 72
   and Chive Dipping Sauce, 209, *209*
Bloody Mary Bar, *68–69,* 69–73
Bloody Marys for a Crowd, 71, *73*
Blueberry(ies)
   Mango, and Kiwi Pavlova Topping,
      236, *237*
   Mixed Berry Coulis, *230,* 231
Blue Cheese
   Dressing, Creamy, 95
   Log with Walnuts and Honey, 24
Boards
   accents and garnishes for, 8
   aesthetic considerations, 10–11
   buffet, about, 5
   focal points, 8
   homemade items for, 8

Boards (cont.)

main types of, 5

matching board types with parties, 14–15

physical options, 6

scaling food for, 6

size options, 6

spreads, about, 5

store-bought items for, 8

styling, steps for, 12–13

traditional, about, 5

unified themes, 8

utensils and containers for, 7

Bockwurst, about, 167

Bonito flakes

Furikake, *120, 121*

Brats, Beer, with Onion and Mustard, 167, *167*

Bread

French, Pizzas, 147, *147*

Olive Oil–Sea Salt Pita Chips, *77, 81*

preparing croutons from, 177

Toasted, for Bruschetta, *82,* 85

Breakfast boards

Bagels and Lox, *54–55, 55–58*

Bloody Mary Bar, *68–69, 69–73*

Breakfast Tacos, *60–61, 61–66*

Granola Parfaits, *40–41, 41–45, 44*

Low-Lift Brunch, *46–47, 47–53*

British-Style Currant Scones, 132, *133*

Brittle, Savory Seed, 256, *257*

Broccoli, preparing for crudités, 34

Broiling, tips for, 194

Brown Sugar and Bourbon Whipped Cream, 229

Brunch Board, Low-Lift, *46–47, 47–53*

Bruschetta Board, *82–83, 83–86*

Bruschetta Toppings

more ideas for, 85

Port-Caramelized Onions, 86, *87*

Smashed Peas with Lemon and Mint, 86, *87*

Tomato-Basil, 85, *87*

Buffalo Wing Sauce, 93

Buttered Popcorn, 105, *105*

Butter(s)

Easy Compound, 189

Garlic, Dipping Sauce, 148

Parsley-Shallot, Easy Steak Frites with, *207, 207*

Butterscotch Sauce, Salted, 230, *231*

C

Cabbage Slaw

Slaw, 194

store-bought mixes, dressing up, 203

Cajun-Spiced Popcorn, 105

Candy Bar Crispy Rice Cereal Treats, 242

Caper(s)

and Garlic, Marinated White Beans with, 182, *182*

Italian Straws, 140

Quick Salsa Verde, 220, *221*

Rémoulade, 220, *221*

-Tarragon Vinaigrette, 175

Capicola, about, 28

Caramel

Salted, and Bacon Crispy Rice Cereal Treats, 242

Salted, –Peanut Granola, 43

Caraway seeds

Everything Bagel Seasoning, 58, *59*

Savory Seed Brittle, 256, *257*

Carrots

Escabeche, 100, *101*

preparing, for crudités, 34

Roasted Zucchini Picnic Sandwich with Olive Spread, 161

Cashew Dip, Whipped, with Roasted Red Peppers and Olives, 36

Cauliflower

Bites, *94,* 95

preparing, for crudités, 34

whole, cutting up, 94

Celery, preparing for crudités, 34

Charcuterie Board, *26–27, 27–31*

Cheddar Cheese Log with Chives, 24

Cheese

Blue, Dressing, Creamy, 95

Blue, Log with Walnuts and Honey, 24

Board, *18–19,* 19–25

Board, Dessert, *252–53,* 253–57

Breakfast Tacos Board, *60–61, 61–66*

Cheddar, Log with Chives, 24

Cheesy Nachos with Refried Beans, *96,* 99

Cheesy Nachos with Spicy Beef Topping, 99

Chorizo, Parsley, and Pepper Jack Frittata Filling, 51

French Bread Pizzas, 147, *147*

Frico Crumble, *176,* 177

Cheese (cont.)

Goat, Asparagus, and Dill Frittata Filling, 51

Goat, Herbed, Baked Potato Topping, 189

Goat, Log with Herbes de Provence, 24

Greek Salad, 148, *149*

and Ham Palmiers, *134,* 135

Improvising Grain Salad, *214,* 215

Macaroni and, Simple Stovetop, 202, *203*

Parmesan-Pepper Popcorn, 105

Prosciutto-Wrapped Asparagus, 37, *37*

Roasted Zucchini Picnic Sandwich with Olive Spread, 161

slicing methods, 22–23

storing, 20

Straws, Easy, 140, *141*

Stuffed Pickled Sweet Peppers, 30

Turkey Picnic Sandwich with Sun-Dried Tomato Spread, 161, *161*

see also Cream Cheese

Cherry–Chocolate Chip Granola, 43

Chicken

Liver Mousse, 125, *125*

Shawarma, 193, *193, 195*

Wings, Fried, 92, *92*

Wings Board, *88–89, 89–95*

Chiles

Escabeche, 100, *101*

Salsa Roja, 66, *67*

Sautéed Poblanos, Beans, and Corn, 66, *67*

Chive(s)

and Black Pepper Dipping Sauce, 209, *209*

Cheddar Cheese Log with, 24

and Garlic Sour Cream Baked Potato Topping, 189

Green Goddess Dip, 36

Herbed Aioli, 111

-Lemon Dressing, 213

and Smoked Salmon Cream Cheese Spread, 57

Chocolate

Chip–Cherry Granola, 43

choosing, for fondue, 241

Classic Hot Fudge Sauce, 229, *230*

Fondue, 241, *241*

Fondue, Five-Spice, 241

Fondue, Orange, 241

Fondue Board, *238–39, 239–43*

-Tahini Sauce, 229

Chopped Salad Board, *170–71, 171–77*
Chorizo, Parsley, and Pepper Jack
    Frittata Filling, 51
Cilantro
    -Chili Vinaigrette, 175
    One-Minute Salsa, *96,* 99
Cinnamon-Sugar Cream Cheese Spread, 57
Citrus
    Glaze, 249
    Soda Syrup, 107
    twists, creating, 141
    see also Grapefruit; Lemon; Lime;
        Orange(s)
Clambake, Indoor, for a Crowd, *216–17,* 219
Clambake Board, *216–17, 217–20*
Clams
    Indoor Clambake for a Crowd, *216–17,* 219
    storing, 219
Classic Hot Fudge Sauce, 229, *230*
Classic Steak Sauce, 209, *209*
Cocktails
    Bellini, 52
    Big Batch Martinis, 139, *139*
    Bloody Mary Bar, *68–69, 69–73*
    Bloody Marys for a Crowd, 71, *73*
    Individual Classic Martinis, 139
    Lemon Drop, 153
    made with tea, 133
    Martinis Board, *136–37, 137–41*
    Micheladas, 100, *101*
    Mimosa, 52, *53*
    Rosé Sangria, 113
    Sangria for a Crowd, *109,* 113
    setting up a brunch cocktail bar, 52
    Shandy, 153
    Tea Liqueur, 133
    Teatini, 133
    White Wine Sangria, 113
Cocktail Sauce, *118,* 119
Coffee Glaze, 249
Compotes
    Strawberry, *40,* 45
    Strawberry-Lime, 45
    Strawberry-Vanilla, 45
Compound Butters, Easy, 189
Cookie Bars, Lemon, 163, *163*
Cookie Decorating Board, *244–45, 245–51*
Cookies
    adding embellishments to, 250
    layering icing on, 250
    piping designs on, 250

Cookies (cont.)
    Roll-and-Cut Sugar, 248, *248*
Corn
    Foolproof Boiled, 202, *203*
    Indoor Clambake for a Crowd, *216–17,* 219
    Poblanos, and Beans, Sautéed, 66, *67*
Coulis, Mixed Berry, *230,* 231
Crackers
    choosing, 20
    Seeded Pumpkin, 25, *25*
Cranberry, Orange, and Mint Pavlova
    Topping, 236, *237*
Cream Cheese
    preparing smoked salmon dip with, 58
    Spread, Cinnamon-Sugar, 57
    Spread, Garlic and Herb, 57, *59*
    Spread, Honey-Rosemary, 57
    Spread, Olive and Scallion, 57
    Spread, Smoked Salmon and Chive, 57
Crema, preparing, 101
Crispy Rice Cereal Treats, 242, *243*
    Bacon and Salted Caramel, 242
    Candy Bar, 242
    Nutella and Hazelnut, 242
    Peanut Butter and Honey, 242
Croutons
    creative, 177
    from-scratch, 177
Crudités Board, *32–33, 33–37*
Crudo, *120,* 121
Cucumbers
    Beet Tzatziki, 36
    Greek Salad, 148, *149*
    preparing, for crudités, 34
Currant Scones, British-Style, 132, *133*

D

Dates, Prosciutto-Wrapped Stuffed,
    140, *141*
Decorating Icing, 249
Dessert boards
    Chocolate Fondue, *238–39, 239–43*
    Cookie Decorating, *244–45, 245–51*
    Dessert Cheese, *252–53, 253–57*
    Ice Cream Sundaes, *226–27, 227–31*
    Pavlovas, *232–33, 233–37*

Dinner-size boards
    Baked Potatoes, *184–85, 185–89*
    Ballpark, *150–51, 151–57*
    Chopped Salad, *170–71, 171–77*
    Clambake, *216–17, 217–20*
    Grilled Vegetable Platter,
        178–79, 179–83
    Oktoberfest, *164–65, 165–68*
    Picnic, *158–59, 159–63*
    Pizza Parlor, *144–45, 145–48*
    Pulled Pork, *196–97, 197–203*
    Salmon Platter, *210–11, 211–15*
    Shawarma, *190–91, 191–95*
    Steak Frites, *204–5, 205–9*
Dips
    Beet Tzatziki, 36
    Belgian-Style Dipping Sauce, 209, *209*
    Chive and Black Pepper Dipping Sauce,
        209, *209*
    Classic Steak Sauce, 209, *209*
    Green Goddess, 36
    Guacamole, *97,* 99
    One-Minute Salsa, *96,* 99
    smoked salmon, preparing, 58
    Ultracreamy Hummus, 79, *79*
    Whipped Cashew, with Roasted
        Red Peppers and Olives, 36
    see also Fondue
DIY Soda Bar, *106,* 107
Dressings
    Basic Vinaigrette, 175, *175*
    Cilantro-Chili Vinaigrette, 175
    Creamy Blue Cheese, 95
    Lemon-Chive, 213
    Lemon-Herb Vinaigrette, 175
    Miso-Ginger, 213
    Ranch, 95
    Tahini, 213
    Tarragon-Caper Vinaigrette, 175
Drinks
    Arnold Palmer, 153
    DIY Soda Bar, *106,* 107
    Grapefruit-Rosemary Spritzer, 52
    more ideas for sodas, 107
    Orange-Thyme Spritzer, 52
    Pitch-Perfect Lemonade, 153, *153*
    Sweet Iced Tea, 202
    see also Cocktails
Drizzles
    Balsamic, 148
    Spicy Honey, 148, *149*

E

Easy Cheese Straws, 140, *141*
Easy-Peel Hard-Cooked Eggs, 176
Easy Steak Frites with Parsley-Shallot
    Butter, 207, *207*
Eggplant
    Grilled Vegetables, *178–79*, 183
Egg(s)
    Easy-Peel Hard-Cooked, 176
    Migas, *61*, 65
    Muffin Tin Frittatas, *50*, 50–51
    and Potato Omelet, Spanish
        (Tortilla Española), *108*, 111
    Scrambled, *64*, 65
    scrambled, tips for, 65
Equipment, 7
Escabeche, 100, *101*
Essential boards
    Charcuterie, *26–27*, 27–31
    Cheese, *18–19*, 19–25
    Crudités, *32–33*, 33–37
Everything Bagel Seasoning, 58, *59*
Everything Straws, 140

F

Farro, cooking directions, 215
Fennel
    -Apple Rémoulade, 168, *169*
    grilling directions, 183
    Quick Pickled, 30
Fig-Balsamic Jam, 24
Finger sandwiches
    filling ideas for, 135
    preparing, 135
Fish
    Crudo, *120*, 121
    Quick Salsa Verde, 220, *221*
    Raw Bar Board, *114–15*, 115–21
    Smoked Trout Pâté, 126, *127*
    sushi grade, buying, 121
    see also Salmon
Five-Spice Chocolate Fondue, 241

Fondue
    Chocolate, 241, *241*
    Chocolate, Board, *238–39*, 239–43
    choosing chocolate for, 241
    choosing dippers for, 242
    Five-Spice Chocolate, 241
    Orange Chocolate, 241
Fondue set, buying, 243
Foolproof Boiled Corn, 202, *203*
Freekeh, cooking directions, 215
French Bread Pizzas, 147, *147*
Frico Crumble, 176, *177*
Fried Chicken Wings, 92, *92*
Frisée
    Bistro Salad, 126, *127*
Frittata Fillings
    Asparagus, Dill, and Goat Cheese, 51
    Chorizo, Parsley, and Pepper Jack, 51
Frittatas, Muffin Tin, *50*, 50–51
Fruit
    Improvising Grain Salad, *214*, 215
    Rosé Sangria, 113
    Sangria for a Crowd, *109*, 113
    White Wine Sangria, 113
    see also specific fruits
Fruit juices, for brunch cocktail bar, 52
Furikake, *120*, 121

G

Garlic
    Aioli, 111
    Butter Dipping Sauce, 148
    and Capers, Marinated White Beans
        with, 182, *182*
    and Chive Sour Cream Baked Potato
        Topping, 189
    Everything Bagel Seasoning, 58, *59*
    and Herb Cream Cheese Spread, 57, *59*
    Herbed Aioli, 111
    and Herb Popcorn, 105
    Italian Straws, 140
    Rémoulade, 220, *221*
    Smoky Aioli, 111
German Potato Salad, 168, *169*

Gin
    Big Batch Martinis, 139, *139*
    Individual Classic Martinis, 139
Ginger
    Mignonette, *118*, 119
    -Miso Dressing, 213
    Soda Syrup, 107
Glazes
    All-Purpose, 249, *249*
    Citrus, 249
    Coffee, 249
    decorating cookies with, 249
Goat Cheese Log with Herbes de
    Provence, 24
Grain(s)
    cooking directions, 215
    Salad, Improvising, *214*, 215
    see also specific grains
Granola
    Almond-Raisin, 43, *43*
    Apricot-Orange, 43
    Cherry–Chocolate Chip, 43
    Honey-Pecan, 43
    Parfaits Board, *40–41*, 41–45, *44*
    Salted Caramel–Peanut, 43
Grapefruit-Rosemary Spritzer, 52
Gravlax, about, 57
Grazing boards
    Afternoon Tea, *128–29*, 129–35
    Bruschetta, *82–83*, 83–86
    Hummus, *76–77*, 77–81
    Martinis, *136–37*, 137–41
    Movie Night, *102–3*, 103–7
    Nachos, *96–97*, 97–101
    Pâté, *122–23*, 123–27
    Raw Bar, *114–15*, 115–21
    Tapas, *108–9*, 109–13
    Wings, *88–89*, 89–95
Greek Salad, 148, *149*
Green Beans
    preparing, for crudités, 34
    Skillet-Roasted, *214*, 214
Green Goddess Dip, 36
Grilled Vegetable Platter, *178–79*, 179–83
Grilled Vegetables, *178–79*, 183
Guacamole, *97*, 99

H

Ham
and Cheese Palmiers, *134*, 135
Serrano, about, 28
see also Prosciutto
**Hazelnut and Nutella Crispy Rice
Cereal Treats, 242**
Herb(s)
Fresh, Skillet Candied Nuts with, 256
and Garlic Cream Cheese Spread, 57, *59*
and Garlic Popcorn, 105
Goat Cheese Log with Herbes de
Provence, 24
Herbed Aioli, 111
Herbed Goat Cheese Baked Potato
Topping, 189
-Lemon Vinaigrette, 175
and Olive Salad Hummus Topping, 80, *81*
Ranch Dressing, 95
Rim Salt, 72, *73*
Soda Syrup, 107
see also specific herbs
Honey
Drizzle, Spicy, 148, *149*
and Peanut Butter Crispy Rice
Cereal Treats, 242
-Pecan Granola, 43
-Rosemary Cream Cheese Spread, 57
and Walnuts, Blue Cheese Log with, 24
Horseradish
Bloody Marys for a Crowd, 71, *73*
Cocktail Sauce, *118*, 119
Hot and Sweet Popcorn, 105
Hot-dog topper ideas, 155
Hot Fudge Sauce
Classic, 229, *230*
store-bought, embellishing, 231
Hummus, Ultracreamy, 79, *79*
Hummus Board, *76–77*, 77–81
Hummus Toppings
Baharat-Spiced Beef, 80, *81*
Herb and Olive Salad, 80, *81*
more ideas for, 80

I

Ice, crushing, 117
**Ice cream, bringing to serving
temperature, 230**
Ice Cream Sundaes Board, *226–27*, 227–31
Iced Tea, Sweet, 202
Icing, Decorating, 249
Improvising Grain Salad, *214*, 215
Individual Classic Martinis, 139
Individual Pavlovas, 235, *237*
Indoor Pulled Pork, 199, *199*
Italian Straws, 140

J

Jam
Bacon, 31, *31*
Fig-Balsamic, 24
Juices, for brunch cocktail bar, 52

K

Ketchup-based sauces
Classic Steak Sauce, 209, *209*
Cocktail Sauce, *118*, 119
Lexington Vinegar Barbecue Sauce,
201, *201*
Smoky Barbecue Wing Sauce, 93
Sweet and Tangy Barbecue Sauce,
201, *201*
**Kiwi, Mango, and Blueberry Pavlova
Topping, 236, *237***
Knackwurst, about, 167

L

Lemon
-Chive Dressing, 213
Citrus Glaze, 249
Citrus Soda Syrup, 107
citrus twists, creating, 141
Cookie Bars, 163, *163*
-Herb Vinaigrette, 175
and Mint, Smashed Peas with, 86, *87*
Quick Salsa Verde, 220, *221*
Rémoulade, 220, *221*
see also Lemonade
Lemonade
Arnold Palmer, 153
Lemon Drop, 153
Pitch-Perfect, 153, *153*
Shandy, 153
Lettuce
Bistro Salad, 126, *127*
Greek Salad, 148, *149*
**Lexington Vinegar Barbecue Sauce,
201, *201***
Lime
Citrus Glaze, 249
Citrus Soda Syrup, 107
Micheladas, 100, *101*
-Strawberry Compote, 45
Liver, Chicken, Mousse, 125, *125*
Liverwurst, about, 167
Lobster
cooking tips, 220
Indoor Clambake for a Crowd,
216–17, 219
meat, removing from shell, 222–23
storing, 219
Low-Lift Brunch Board, *46–47*, 47–53
Lox, about, 57

M

Macaroni and Cheese, Simple Stovetop, 202, *203*

Mango, Kiwi, and Blueberry Pavlova Topping, 236, *237*

Mango Chutney Wing Sauce, 93

Maple Whipped Cream, 229

Marinated White Beans with Garlic and Capers, 182, *182*

Marshmallows
  Bacon and Salted Caramel Crispy Rice Cereal Treats, 242
  Candy Bar Crispy Rice Cereal Treats, 242
  Crispy Rice Cereal Treats, 242, *243*
  Nutella and Hazelnut Crispy Rice Cereal Treats, 242
  Peanut Butter and Honey Crispy Rice Cereal Treats, 242

Martinis
  Big Batch, 139, *139*
  Board, *136–37*, 137–41
  customizing, 139
  garnish ideas, 139
  Individual Classic, 139

Meat
  Charcuterie Board, *26–27*, 27–31
  cured and fermented, primer on, 28
  veal sausages, types of, 167
  see also Beef; Pork

Meatballs in Almond Sauce (Albóndigas en Salsa de Almendras), 112, *113*

Micheladas, 100, *101*

Microwave-Fried Shallots Baked Potato Topping, 189

Migas, *61*, 65

Mignonette, *118*, 119

Mignonette, Ginger, *118*, 119

Mimosa, 52, *53*

Mint
  Cranberry, and Orange Pavlova Topping, 236, *237*
  and Lemon, Smashed Peas with, 86, *87*
  Lemon-Herb Vinaigrette, 175

Miso-Ginger Dressing, 213

Mixed Berry Coulis, *230*, 231

Mortadella, about, 28

Mousse, Chicken Liver, 125, *125*

Movie Night Board, *102–3*, 103–7

Muffin Tin Frittatas, *50*, 50–51

Mushrooms, grilling directions, 183

Mussels
  debearding, 221
  Indoor Clambake for a Crowd, *216–17*, 219
  storing, 219

Mustard
  Barbecue Sauce, South Carolina, 201, *201*
  and Onion, Beer Brats with, 167, *167*
  Rémoulade, 220, *221*

N

Nachos
  Board, *96–97*, 97–101
  Cheesy, with Refried Beans, 96, 99
  Cheesy, with Spicy Beef Topping, 99

'Nduja, about, 28

Nori
  Furikake, *120*, 121

Nova lox, about, 57

Nutella and Hazelnut Crispy Rice Cereal Treats, 242

Nuts
  Albóndigas en Salsa de Almendras (Meatballs in Almond Sauce), 112, *113*
  Almond-Raisin Granola, 43, *43*
  Baharat-Spiced Beef Hummus Topping, 80, *81*
  Blue Cheese Log with Walnuts and Honey, 24
  Cherry–Chocolate Chip Granola, 43
  Honey-Pecan Granola, 43
  Improvising Grain Salad, *214*, 215
  Nutella and Hazelnut Crispy Rice Cereal Treats, 242
  Prosciutto-Wrapped Stuffed Dates, 140, *141*
  Salted Caramel–Peanut Granola, 43
  Seeded Pumpkin Crackers, 25, *25*
  Skillet Candied, 256, *257*
  Skillet Candied, with Fresh Herbs, 256

Nuts *(cont.)*
  Spiced Skillet Candied, 256
  Whipped Cashew Dip with Roasted Red Peppers and Olives, 36

O

Oats
  Almond-Raisin Granola, 43, *43*
  Apricot-Orange Granola, 43
  Cherry–Chocolate Chip Granola, 43
  Honey-Pecan Granola, 43
  Salted Caramel–Peanut Granola, 43
  Savory Seed Brittle, 256, *257*

Oktoberfest Board, *164–65*, 165–68

Olive Oil–Sea Salt Pita Chips, *77*, 81

Olive(s)
  Greek Salad, 148, *149*
  and Herb Salad Hummus Topping, 80, *81*
  and Roasted Red Peppers, Whipped Cashew Dip with, 36
  and Scallion Cream Cheese Spread, 57
  Spread, Roasted Zucchini Picnic Sandwich with, 161

Omelet, Spanish Egg and Potato (Tortilla Española), *108*, 111

One-Minute Salsa, *96*, 99

Onion(s)
  Bacon Jam, 31, *31*
  Escabeche, 100, *101*
  Everything Bagel Seasoning, 58, *59*
  Grilled Vegetables, *178–79*, 183
  and Mustard, Beer Brats with, 167, *167*
  Pickled Red, 58, *59*
  Port-Caramelized, 86, *87*
  Sumac, 194

Orange(s)
  Chocolate Fondue, 241
  Citrus Glaze, 249
  Cranberry, and Mint Pavlova Topping, 236, *237*
  Mimosa, 52, *53*
  -Thyme Spritzer, 52
  Whipped Cream, 229

Oysters, shucking, 119

P

Palmiers, Ham and Cheese, *134,* **135**
Parfaits, Granola, Board, *40–41, 41–45, 44*
Parmesan-Pepper Popcorn, 105
Parsley
    Garlic and Herb Cream Cheese Spread,
        57, 59
    Green Goddess Dip, 36
    Herb and Olive Salad Hummus Topping,
        80, *81*
    Herbed Aioli, 111
    Quick Salsa Verde, 220, *221*
    -Shallot Butter, Easy Steak Frites with,
        207, *207*
Pasta. *See* **Macaroni and Cheese**
Pastry bag and tip, substitute for, 251
Pâté
    Board, *122–23, 123–27*
    Chicken Liver Mousse, 125, *125*
    country-style, about, 127
    en croute, about, 127
    leftover, uses for, 126
    primer on, 127
    rillettes, about, 127
    Smoked Trout, 126, *127*
    smooth, about, 127
    terrines, about, 127
Pavlovas, Individual, 235, *237*
Pavlovas Board, *232–33, 233–37*
Pavlova Toppings
    Cranberry, Orange, and Mint Pavlova
        Topping, 236, *237*
    Mango, Kiwi, and Blueberry Pavlova
        Topping, 236, *237*
    Strawberry, Lime, and Basil Pavlova
        Topping, 236, *237*
Peach(es)
    Bellini, 52
    and Tomato Salad, 162, *162*
Peanut Butter
    and Honey Crispy Rice Cereal
        Treats, 242
    Whipped Cream, 229
Peanut–Salted Caramel Granola, 43
Peas, Smashed, with Lemon and Mint,
    86, *87*
Pecan-Honey Granola, 43

Pepitas
    Apricot-Orange Granola, 43
    Herb and Olive Salad Hummus Topping,
        80, *81*
    Savory Seed Brittle, 256, *257*
Peppers
    Grilled Vegetables, *178–79,* 183
    Migas, *61,* 65
    preparing, for crudités, 34
    Roasted Red, and Olives, Whipped
        Cashew Dip with, 36
    Sweet, Stuffed Pickled, 30
    Turkey Picnic Sandwich with Sun-Dried
        Tomato Spread, 161, *161*
    see also Chiles
Pickled Fennel, Quick, 30
Pickled Red Onion, 58, *59*
Pickled Stuffed Sweet Peppers, 30
Picnic Board, *158–59, 159–63*
Pineapple Soda Syrup, 107
Pine nuts
    Baharat-Spiced Beef Hummus Topping,
        80, *81*
Pistachios
    Seeded Pumpkin Crackers, 25, *25*
Pita Chips, Olive Oil–Sea Salt, *77, 81*
Pitch-Perfect Lemonade, 153, *153*
Pizza Parlor Board, *144–45, 145–48*
Pizzas
    French Bread, 147, *147*
    guidelines for toppings, 147
Poached Shrimp, 117, *117*
Popcorn
    Buttered, 105, *105*
    Cajun-Spiced, 105
    Garlic and Herb, 105
    Hot and Sweet, 105
    more flavoring ideas, 105
    Parmesan-Pepper, 105
Pork
    Albóndigas en Salsa de Almendras
        (Meatballs in Almond Sauce),
        112, *113*
    Pulled, Board, *196–97, 197–203*
    Pulled, Indoor, 199, *199*
    pulled, sauces for, 201, *201*
    see also Bacon; Ham; Sausage
Port-Caramelized Onions, 86, *87*

Potato(es)
    Asparagus, Dill, and Goat Cheese
        Frittata Filling, 51
    Chorizo, Parsley, and Pepper Jack
        Frittata Filling, 51
    cutting, for French fries, 208
    Easy Steak Frites with Parsley-Shallot
        Butter, 207, *207*
    and Egg Omelet, Spanish (Tortilla
        Española), *108,* 111
    Indoor Clambake for a Crowd,
        216–17, 219
    Salad, German, 168, *169*
Potatoes, Baked
    Board, *184–85, 185–89*
    Easy Compound Butters Topping, 189
    Garlic and Chive Sour Cream
        Topping, 189
    Herbed Goat Cheese Topping, 189
    Microwave-Fried Shallots Topping, 189
    more topping ideas, 187
    Simple, 187–88, *188*
Pretzels, Ballpark, 154–57, *155*
Prosciutto
    about, 28
    Stuffed Pickled Sweet Peppers, 30
    -Wrapped Asparagus, 37, *37*
    -Wrapped Stuffed Dates, 140, *141*
Puff pastry
    Easy Cheese Straws, 140, *141*
    Everything Straws, 140
    Ham and Cheese Palmiers, *134,* 135
    Italian Straws, 140
    Sweet and Spicy Straws, 140
Pulled Pork
    Board, *196–97, 197–203*
    Indoor, 199, *199*
    sauces for, 201, *201*
Pumpkin Crackers, Seeded, 25, *25*

Q

Quick Pickled Fennel, 30
Quick Salsa Verde, 220, *221*

R

Radicchio, grilling directions, 183
Radishes, preparing for crudités, 34
Raisin(s)
    -Almond Granola, 43, *43*
    Classic Steak Sauce, 209, *209*
    Honey-Pecan Granola, 43
Ranch Dressing, 95
Raspberries
    Berry Soda Syrup, 107
    Mixed Berry Coulis, *230*, 231
Raw Bar Board, *114–15*, *115–21*
Rémoulade, 220, *221*
Rémoulade, Apple-Fennel, 168, *169*
Rice, cooking directions, 215
Rillettes, about, 127
Rim Salt
    Herb, 72, *73*
    Sriracha, 72
Roasted Zucchini Picnic Sandwich with
    Olive Spread, 161
Roll-and-Cut Sugar Cookies, 248, *248*
Rosemary
    -Grapefruit Spritzer, 52
    -Honey Cream Cheese Spread, 57
Rosé Sangria, 113

S

Salads
    Apple-Fennel Rémoulade, 168, *169*
    Bistro, 126, *127*
    Chopped, Board, *170–71*, *171–77*
    chopped, ideas for, 177
    croutons for, 177
    Grain, Improvising, *214*, 215
    Greek, 148, *149*
    Peach and Tomato, 162, *162*
    Potato, German, 168, *169*
    suggested salad bar ingredients, 174

Salami
    about, 28
    "rose," preparing, 29
Salmon
    gravlax, about, 57
    lox, about, 57
    Salmon Platter, *210–11*, *211–15*
    Slow-Roasted, 213, *213*
    smoked, about, 57
    Smoked, and Chive Cream Cheese
        Spread, 57
    smoked, preparing dip with, 58
Salsa
    One-Minute, *96*, 99
    Roja, 66, *67*
    Verde, Quick, 220, *221*
Salt, Rim
    Herb, 72, *73*
    Sriracha, 72
Salted Butterscotch Sauce, *230*, 231
Salted Caramel–Peanut Granola, 43
Sandwiches
    Chicken Shawarma, 193, *193*, 195
    finger, filling ideas for, 135
    finger, preparing, 135
    pocketless pita, folding, 195
    Roasted Zucchini Picnic, with Olive
        Spread, 161
    Tofu Shawarma, 193
    Turkey Picnic, with Sun-Dried
        Tomato Spread, 161, *161*
Sangria
    for a Crowd, *109*, 113
    Rosé, 113
    White Wine, 113
Sauces
    Aioli, 111
    Belgian-Style Dipping, 209, *209*
    Buffalo Wing, 93
    Chive and Black Pepper Dipping,
        209, *209*
    Chocolate-Tahini, 229
    Classic Steak, 209, *209*
    Cocktail, *118*, 119
    crema, preparing, 101
    Garlic Butter Dipping, 148
    Ginger Mignonette, *118*, 119

Sauces (*cont.*)
    Herbed Aioli, 111
    Hot Fudge, Classic, 229, *230*
    Lexington Vinegar Barbecue, 201, *201*
    Mango Chutney Wing, 93
    Mignonette, *118*, 119
    Mixed Berry Coulis, *230*, 231
    One-Minute Salsa, *96*, 99
    Quick Salsa Verde, 220, *221*
    Rémoulade, 220, *221*
    Salsa Roja, 66, *67*
    Salted Butterscotch, *230*, 231
    Smoky Aioli, 111
    Smoky Barbecue Wing, 93
    South Carolina Mustard Barbecue,
        201, *201*
    store-bought hot fudge, embellishing, 231
    Sweet and Tangy Barbecue, 201, *201*
    wing, leftover, uses for, 92
    Yogurt, 193
Sausage
    Beer Brats with Onion and Mustard,
        167, *167*
    bockwurst, about, 167
    capicola, about, 28
    Chorizo, Parsley, and Pepper Jack
        Frittata Filling, 51
    German, types of, 167
    Indoor Clambake for a Crowd,
        216–17, 219
    knackwurst, about, 167
    liverwurst, about, 167
    mortadella, about, 28
    'nduja, about, 28
    salami, about, 28
    salami "rose," preparing, 29
    weisswurst, about, 167
Sautéed Poblanos, Beans, and Corn, 66, *67*
Savory Seed Brittle, 256, *257*
Scallion and Olive Cream Cheese
    Spread, 57
Scones, British-Style Currant, 132, *133*
Scrambled Eggs, *64*, 65
Seasonings
    Everything Bagel, 58, *59*
    Furikake, *120*, 121
    for raw fish, ideas for, 121

Seed(s)
Apricot-Orange Granola, 43
Brittle, Savory, 256, *257*
Everything Bagel Seasoning, 58, *59*
Furikake, *120*, 121
Herb and Olive Salad Hummus Topping, 80, *81*
Improvising Grain Salad, *214*, 215
Seeded Pumpkin Crackers, 25, *25*

Sesame seeds
Everything Bagel Seasoning, 58, *59*
Furikake, *120*, 121
Herb and Olive Salad Hummus Topping, 80, *81*
Savory Seed Brittle, 256, *257*
Seeded Pumpkin Crackers, 25, *25*

Shallot(s)
Microwave-Fried, Baked Potato Topping, 189
-Parsley Butter, Easy Steak Frites with, 207, *207*

Shandy, 153
Shawarma
Board, *190–91*, 191–95
Chicken, 193, *193*, 195
Tofu, 193

Shellfish
Clambake Board, *216–17*, 217–20
debearding mussels, 221
Indoor Clambake for a Crowd, *216–17*, 219
lobster cooking tips, 220
Poached Shrimp, 117, *117*
Raw Bar Board, *114–15*, 115–21
removing lobster meat from the shell, 222–23
shucking oysters, 119
storing, 219

Shrimp, Poached, 117, *117*
Simple Baked Potatoes, 187–88, *188*
Simple Stovetop Macaroni and Cheese, 202, *203*
Skewered Bloody Mary garnishes, 71
Skillet Candied Nuts, 256, *257*
with Fresh Herbs, 256
Spiced, 256

Skillet-Roasted Green Beans, 214, *214*
Slaw(s)
Cabbage, 194
store-bought, dressing up, 203

Slow-Roasted Salmon, 213, *213*
Smashed Peas with Lemon and Mint, 86, *87*
Smoked Salmon
about, 57
and Chive Cream Cheese Spread, 57
dip, preparing, 58

Smoked Trout Pâté, 126, *127*
Smoky Aioli, 111
Smoky Barbecue Wing Sauce, 93
Soda Bar, DIY, *106*, 107
Soda Syrups
Berry, 107
Citrus, 107
drink ideas for, 107
Ginger, 107
Herb, 107
Pineapple, 107
Watermelon, 107

Sour Cream
Garlic and Chive, Baked Potato Topping, 189
Ranch Dressing, 95

South Carolina Mustard Barbecue Sauce, 201, *201*
Spanish Egg and Potato Omelet (Tortilla Española), *108*, 111
Spiced Skillet Candied Nuts, 256
Spicy Honey Drizzle, 148, *149*
Spreads
Cinnamon-Sugar Cream Cheese, 57
Garlic and Herb Cream Cheese, 57, *59*
Honey-Rosemary Cream Cheese, 57
Olive, Roasted Zucchini Picnic Sandwich with, 161
Olive and Scallion Cream Cheese, 57
Smoked Salmon and Chive Cream Cheese, 57
Sun-Dried Tomato, Turkey Picnic Sandwich with, 161, *161*

Spritzers
Grapefruit-Rosemary, 52
Orange-Thyme, 52

Squash. *See* Pumpkin; Zucchini
Sriracha Rim Salt, 72
Steak Frites Board, 204–5, 205–9
Steak Sauce, Classic, 209, *209*
Strawberry(ies)
Berry Soda Syrup, 107
Compote, *40*, 45
Lime, and Basil Pavlova Topping, 236, *237*
-Lime Compote, 45
-Vanilla Compote, 45

Stuffed Pickled Sweet Peppers, 30
Sugar, coloring, 250
Sugar Cookies, Roll-and-Cut, 248, *248*
Sumac Onions, 194
Sunflower seeds
Herb and Olive Salad Hummus Topping, 80, *81*
Savory Seed Brittle, 256, *257*

Sweet and Spicy Straws, 140
Sweet and Tangy Barbecue Sauce, 201, *201*
Sweet Iced Tea, 202

T

Tacos Board for Breakfast, *60–61*, 61–66
Tahini
-Chocolate Sauce, 229
Dressing, 213
Ultracreamy Hummus, 79, *79*

Tapas Board, *108–9*, 109–13
Tarragon
-Caper Vinaigrette, 175
Green Goddess Dip, 36

Tea
Arnold Palmer, 153
brewing, tips for, 132
cocktails made with, 133
Liqueur, 133
Sweet Iced, 202
Teatini, 133

Terrines, about, 127
Thyme
    Lemon-Herb Vinaigrette, 175
    -Orange Spritzer, 52
Tofu Shawarma, 193
Tomato(es)
    -Basil Bruschetta Topping, 85, 87
    French Bread Pizzas, 147, 147
    Greek Salad, 148, 149
    Grilled Vegetables, 178–79, 183
    Italian Straws, 140
    One-Minute Salsa, 96, 99
    and Peach Salad, 162, 162
    Salsa Roja, 66, 67
    Sun-Dried, Spread, Turkey Picnic
        Sandwich with, 161, 161
Tomato juice
    Bloody Marys for a Crowd, 71, 73
Tortilla chips
    Cheesy Nachos with Refried Beans,
        96, 99
    Cheesy Nachos with Spicy Beef
        Topping, 99
Tortilla Española (Spanish Egg and Potato
    Omelet), 108, 111
Tortillas
    Breakfast Tacos Board, 60–61, 61–66
    charring, 64
    Migas, 61, 65
Trout, Smoked, Pâté, 126, 127
Turkey Picnic Sandwich with Sun-Dried
    Tomato Spread, 161, 161
Tzatziki, Beet, 36

V

Vanilla-Strawberry Compote, 45
Veal sausages, types of, 167
Vegetables
    blanching directions, 35
    Crudités Board, 32–33, 33–37
    Grilled, 178–79, 183
    Grilled Vegetable Platter,
        178–79, 179–83
    Improvising Grain Salad, 214, 215
    preparing, for crudités, 34
    see also specific vegetables
Vermouth
    Big Batch Martinis, 139, 139
    Individual Classic Martinis, 139
Vinaigrettes
    Basic, 175, 175
    Cilantro-Chili, 175
    Lemon-Herb, 175
    Tarragon-Caper, 175
Vinegar
    Barbecue Sauce, Lexington, 201, 201
    Ginger Mignonette, 118, 119
    Mignonette, 118, 119
Vodka
    Big Batch Martinis, 139, 139
    Bloody Marys for a Crowd, 71, 73
    Individual Classic Martinis, 139
    Lemon Drop, 153
    Tea Liqueur, 133
    Teatini, 133

Wheat berries, cooking directions, 215
Whipped Cashew Dip with Roasted
    Red Peppers and Olives, 36
Whipped Cream, 229
    Brown Sugar and Bourbon, 229
    Maple, 229
    Orange, 229
    Peanut Butter, 229
White Wine Sangria, 113
Wild rice, cooking directions, 215
Wine
    Bellini, 52
    Mimosa, 52, 53
    Port-Caramelized Onions, 86, 87
    Rosé Sangria, 113
    Sangria for a Crowd, 109, 113
    sparkling, for brunch cocktail bar, 52
    sparkling, leftover, uses for, 53
    White, Sangria, 113
Wing Sauces
    Buffalo, 93
    leftover, uses for, 92
    Mango Chutney, 93
    Smoky Barbecue, 93
Wings Board, 88–89, 89–95

Y

Yogurt
    Beet Tzatziki, 36
    Sauce, 193

U

Ultracreamy Hummus, 79, 79

W

Walnuts
    and Honey, Blue Cheese Log with, 24
    Prosciutto-Wrapped Stuffed Dates,
        140, 141
Watermelon Soda Syrup, 107
Weisswurst, about, 167

Z

Zucchini
    Grilled Vegetables, 178–79, 183
    Roasted, Picnic Sandwich with
        Olive Spread, 161